FINANCIAL INSTITUTIONS AND SERVICES

THE INTERNATIONAL MONETARY FUND (IMF): FINANCIAL CRISIS AND SELECT ISSUES

FINANCIAL INSTITUTIONS AND SERVICES

Additional books in this series can be found on Nova's website under the Series tab.

Additional E-books in this series can be found on Nova's website under the E-books tab.

FINANCIAL INSTITUTIONS AND SERVICES

THE INTERNATIONAL MONETARY FUND (IMF): FINANCIAL CRISIS AND SELECT ISSUES

RACHEL E. LAYTON
EDITOR

Nova Science Publishers, Inc.
New York

For permission to use material from this book please contact us:
Telephone 631-231-7269; Fax 631-231-8175
Web Site: http://www.novapublishers.com

LIBRARY OF CONGRESS CATALOGING-IN-PUBLICATION DATA

The International Monetary Fund (IMF) financial crisis and select issues /
editor, Rachel E. Layton.
p. cm.
Includes index.
ISBN 978-1-61728-499-1 (hbk.)
1. International Monetary Fund. 2. Global Financial Crisis, 2008-2009.
I. Layton, Rachel E.
HG3881.5.I58I5747 2009
332.1'52--dc22
2010025407

Published by Nova Science Publishers, Inc. ✢ New York

CONTENTS

PREFACE

The current global financial crisis, which began with the downturn of the U.S. subprime housing market in 2007, is testing the ability of the International Monetary Fund (IMF) in its role as the central international institution for oversight of the global monetary system. Though the IMF is unlikely to lend to the developed countries most affected by the crisis and must compete with other international financial institutions as a source of ideas and global macroeconomic policy coordination, the spillover effects of the crisis on emerging and less-developed economics gives the IMF an opportunity to reassert its role in the international economy. This book discusses the potential roles that the IMF may have in helping to resolve the current global financial crisis

Chapter 1- At their meeting in London on April 2, 2009, the leaders of the 20 systemically important industrialized and developing countries (G-20) agreed on several initiatives to bolster the International Monetary Fund's (IMF) resources, improving its ability to provide financial assistance to countries impacted by the ongoing financial crisis. These included increasing the resources of the IMF and international development banks by $1.1 trillion including $750 billion more for the IMF, $250 billion to boost global trade, and $100 billion for multilateral development banks. For the additional IMF resources, $250 billion was to be made available immediately through bilateral arrangements between the IMF and individual countries, while an additional $250 billion would become available as additional countries pledged their participation.

Chapter 2-This chapter discusses two potential roles the International Monetary Fund (IMF) may have in helping to resolve the current global financial crisis: (1) immediate crisis control through balance of payments lending to emerging market and less-developed countries and (2) increased surveillance of the global economy through better coordination with the international financial regulatory agencies.

The current global financial crisis, which began with the downturn of the U.S. subprime housing market in 2007, is testing the ability of the International Monetary Fund (IMF), in its role as the central international institution for oversight of the global monetary system. Though the IMF is unlikely to lend to the developed countries most affected by the crisis and must compete with other international financial institutions[1] as a source of ideas and global macroeconomic policy coordination, the spillover effects of the crisis on emerging and less-developed economies gives the IMF an opportunity to reassert its role in the international economy on two key dimensions of the global financial crisis: (1) immediate crisis management and (2) long-term systemic reform of the international financial system

Chapter 3- The International Monetary Fund faces a unique set of challenges in the current economic environment. With the continuing growth in the emerging market economies, the demand for IMF assistance has shrunk dramatically. In order to prevent a future need for an IMF-bailout, many emerging market countries are accumulating vast amounts of foreign exchange reserves. In 2006, IMF Managing Director Rodrigo de Rato created a panel of "eminent persons" to advise the IMF about reform of its income model, given the lower demand for IMF lending. The panel proposed the creation of an endowment that would be funded either with quota resources or through the sale of gold from the IMF reserves. This has raised questions among Members of Congress about the benefits of selling IMF gold and the presumed need for reform of the IMF 's income model.

Chapter 4 -Many developing countries have long argued that they deserve an increase in the influence that they wield at the International Monetary Fund (IMF). They point out that after years of sustained economic growth, their representation does not reflect their current economic position in the world economy. Proposed changes would give these emerging economies as well as poor borrowers and countries that do not significantly contribute to funding IMFoperations greater say in order to enhance the perceived legitimacy and effectiveness of the institution.

At the spring 2006 IMF meetings, IMF Managing Director Rodrigo de Rato presented a loosely fleshed out proposal that would provide for a two-step process. In the first step, there would be a so-called ad hoc quota increase that would immediately raise the representation of a few select countries who it is commonly agreed are under-represented at the Fund and follow with fundamental reform of the IMF quota system

Chapter 5- The International Monetary Fund (IMF) and World Trade Organization (WTO) approach the issue of "currency manipulation" differently. The IMF Articles of Agreement prohibit countries from manipulating their currency for the purpose of gaining unfair trade advantage, but the IMF cannot force a country to change its exchange rate policies. The WTO has rules against subsidies, but these are very narrow and specific and do not seem to encompass currency manipulation. Several options might be considered for addressing this matter in the future, if policymakers deem this a wise course of action.

This chapter describes how the International Monetary Fund (IMF) and World Trade Organization (WTO) deal with the issue of currency manipulation. It also discusses apparent discrepancies in their charters and ways those differences might be addressed.

Chapter 6 - Governments discuss and coordinate economic policies using a mix of formal institutions, such as the World Trade Organization (WTO) and International Monetary Fund (IMF), and more informal economic forums, like the Group of Seven, or G-7, and the Group of 20, or G-20. This chapter focuses on informal economic forums, and, specifically, the role of the G-20 in coordinating governments' responses to the current economic crisis. The members of the G-7 are Canada, France, Germany, Italy, Japan, the United Kingdom, and the United States. The G-20 includes the G-7 members plus Argentina, Australia, Brazil, China, India, Indonesia, Mexico, Russia, Saudi Arabia, South Africa, South Korea, Turkey, and the European Union (EU)

Since the mid-1970s, leaders from the G-7, a small group of developed countries, have gathered annually to discuss and coordinate financial and economic policies. Large emerging-market economies such as China started to have more sway in financial markets in the 1990s, and the Asian Financial Crisis in 1997-1998 showed that emerging markets were too important to exclude from international economic discussions. The G-20 was formed in 1999 as an opportunity for finance ministers and central bank governors from both developed and emerging-market countries to discuss financial issues. The G-20 remained a less prominent forum than the G-7, as it involved meetings among finance ministers while the G-7 sessions also involved summit meetings among heads of governments or heads of state.

Chapter 7 -The International Monetary Fund (IMF) has significantly increased its total committed lending to countries from about $3.5 billion in August 2008 to about $170.4 billion in August 2009, as countries have been severely affected by the global economic crisis. IMFsupported programs are intended to help countries overcome balance-of-payments problems, stabilize their economies, and restore sustainable economic growth. Critics have long-standing concerns that the IMF has an overly austere approach to macroeconomic policy that does not sufficiently heed country viewpoints. To help address these concerns, the IMF recently stated that it has changed its policies, including by increasing its flexibility

In: The International Monetary Fund (IMF) Financial Crisis and... ISBN: 978-1-61728-499-1
Editor: Rachel E. Layton

Chapter 1

THE GLOBAL FINANCIAL CRISIS: INCREASING IMF RESOURCES AND THE ROLE OF CONGRESS

Jonathan E. Sanford and Martin A. Weiss

SUMMARY

At their meeting in London on April 2, 2009, the leaders of the 20 systemically important industrialized and developing countries (G-20) agreed on several initiatives to bolster the International Monetary Fund's (IMF) resources, improving its ability to provide financial assistance to countries impacted by the ongoing financial crisis. These included increasing the resources of the IMF and international development banks by $1.1 trillion including $750 billion more for the IMF, $250 billion to boost global trade, and $100 billion for multilateral development banks. For the additional IMF resources, $250 billion was to be made available immediately through bilateral arrangements between the IMF and individual countries, while an additional $250 billion would become available as additional countries pledged their participation.

In June 2009, Congress enacted legislation authorizing U.S. participation in this new increase in IMF resources. The White House formally requested on May 12 that Congress consider increasing the U.S. contribution to the IMF based on commitments made by the Bush Administration in 2008 and by the Obama Administration at the London meeting of the G-20 countries in April 2009. At the meeting, G-20 leaders agreed that the IMF's New Arrangements to Borrow (NAB), a supplemental fund to bolster IMF resources, should be increased by up to $500 billion from its present level of $50 billion. The Obama Administration proposed that the United States contribute up to $100 billion. The G-20 also agreed that the IMF should create $250 billion in new Special Drawing Rights (SDR) and allocate them to its members through its SDR Department.

Already pending at the time of the G-20 meeting was a proposal for a new increase in IMF quota resources. Negotiations on a package of reforms and a new quota increase were completed in April 2008, and the proposals were submitted to the House and Senate by the Bush Administration in November 2008. The U.S. share is about $8 billion. The package includes reform of IMF governance, finances, and procedures. It also includes a proposal that the IMF sell 403 metric tons of gold to create a facility that would cover the costs of its country and global surveillance, technical assistance, research, and other non-lending operations.

U.S. participation in the new IMF quota increase and a U.S. subscription of $100 billion for the NAB required congressional approval. Likewise, amendments to the IMF Articles—including the prospective Fourth Amendment for a new SDR allocation—required congressional approval. On the other hand, the proposed $250 billion allocation of SDRs (which is being made under a different provision of the IMF Articles) was too small to trigger the legal requirement that Congress give its assent. Any contributions to the IMF, to fund increases in the U.S. quota or to subscribe new resources to the NAB, must be authorized by Congress.

Despite concerns about the process of authorizing and appropriating contributions to the IMF, and the impact on the global economy of creating a large of amount of SDRs, U.S. participation in the funding agreement, and the requisite authorizations for IMF reform efforts, were included in the FY2009 Spring Supplemental Appropriations for Overseas Contingency Operations (P.L. 111-32).

On May 12, 2009, the Obama Administration formally requested that Congress consider increasing the U.S. contribution to the International Monetary Fund (IMF) based on commitments made by the Bush Administration in 2008 and by the Obama Administration at the London meeting of the G-20 countries in April 2009.[1] At the meeting, G-20 leaders agreed that the IMF's New Arrangements to Borrow (NAB), a supplemental fund to bolster IMF resources, should be increased by up to $500 billion from its then current level of $50 billion.[2] The Obama Administration proposed that the United States contribute up to $100 billion. Pledges totaling $411.5 billion have since been received from several countries.[3] The G-20 also agreed that the IMF should create $250 billion in new Special Drawing Rights (SDR) and allocate them to its members through its SDR Department. These new resources would expand world foreign exchange reserves by about 4%.

Already pending at the time of the G-20 meeting was an IMF reform package comprising a modest quota increase to boost the relative share of underrepresented developing countries and several governance reforms. The U.S. share of the quota increase is around $8 billion, the amount required to maintain the existing 16.77% U.S. voting share, which provides a veto on major IMF decisions requiring an 85% majority. The reform package also included a proposal to sell 403 metric tons of gold held by the IMF to create an income-generating fund to partially finance the IMF 's country and global surveillance, technical assistance, research, and other non-lending operations.[4]

U.S. participation in the funding agreement, and the requisite authorizations for IMF reform efforts, were included in the FY2009 Spring Supplemental Appropriations for Overseas Contingency Operations (P.L. 111-32). This chapter provides information on (1) the role the IMF has played in the financial crisis, (2) international agreement to increase the financial resources of the IMF, and (3) the role of Congress in increasing the Fund's resources.

THE FINANCIAL CRISIS AND DEVELOPING COUNTRIES[5]

What began as a bursting of the U.S. housing market bubble and a rise in foreclosures has ballooned into a global financial and economic crisis. The crisis has exposed fundamental weaknesses in financial systems worldwide. Despite coordinated easing of monetary policy and trillions of dollars in intervention by central banks and governments, economies continue to decline into what is turning out to be the most severe global recession since the Great Depression of the 1930s.

On April 22, 2009, coinciding with the London G-20 meeting, the IMF forecasted economic growth of -1.3% for 2009—the lowest since World War II. Lower global growth, weak demand for exports, a precipitous drop in commodity prices, and increased risk aversion in the developed markets have all contributed to weak economic growth in developing countries (Figure 1). Central and Eastern Europe and Latin America have been particularly hard-hit.

The crisis is impacting developing countries through several channels. First, economic slowdown in the advanced economies is leading to decreased demand for developing country exports (Figure 2) and a contraction of capital flows (Figure 3). Developing countries also suffer from the collapse of commodity prices. Rapid economic growth in China and India over the past decade led to record prices for petroleum, minerals, and other commodities. Between 2003 and 2008, oil prices rose by 320% and food prices by 138%. Since mid-2008, however, weakening demand for these exports has led to a rapid decline in the price of many of these commodities. The combination of declining foreign direct investment, portfolio investment, weak export demand, and a more constrained environment for remittances and foreign aid, has put pressure on many countries' government fiscal balances (Figure 4).

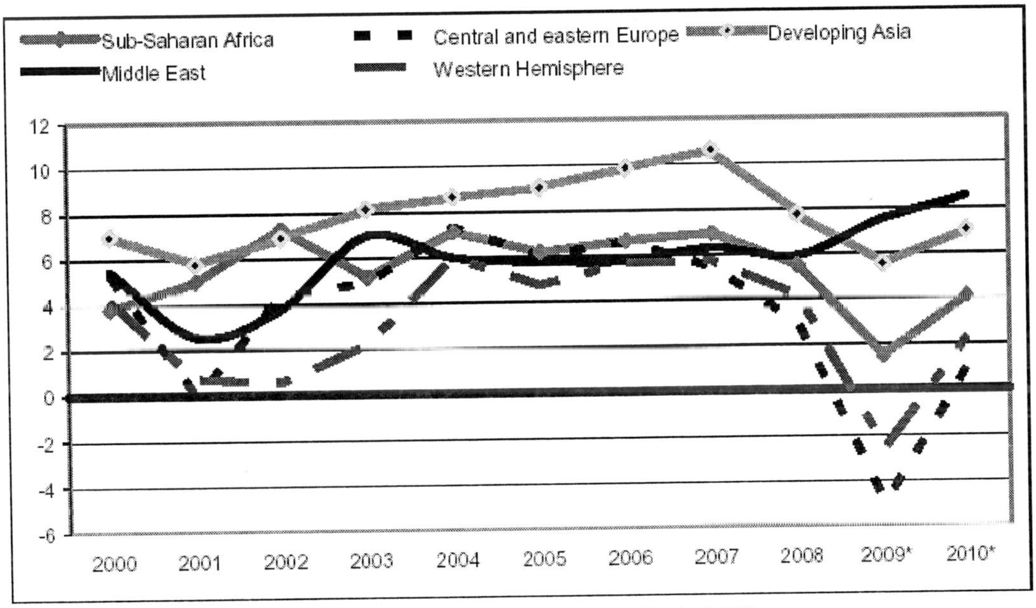

Source: IMF World Economic Outlook Database, estimates as of July 2009.

Figure 1. Impact of the Crisis on Developing Regions Annual GDP Growth Rate.

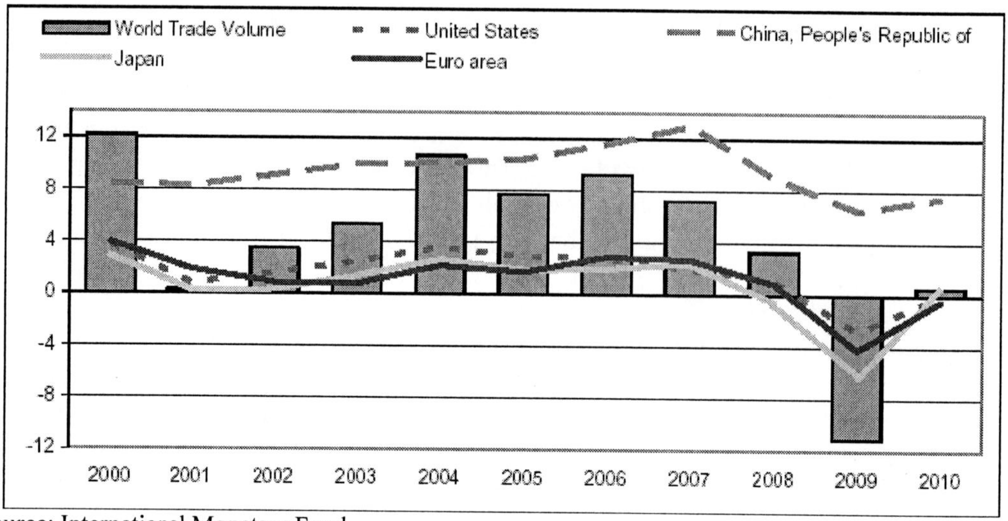

Source: International Monetary Fund

Figure 2. GDP Growth in Major Export Markets and World Trade
Annual Percentage Change

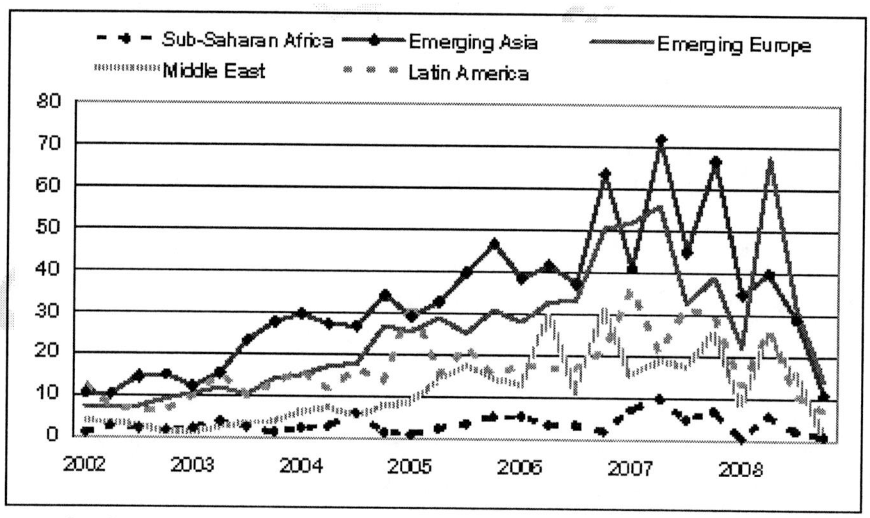

Source: International Monetary Fund

Figure 3. Private Capital Flows
Bond, equity, and loan issuances ($ billion)

IMPACT OF THE CRISIS ON THE IMF

The severity of the current financial crisis presented a challenge for the IMF, whose financial resources had not kept pace with the global economy over the past decade. The IMF reported in early 2009 that its resources would need to grow by 55% to match the level of its resources (relative to global output) that it held during the Asian financial crisis of 1997-1998.

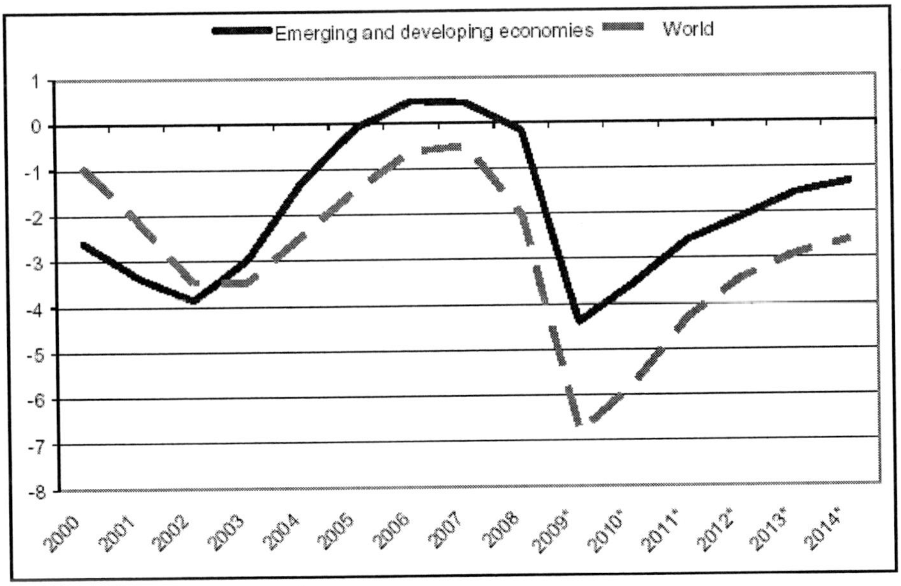

Source: International Monetary Fund

Figure 4. General Government Fiscal Balances
Percent of GDP

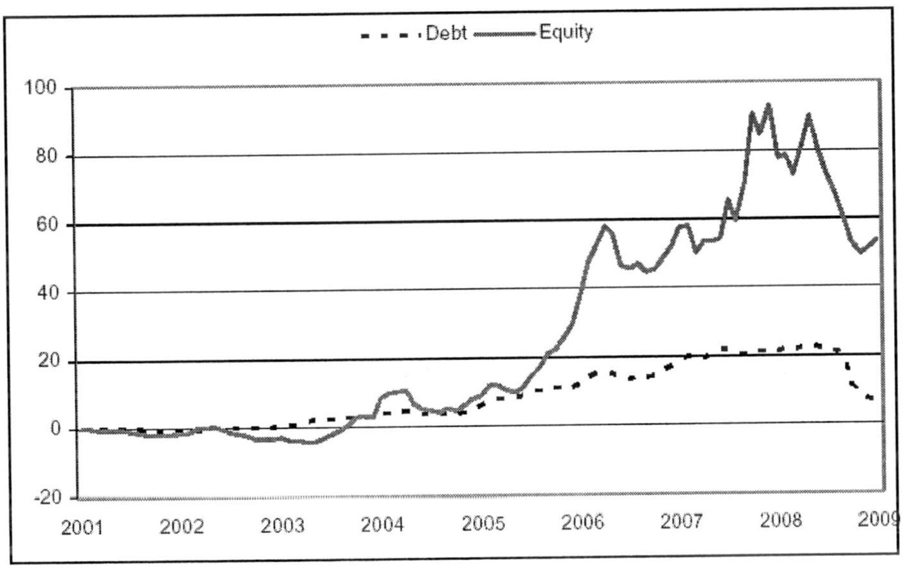

Source: International Monetary Fund

Figure 5. Capital Flows to Emerging Economies
Billions of U.S. Dollars

Demand for IMF resources in late 2008-2009 has been strong. Between October and December 2008, lending almost doubled, from $17.1 billion to $32.54 billion. As of July 2009, IMF lending commitments are $157 billion, a record high.[6] The recent rise in IMF lending, however, was preceded by historic lows. On August 31, 2008, total IMF lending was $16.65 billion, down from a peak of $116 billion in September 2003.[7] Since the IMF's main source of income is the interest paid on its loans, weak demand for IMF loans between 2000 and 2008 resulted in shortfalls in the IMF 's administrative budget and a roughly 20% reduction in IMF staff during 2007-2008.

Given the IMF 's constrained financial situation, many analysts raised concerns that the institution did not have the necessary resources should there be widespread demand for IMF financial support. Total IMF quota, resources ($337.2. billion as of July 2009) were small compared to the growth of capital flows to emerging economies, let alone the advanced economies.

If the G-20 pledges of $500 billion in new resources are realized, many argue that the IMF will once again have the financial resources to credibly lend to developing countries impacted by the crisis.

INCREASING FUND RESOURCES

New Arrangements to Borrow (NAB)

The NAB are a set of credit arrangements, created in 1998, between the IMF and 26 developed country members and institutions to provide supplementary resources that the IMF can use to help financial crises in countries of major significance to the world financial system.[8] The NAB was activated once, in December 1998, to finance a loan for Brazil.

At the G-20 meeting in April 2009, the major countries agreed that the resources of the NAB should be expanded by about $500 billion. The G-20 agreed that $250 billion should be made available immediately to the IMF through bilateral arrangements between the IMF and individual countries. The G-20 also agreed that the NAB would be expanded by an additional $250 billion as more countries pledged their participation. To date, pledges totaling $411.5 billion have been received from several countries.[9]

The NAB is a supplemental, emergency mechanism intended to provide temporary financing for the IMF only when necessary. Thus, it is a non-quota based source of financing for the IMF. The NAB is not, therefore, intended to substitute for a quota or capital increase. If activated, participating donor countries make loans to the IMF, and the IMF uses those funds to provide loans to eligible countries. Repayments flow from the country to the IMF and then from the IMF to the NAB.

Under current NAB rules, before the IMF can draw against NAB resources, an 85% majority of the IMF Executive Board and countries representing 80% share of the NAB credit volume must agree. The IMF must repay the NAB creditors within five years.

SDR Allocation

As noted above, G-20 leaders agreed in April that the IMF create $250 billion worth of new SDRs and allocate them to its member countries. SDRs are created and allocated solely by the IMF. Separately, the Obama Administration requested that Congress approve an amendment to the IMF Articles of Agreement, originally proposed in 1997, that would permit a special allocation of SDRs to IMF member countries that joined the IMF following the initial allocation. None of the funds being contributed by the United States or other countries to expand the NAB will be used to fund the new allocation of SDRs.

The First Amendment to the IMF Articles, which went into effect in 1969, authorized the IMF to create a new international reserve asset that could be used to supplement its member country's foreign exchange reserves. This asset, known as special drawing rights (SDRs), is neither a currency, nor a claim on the IMF. Rather, it is a potential claim on the freely usable currencies of IMF members. SDRs are created by fiat, and are not "paid for" by any foreign contributions or backed by any national currency.

SDRs are not a global reserve currency. However, they may be exchanged for hard convertible currency among IMF member nations. Established rules govern how a country may exercise its claim and convert its share of SDRs into another country's hard currency. The SDR serves as the IMF 's standard unit of account.[10]

IMF Bond Sales

Several developing countries with considerable foreign exchange reserve holdings have been approached about contributing to the G-20 pledge to increase IMF resources. Many have expressed their unwillingness to lend money to the institution until broader governance reform at the institution is achieved. While some changes in quota share were agreed to at the April 2008 IMF spring meetings that will increase developing country representation, they have been widely characterized as modest. Many developing countries have thus sought a temporary means to provide assistance to the IMF, while delaying a more permanent contribution until more substantial governance reforms give them a larger representation in the institution.[11] For countries with large reserves, these bonds are attractive since they provide an additional vehicle for diversifying the currency composition of their foreign exchange reserves. (Most foreign exchange reserves are currently held in only a few currencies including U.S. dollars, euros, and Japanese yen.)

Article 7 of the IMF 's Articles of Agreement provides the IMF the authority to issue bonds and notes. Neither U.S. Treasury consent, nor congressional authorization, is needed. The IMF has never issued bonds or notes in its 60-year history; however, on July 1, 2009, the IMF approved a framework for issuing bonds and notes to member countries and their central banks.[12] These would be sold only to member countries, which may trade them only among themselves. Countries would not be allowed to sell the bonds or notes to private firms or individuals on the secondary market. Several members have indicated their intent or have already bought IMF notes. China has said it will buy up to $50 billion in IMF notes, while Brazil, India and Russia have said they will buy up to US$10 billion each.[13] The notes have a maximum maturity of five years and will be denominated in SDRs.

The implication for the United States of the proposal would be mixed. If successful, the proposal could lead to greater international macroeconomic security. One concern, however, about the bond sales is that if increasing amounts of foreign exchange reserves are transferred out of dollars into IMF bonds, the future demand for U.S. Treasury bills and agency instruments (traditional reserve instruments) may decline, thus increasing the yield on low-risk assets. This would raise the cost to the United States of future debt placements and possibly accentuate a trend of countries slowly diversifying their reserves out of the dollar.

Many analysts have argued that since the Asian financial crisis (and during the current crisis), foreign demand for U.S. Treasury assets (largely from central banks) has played a crucial role in depressing U.S. interest rates. Should demand for U.S. Treasury assets decrease because of asset allocation decisions by foreign central banks, or because foreign governments need to spend more of the reserves domestically and have less to invest, there could be upward pressure on U.S. interest rates. However, the overall demand for U.S. Treasury bonds may also be minimally impacted if they are held instead by an emerging market country that receives IMF loans rather than by an emerging market country purchasing IMF bonds.

IMF Governance Reforms

Several IMF proposals were already pending at the time of the G-20 meeting on April 2, 2009. These proposals are part of an IMF governance reform package negotiated between 2006 and 2008. The George W. Bush Administration submitted proposed legislation regarding these reforms in November 2008, but it was not taken up by the 110th Congress. The reforms included plans for an increase in IMF quotas for selected members and several procedural, policy, and financial reforms.

The quota increase involved a targeted realignment in the voting shares of member countries in order to give poor countries and dynamic emerging market countries more say in the organization. The U.S. voting share in the IMF would remain at its present 16.77% and the United States would retain the capacity to block the 85% vote that is required to approve most major initiatives in the Fund. Under this reform of IMF quotas, 54 under-represented countries would see their combined quota share in the Fund increase by about 5% of the total.

Other reforms included in the governance reform package include (1) a new formula for determining country quotas, giving much more weight to GDP and thus better reflecting countries' weight in the world economy; (2) a tripling of "basic votes"—equally allocated votes—thus giving the poor countries an increased voice in the organization; (3) an additional Alternate Executive Director for the two constituencies of the Executive Board representing countries in sub-Saharan Africa; and (4) changes in the IMF 's investment and financial procedures, including the sale of gold to finance the establishment of an income-generating endowment fund to help pay for the IMF 's activities (research, policy and technical assistance, etc.) that are not related to its loan operations. Those reforms requiring congressional action, were authorized in the FY2009 Spring Supplemental Appropriations for Overseas Contingency Operations (P.L. 111-32), signed by President Obama on June 24, 2009.

Congressional Action

Some of the provisions discussed above required congressional assent and some did not. Congressional action is required before the United States can vote for amendments to the IMF Articles, for gold sales, or for quota increases that involve contributions by the United States.

Congress and the New Allocations of SDRs

As noted above, G-20 leaders agreed that IMF create $250 billion worth of new SDRs and allocate them to its member countries. Separately, the Obama Administration requested that Congress approve an amendment to the IMF Articles of Agreement, originally proposed in 1997, that would permit a special allocation of SDRs (around $32 billion) to IMF member countries that joined the IMF following the initial allocation.

U.S. contributions to the IMF, either for the $8 billion increase in the U.S. quota or the $100 billion increase in the U.S. line of credit to the NAB facility, are not linked to the forthcoming allocation of $250 billion worth of SDRs. No funds provided by the United States are being used to facilitate the new allocation of Special Drawing Rights (SDRs).

New Allocation of $250 billion of SDRs

If an 85% majority of the IMF membership agrees, the IMF can unilaterally create new SDRs and allocate them to its member countries. Article XXVIII of the Fund's Articles of Agreement specifies the procedure that is to be used. The SDR Department handles these operations. The resources of the SDR Department and the IMF 's General Reserve are not co-mingled, and the two accounts have different rules. (The IMF uses the resources of its General Reserve to fund its loans to borrower countries.) SDRs held in the SDR Department belong to the countries holding them and not to the IMF. Countries may use these SDRs to settle accounts with other IMF member countries, or they may transfer ownership to other countries in exchange for an equivalent value of the purchaser country's currency. The IMF serves as broker for these exchanges. Through the IMF, countries pay or receive interest when they sell or buy each other's SDRs.

No congressional action is needed for this allocation to take effect. In the Special Drawing Rights Act of 1968, Congress gave the Administration authority to vote for the First Amendment to the IMF's Articles of Agreement creating the SDR, and set forth the guidelines for U.S. participation in the SDR Department. Section 6 of the Act says that Congress must give its consent before the United States can vote for any allocation of SDRs that would be equal to or greater than the existing U.S. quota in the IMF. However, the Act also says that if the U.S. share of a new allocation of SDRs is less than the size of the U.S. quota, the United States can support an SDR allocation as long as the Treasury Department consults with leaders of the House and Senate authorizing committees at least 90 days in prior to the vote. The 90-day period began on April 13, 2009, when a Treasury official notified Congress that the United States planned to vote in favor of the proposed new allocation of SDRs.

Special SDR Allocation for New IMF Members

Separately, a proposal was been pending since 1997 to grant SDRs to countries that joined the IMF since the IMF 's last designation of SDRs in 1979-81. When a country joins the IMF, they do not automatically receive a share of SDRs since any increase of IMF SDRs that is not proportional for all members requires an amendment to the IMF's Articles of Agreement. Currently, over one-fifth of the IMF's membership is ineligible to participate in the SDR Department.

Since this allocation is not equi-proportional (all countries receiving a share equal to their quota share), it requires an Amendment to the IMF 's charter, what has come to be known as the "Fourth Amendment." To be enacted, the Fourth Amendment (or any IMF amendment) requires an affirmative vote of three-fifths of the IMF membership with 85% of the total voting power. Prior to passage of the FY2009 Spring Supplemental Appropriations for Overseas Contingency Operations (P.L. 111-32), the United States had not voted to accept the amendment. Approval by the United States in the legislation, with a 16.77% voting share, put the Fourth Amendment into effect.

SDRs and Inflation

Some Members of Congress have questioned whether the SDR increase will have an impact on global inflation.[14] The impact of the SDR allocation on global inflation is expected to be modest for several reasons. First, SDRs represent a small percentage of the amount of global foreign reserves. Currently, total SDRs allocated by the IMF are worth approximately $33.5 billion or 0.51% of total foreign exchange reserves of $6.5 trillion as of the first quarter of 2009.[15] An increase of SDRs worth $250 billion would increase the ratio of SDRs to total foreign reserves to 4.3% of total foreign reserves, still a relatively small percentage. The $250 billion increase in potential spending power would be almost indistinguishable compared to the size of the world economy or the value of world trade.

Second, the SDR increase is small compared to other injections of liquidity in the global economy taken by global central banks. Since the beginning of the crisis, the United States, European countries, China and others have injected or are injecting much more spending power into their economies than the IMF will be creating through this new allocation of SDRs. Stimulus measures for the G-20 countries are expected to total 2% of global GDP in 2009 and 1.5% of global GDP in 2010.[16] These measures are likely to have significantly greater inflationary impact than the SDR increase.

Third, the IMF 's SDR allocation is to be distributed proportionally among all the IMF member nations, thus muting any inflationary impact it might have. Furthermore, the impact of the global economic crisis on the output of goods and services is expected to linger for several years. However, any additional spending due to an immediate encashment of a country's SDR allocation would likely occur now, rather than in the future. (Otherwise, there would be no need to exchange their SDRs for hard currency.) It is expected that by the time the global economy fully recovers, any potential inflationary pressure from increased spending resulting from the encashment of SDRs will have subsided.

Fourth, since the $250 billion SDR increase is distributed according to countries' quotas, the majority of it will be allocated to advanced economies, which are unlikely to ever use their SDRs.[17] Advanced economies such as the United States, Japan, and the Eurozone countries will receive the majority of the SDRs.[18] These countries could buy and sell SDRs among themselves in order to get useable foreign exchange, but they can do this already—and much more easily— through central bank swaps and other such devices. Lastly, it is unlikely that the United States would sell its SDRs to emerging market countries, partly because it cannot use their currencies to settle obligations to third countries. Moreover, it is unlikely that developing countries willingly purchase U.S. SDRs, since their interest is in selling their SDRs for U.S. dollars and not acquiring additional SDRs.

Gold Sales

Another major component of President Obama's request was for congressional authorization for the Administration to vote in favor of selling 403 metric tons of IMF gold for the purpose of increasing the Fund's liquid reserves. Income earned on these reserves, in turn, would finance a portion of the IMF budget related to its provision of global public goods, such as economic and financial surveillance. The gold sales to benefit poor countries, announced by the G-20 leaders, would be included in this agreed total, as it is expected that the currently high price of gold may provide some additional income beyond what is expected for budget financing. However, any additional income would likely be modest since the current price of gold (around $946 per ounce) is not significantly different from the assumption on which the new income model was based ($850 per ounce). The IMF Articles of Agreement specify that any sale of IMF gold must receive an 85% affirmative vote by the member countries.

Under Article V, Sec. 12 of the IMF 's Articles of Agreement, approval of gold sales by the IMF requires an 85% IMF voting majority. The United States has almost a 16.77% vote and could thus block any sale of IMF gold. Understanding this "virtual" veto, Congress enacted legislation in 1999, in the FY 2000 Consolidated Appropriations Act, authorizing the United States to vote at the IMF in favor of a limited sale of IMF gold to fund the IMF 's participation in the multilateral Debt Relief Initiative for Heavily Indebted Poor Countries (HIPC).[19] The act amending section 5 of the Bretton Woods Agreements Act (22 U.S.C. 286c), requires the explicit consent of Congress before the executive branch can support future gold sales. However, the law provides that the United States may support the sale of IMF gold without congressional action if the Secretary of the Treasury certifies to Congress that the sale of gold is necessary for the Fund to restitute gold to its members, or to provide liquidity that will enable the Fund to meet member countries' claims on it or to meet threats to the systemic stability of the international financial system.[20]

IMF Quota and NAB Contributions

When the Obama Administration initially requested that Congress approve increasing U.S. contributions to the IMF by $108 billion following the April 2009 G-20 Summit, it did not request new appropriations to cover the cost of U.S. contributions to the IMF. This strategy contradicted the precedent used since 1980 for budgeting for U.S. contributions to the IMF (Appendix).

In 2009, there was concern that the procedural aspects of the budget process may have an impact on congressional consideration of the proposed new U.S. subscriptions to the IMF. The Obama Administration did not follow the immediate precedent and proposed to increase U.S. contributions to the IMF through only an authorization, with no corresponding appropriating legislation. Peter Orszag, director of the Office of Management and Budget (OMB), was quoted in April 2009 as saying that he cannot see "any analytical rationale for why something would score zero as an outlay but then score as something in budget authority."[21] Furthermore, the United States actually profited from its participation in the IMF. The Treasury Department is required by law to report to Congress quarterly the financial cost of U.S. participation in the IMF. The most recent report, current through 2007, was submitted in April 2009.[22] The Department reports that, in 2007, the United States earned a net $68 million from its participation in the SDR Department, and it earned a net $362 million from its transactions with the IMF General Department (which deals with quota accounts).

Nonetheless, some Members of Congress raised concerns that the exchange of assets approach, which led to no budgetary cost to the United States for its IMF contribution, did not correctly reflect the degree of risk of the IMF defaulting on the U.S. contribution, given the current economic turmoil. Supporters of the increased U.S. contribution were also concerned that reverting to the earlier budget procedures, rather than using the one employed since 1980, would be seen as an effort to change the rules in the face of controversy or a signal that the Obama Administration feared that it may not have the votes to approve the measure through the established process.

After several months of negotiations, on May 12, 2009, the White House and Congress reached an agreement to treat the U.S. subscription to the IMF as a line of credit for budgetary purposes, after which the President made the formal request to include authorization and appropriations for the IMF in the FY2010 defense supplemental request. Reminiscent of the method used for the 1966 quota increase, Congress was asked by the Administration to authorize the United States to extend a line of credit for the U.S. contributions to the IMF, which totals $108 billion. Unlike IMF quota increases since 1967, the U.S. contribution would be scored as a loan for budgetary purposes under the existing credit reform legislation with a commensurate budgetary impact.

The Federal Credit Reform Act of 1992 (P.L. 101-508) provides that when the U.S. Government makes a loan, it does not need to include the full face value of the loan in the federal budget. Rather, Congress must appropriate, as a potential loan loss reserve, an amount equal to the amount the U.S. Government might lose from these loans as a consequence of defaults. This procedure is used throughout the federal budgeting process.

CBO is responsible for determining what the prospective loan loss rate might be for any federal loan program. When there are several alternative calculations of the probability of loss, CBO typically uses an average of the possibilities as the figure used to estimate potential loss. This is what CBO did when it determined that the loan loss risk from these payments to the IMF was $5 billion.[23] In the law authorizing U.S. participation in the new IMF funding plans, the FY2009 Spring Supplemental Appropriations for Overseas Contingency Operations (P.L. 111-32), Congress subsequently appropriated $5 billion as a loan loss reserve to cover the risk associated with the new U.S. payments to the IMF.

Congress and Other IMF Issues, 2009

In 2009, Congress enacted two laws that contained provisions applicable to the IMF or to U.S. participation in the IMF. The first was the Supplemental Appropriations Act, 2009 (P.L. 111-32), which is discussed above. Signed into law on June 24, 2009, it included authorizations for U.S. participation in the new quota increase, the loan to the NAB, approval of amendments to the IMF Articles of Agreement and other matters. Some but not all of these were discussed above. The second was the Consolidated Appropriations Act, 2010 (P.L. 111-

117), which was signed into law on December 16, 2009. The IMF provisions in this law addressed some new topics and they also dealt with some issues concerning U.S. participation in the NAB and the allocation of SDRs that had not been settled the previous June.

Issues Relating to the NAB and SDR Allocation

There had been debate in Congress, during its consideration of the IMF legislation in early 2009, whether Congress should limit the time period during which the United States could participate in the NAB or whether there should be no such statutory limitations. Some Members of Congress wanted to sunset U.S. involvement in the newly expanded NAB by requiring that the $100 billion should be returned to the U.S. Treasury after five years. This effectively would make the NAB a five-year program, since other countries would likely withdraw then as well. Other Members believed that a formal limitation on the time period for U.S. participation would send the wrong signals to capital markets during the financial crisis. They also worried that, in five years, there might still be a need for a facility like the NAB and statutory sunset legislation could complicate future negotiations aimed at addressing that issue.

No sunset provision was included in the June legislation. Towards the end of the year, however, sentiment in Congress in favor of a sunset provision was much stronger and a new debate about the issue ensued. In December, Congress enacted conditional sunset legislation in section 7090(b) of P.L. 111-117 that authorized the Secretary of the Treasury to agree to an extension of the NAB after five years, provided that he certified to the appropriate congressional committees that certain conditions had been met. In the main, these conditions were consistent with the purposes for which the NAB was established and the principles on which it was supposed to operate.[24] Even if those conditions were not met, the law allowed the Secretary to continue U.S. participation in the NAB if he certified that it was in the strategic economic interest of the United States.

Many Members of Congress were also distressed that countries that supported international terrorism would be eligible to receive funds through the IMF as a result of the new $250 billion allocation of SDRs. Language had been included in the law adopted in June (Section 1404 of P.L. 111-32) directing the Secretary of the Treasury to instruct the U.S. executive directors at the IMF and all the multilateral development banks to oppose any loans or other assistance by those institutions to any country that the Secretary of the Treasury had determined had repeatedly provided support for acts of international terrorism.

In December, Congress enacted language that appeared on its face to be aimed at blocking terrorist countries from receiving SDRs from the new IMF allocation. This legislation (Section 7090a of P.L. 111-117) directed the Secretary to instruct the U.S. executive director at the IMF to oppose any provision of dollars, euros or Japanese yen to terrorist countries that wished to encash some of their new SDRs for foreign exchange. As a practical matter, this legislation will have little or no effect. The IMF board of governors had already approved the new $250 billion allocation of SDRs and its implementation—as specified in the IMF Articles of Agreement—is automatic. No subsequent action by the IMF board of executive directors is required for the allocation to proceed and no action by the IMF executive board would be sufficient to stop any country from getting SDRs through the allocation process or from using them. The Secretary of the Treasury may instruct the U.S. executive director to oppose such action but individual country allocations of SDRs will not be considered by the executive board. Also, opposition by the U.S. executive director cannot stop the IMF 's SDR department from implementing the new allocation arrangement once it has been approved by the IMF governors.

Some Members of Congress were also concerned that, even though the expansion plan for the NAB provided that the United States would provide only 20% of the new money, other countries might renege on their commitments. In that case, if the United States contributed the full $100 billion approved in June 2009, the U.S. share of the expanded NAB would exceed 20%. To address this concern, Congress approved Section 7090(c) of P.L. 111-117, specifying that the U.S. share of the new NAB money must not exceed 20%. Subsequently, enough countries subscribed their shares in the NAB or otherwise agreed to provide new funding, so that the original $500 billion goal was met or exceeded and the U.S. share did not exceed that limit.

The same section of the law also required the Secretary of the Treasury to report to the House and Senate Appropriations Committees within 60 days of enactment and annually thereafter indicating what countries had received assistance through use of the NAB. The report must also include information about the economic policies of those countries, a description of the reform policies those countries were required to adopt, a detailed summary of their trade policies (including any unfair trade practices that adversely affected the United States), and the amounts, disbursement and repayment schedules, and interest rates for all NAB loans.

Other IMF Issues

Congress also took the opportunity, in the IMF portions of the legislation it adopted in June and December 2009, to address several other matters concerning the IMF that did not relate to the quota increase, amendments to the Articles of Agreement, or other funding concerns.

Section 1403(a) of the Supplemental Appropriations Act, 2009 (P.L. 111-32), adopted in June, requires the Secretary of the Treasury to submit a report to the appropriate congressional committees within 30 days of enactment, showing the steps being taken to coordinate the activities of the World Bank and IMF in order to avoid duplication of activities. The Secretary is also required to discuss in this chapter steps that the Treasury Department and IMF have taken to increase the oversight and accountability of the fund's activities.

Section 1403(c) of the same Act requires the Secretary to include, in his next semi-annual report to Congress on international and exchange rate policies, a discussion of ways the IMF's surveillance of country exchange rates under Article IV of its charter could be enhanced and made more effective for avoiding currency manipulation. The report must also discuss steps the Fund can take to promote global financial stability and to conduct effective multilateral surveillance.

Additionally, the report must assess the feasibility and usefulness of publishing the Fund's own internal calculations of indicative exchange rates for the currencies of individual countries. These are the IMF's calculations as to what the approximate "correct" exchange rates might be if market distortions and manipulation were eliminated from the equation. Without calculations of this sort, the IMF staff would have a difficult time discussing effectively with country officials whether their national currency is over-valued or under-valued. The IMF's publication of these numbers might put pressure on countries to revalue their currencies. On the other hand, it would put the IMF in the awkward position of asserting that it knows what the "correct" value of a currency might be, without any way of requiring countries to put the IMF-calculated exchange rate into effect.

Section 1403(d) of the June legislation requires the Secretary to direct the U.S. executive director at IMF to oppose any loan, assistance, agreement or plan of the Fund relating to a Heavily Indebted Poor Country (HIPC) if it would not allow the country's government to maintain or increase its spending for health care, education, food aid, or other safety net programs. Critics of the IMF have been concerned for years that, when the IMF mandates budget cuts as a condition for one of its stabilization loans, expenditures for health, education and services for the needy are often the first to go. The IMF has been seeking to address these concerns in recent years. The new legislation would have the United States push for more progress on these concerns.

Later in 2009, Congress adopted addition legislation affecting U.S. participation in the IMF and other multilateral institutions. In Section 7086(b) of P.L. 111-117, Congress directed the Secretary of the Treasury to instruct the U.S. executive director at the IMF to promote greater transparency in public access to IMF documents and minutes of executive board meetings. The IMF's Independent Evaluation Office had recently recommended adoption of such transparency procedures.

Congress also directed the Secretary to instruct the U.S. executive director at the Fund to promote greater transparency and accountability of the policy making and budgetary procedures of IMF member country governments, greater participation by citizens and non-governmental organizations (NGOs) in the economic policy decisions of those governments, and the adoption of IMF loan agreements and programs by the borrower country's legislature or by other participatory and transparent procedures rather than by administrative fiat by the borrower country government.

In the same section of P.L. 111-117, Congress required the Secretary to instruct the U.S. executive director at the IMF to promote policies and practices that would reduce the worst forms of child labor in IMF member countries. The Secretary was also required to report to the appropriate authorization and appropriation committees of Congress, within one year, on the efforts being made by the IMF to reduce the worst forms of child labor. A similar requirement was not levied on the U.S. executive directors at the multilateral development banks.

Congress also provided, in Section 7086(d) of the Act, that 10% of the money being appropriated in that legislation for contribution to the Asian Development Fund (AsDF) would be withheld until the Secretary of the Treasury reports the appropriations committees that the Asian Development Bank (ADB) had implemented an independent review and strengthened its internal and external controls and other potentially vulnerable safeguards against corruption. The Secretary must also report whether the ADB has resolved to seek restitution, including criminal prosecution if appropriate, in cases where the Bank experiences losses from fraud or corruption.

APPENDIX. PAST BUDGETARY TREATMENT OF U.S. CONTRIBUTIONS

In the past 60 years, Congress has handled the bookkeeping aspects for U.S. participation in the IMF in a variety of ways. This system was the result of a compromise among the leading figures on the relevant congressional committees in 1980.

Payments to the IMF were considered to be an exchange of assets because the United States receives back from the IMF a monetary instrument of equal value which it adds to its foreign exchange reserves. The United States receives an increased holding of SDRs in the Fund's SDR Department whenever it purchases SDRs from another country, and an increased reserve tranche position whenever the IMF draws on the U.S. quota to finance loans to borrower countries. Both the SDR and reserve tranche positions are liquid interest bearing assets. SDRs cannot be used to make purchases in the marketplace, but they can be exchanged with other IMF members for currencies or used to satisfy international obligations which in most cases involve the Fund. In the case of loans through the NAB, the United States receives a promissory note from the IMF pledging to repay the loan with interest at a certain time. Credits provided to the IMF through the NAB are considered to be monetary assets and are included in countries' foreign exchange reserves. The proceeds are considered to be readily available because NAB participants can obtain immediate early repayment from the IMF if they have a balance of payments need.

The United States has used various methods over the years to account for the cost of its participation in the IMF. Before 1967, the United States funded its participation in the IMF through a variety of procedures, including public debt transactions and payments from the Exchange Stabilization Fund. In the 1966 quota increase, the U.S. payment took the form of a letter of credit to the IMF which, for technical reasons, the United States mostly borrowed back during the following years.

In 1967, the U.S. Government adopted a unified federal budget that consolidated the operating budget of the government with other previously off-budget accounts. This was intended to improve clarity and to enhance the government's management of fiscal policy. In the process, the President's Commission on Budget Concepts (PCBC) also examined the procedures by which the United States managed its payments to the IMF. It recommended that payments to the IMF should be treated as monetary exchanges akin to bank withdrawals and deposits rather than as international lending operations. As such, these payments would be handled as an exchange of assets and would be excluded from budget receipts and expenditures. Congress would be asked to authorize new U.S. payments to the IMF, but the cost of those payments would not be included in the federal budget.

The new budget concept was not fully implemented when the next quota increase was considered by Congress. In addition to legislation authorizing U.S. participation, the Nixon Administration sought and Congress approved appropriations to effect U.S. participation in the plan. They agreed, however, that the exchange of assets concept was sufficient to cover the resulting payments, and they would have no net outlay impact on the U.S. budget.[25] In 1976, when the following quota increase was considered, the Ford Administration proposed and Congress agreed that the transaction would be treated solely as an exchange of assets. Legislation was enacted authorizing U.S. participation in the plan, but no appropriations were required. The same procedure was used the following year to approve a loan by the United States to the IMF 's Supplemental Financing Facility ("Witteveen Facility").[26] CBO found, in a study of the budgetary scorekeeping issue in 1978, that any procedure—appropriated, exchanged, on-budget, offbudget—is intrinsically arbitrary and not consistent with similar or comparable programs that are treated differently from a scorekeeping perspective elsewhere in the U.S. budget process.[27]

Many Members of Congress, reportedly, were not happy with this arrangement. Some argued, citing the provision of the U.S. Constitution which says that no money shall be drawn from the Treasury except through an appropriation by law, that the funding for U.S. participation in the IMF must be appropriated. Some also said that treating the U.S. payments to the IMF as an off- budget transaction was inconsistent with the principle of budgetary unity which underlay the work of the Presidential budget commission in 1967 and a violation of the prohibition against "backdoor spending" in the Congressional Budget Act of 1974.

The issue came to a head in 1980 during congressional consideration of legislation to approve U.S. participation in a new quota increase for the IMF. A compromise was ultimately agreed to. Under this arrangement, the full amount of the U.S. subscription to the IMF would be appropriated as budget authority.[28] This gave Congress control over the size of the U.S. payments and the amount of contingent liability the United States undertook through its participation in the IMF. However, consistent with the exchange of assets concept, no outlays would be counted and the payments to the IMF would be deemed to have no net impact on the U.S. budget. This procedure remains in effect to this day.

Congress has taken a different approach in its budgetary treatment of the contingent liability associated with U.S. participation in the multilateral development banks (MDBs). The MDBs fund their market-rate loan programs with money borrowed in commercial markets. Because they are backed by substantial reserves and by the callable capital subscriptions of their member countries, the banks can sell their bonds and notes at favorable interest rates, and they pass these relatively low rates on to their borrower countries. MDB member countries subscribe some of their purchases of capital stock in callable capital and some (a fixed ratio, now a very small percent of the cost for each share) in paid-in capital. Callable capital is a type of full faith and credit guarantee to the banks' bondholders from their member countries. Most analysts believe that it is very unlikely that one of the MDBs would go bankrupt, exhausting all its resources, and needing to call on the callable capital of its members in order to satisfy its creditors.

Before 1982, Congress appropriated the full amount necessary for the callable portion of U.S. subscriptions to capital stock in the multilateral development banks (MDB). About $12 billion for callable capital had been appropriated by that time, roughly $8 billion for the World Bank and $4 billion for the regional development banks. No outlays were associated with this budget authority and it had no impact on the budget or the budget deficit. During the 1970s, however, cuts were adopted reducing the appropriations for MDB callable capital. The proponents of these cuts often claimed that they were saving the taxpayers and reducing the budget deficit by hundreds of millions of dollars. The cuts in callable capital were not program oriented, since the full paid-in portion of the subscriptions for MDB capital stock was generally appropriated. The resulting mismatch in appropriations had a negative effect on U.S. participation in the banks.

Consequently, in 1981, Congress decided that funds would no longer need to be appropriated for new U.S. subscriptions to callable capital. Instead, as is now the current arrangement, the size of the annual U.S. subscription is regulated through program limitations in appropriations acts.[29] No formal appropriations are required, though appropriations would be required if there ever were to be a call on callable capital. In the case of the IMF, neither the Balanced Budget Act of 1977 nor Sec. 17 of the BWAA require that budget authority must be appropriated to facilitate future increases in the U.S. quota in the IMF or future loans to the IMF through the NAB. The law is silent as to the budgetary procedures that Congress should use on such occasions.

The procedures are different for the IMF and the multilateral banks, but the budgeting issue in both situations is essentially the same. Should the outlay effect of the U.S. commitment to these institutions be counted as zero or is there a likelihood that the IMF will not pay the United States back or a possibility that a call might be made on callable capital? Congress has used a variety of mechanisms to effect the U.S. payments to international financial institutions—in some cases appropriating the full amount in budget authority, in other cases setting a program limitation on new liability, and in other cases treating the entire transaction as an off-budget exchange of assets. None of these arrangements seems to be superior to the others, either in terms of maintaining congressional control or in reflecting or controlling the liabilities that the United States faces through its participation in international financial programs.

In 2004, CBO Director Douglas Holtz-Eakin told the Senate Banking Committee that, "The current budgetary treatment does not fully reflect the U.S. share of the credit risk associated with the lending and other transactions of the international financial institutions." He had no recommendations for change, however. He said that CBO hoped to discuss these issues further in a future paper.[30] For various reasons, that study was never completed and no paper was released. It may be difficult, in the present moment, for Congress to determine what the "right" budgeting procedure might be in this situation. Over the longer term, however, Congress may want to consider whether an analysis of these budgetary issues might be desirable and whether some changes in the scorekeeping system for international financial institutions might be appropriate.

End Notes

[1] For background on the IMF, see: "Financial Organization and Operations of the IMF," *International Monetary Fund*, 2001. The document is available at: http://www.imf.org/external/pubs/ft/pam/pam45/contents.htm.

[2] "Global plan for recovery and reform: the Communiqué from the London Summit," April 2, 2009. The communiqué is available at: http://www.londonsummit.gov.uk/en/summit-aims/summit-communique/.

[3] They include: Japan - $100 billion; European Union - $100 billion; Norway - $4.5 billion; Canada - $10 billion; Switzerland - $10 billion; Korea - at least $10 billion; Australia - $7 billion; Russia - up to $10 billion; China - up to $50 billion, and Brazil - up to $10 billion. "Bolstering the IMF's Lending Capacity," *International Monetary Fund*, July 8, 2009. Webpage is available at: http://www.imf.org/external/np /exr/faq/contribution.htm.

[4] Edwin M. Truman, "On What Terms is the IMF Worth Funding," *Peterson Institute for International Economics*, December 2008. The working paper is available at: http://www.piie.com/publications/wp/wp08-11.pdf.

[5] CRS Report RL34742, The Global Financial Crisis: Analysis and Policy Implications, coordinated by Dick K. Nanto.

[6] "A Changing IMF—Responding to the Crisis," *International Monetary Fund*, July 2009. Factsheet is available at: http://www.imf.org/external/np/exr/facts/changing.htm.

[7] Total IMF Credit Outstanding for all members from 1984-2008, available at: http://www.imf.org/external/ np/fin/tad/ extcred1.aspx.

[8] An earlier facility, the General Arrangement to Borrow, was created for a similar purpose in 1962.

[9] They include: Japan - $100 billion; European Union - $100 billion; Norway - $4.5 billion; Canada - $10 billion; Switzerland - $10 billion; Korea - at least $10 billion; Australia - $7 billion; Russia - up to $10 billion; China - up to $50 billion, and Brazil - up to $10 billion. "Bolstering the IMF's Lending Capacity," *International*

Monetary Fund, July 8, 2009. Webpage is available at: http://www.imf.org/external/np/exr/faq/contribution.htm.

[10] The currency value of the SDR is determined by summing the values in U.S. dollars, based on market exchange rates, of a basket of major currencies (the U.S. dollar, euro, Japanese yen, and pound sterling). The SDR currency value is calculated daily and the valuation basket is reviewed and adjusted every five years. For example, on August 4, 2009, $1.00 equaled SDR 0.637. "Exchange Rate Archives by Month," *International Monetary Fund,* accessed August 5, 2009. The Webpage is located at: http://www.imf.org/external/np/fin/data/param_rms_mth.aspx.

[11] For background, see: CRS Report RL33626, *International Monetary Fund: Reforming Country Representation,* by Martin A. Weiss.

[12] "IMF Approves Framework for Issuing Notes to the Official Sector," *International Monetary Fund,* July 1, 2009. Press Release is available at: http://www.imf.org/external/np/sec/pr/2009/pr09248.htm.

[13] Ibid.

[14] There is an active and ongoing debate among economists over what causes inflation that is beyond the scope of this chapter. The assertion that an increase in SDRs will lead to inflation derives from one school of thought, *monetarism,* which posits a strong link between an increase in the global money supply (such as an increase in the total amount of SDRs, which count toward a country's foreign reserve levels) and the level of prices. For more information, see: CRS Report RL3 0344, *Inflation: Causes, Costs, and Current Status,* by Marc Labonte.

[15] "Currency Composition of Official Foreign Exchange Reserves (COFER)" *International Monetary Fund,* June 30, 2009. Available at: http://www.imf.org/external/np/sta/cofer/eng/cofer.pdf.

[16] World Economic Outlook: Crisis and Recovery, *International Monetary Fund,* April, 2009. Available at: http://www.imf.org/external/pubs/ft/weo/2009/01/pdf/text.pdf.

[17] While this may beg the question why the SDR increase is necessary in the first place, for emerging and least-developed countries, the SDR allocation will provide a significant increase in their foreign reserves, may help remove immediate funding pressures, and may help prevent extensive foreign reserve accumulation, which contributed to global imbalances over the past several years. "Allocation of Special Drawing Rights for the Ninth Basic Period: Draft Executive Board Decision and Managing Director Report to the Board of Governors," *International Monetary Fund,* July 16, 2009. The Decision and Report are available at: http://www.imf.org/external/np/pp/eng/2009/071609.pdf.

[18] The *Eurozone,* or *Euro Area,* consists of the European Union member state that have adopted the Euro is their currency. To date, 16 countries have adopted the Euro as their sole legal tender: Austria, Belgium, Cyprus, Finland, France, Germany, Greece, Ireland, Italy, Luxembourg, Malta, the Netherlands, Portugal, Slovakia, Slovenia and Spain.

[19] CRS Report RL34644, *Debt Relief for Poor Countries,* by Jonathan E. Sanford and Martin A. Weiss.

[20] P.L. 106-113, Consolidated Appropriations Act, 2000, Sec. 504(d).

[21] David Rogers, "How to spend without 'spending,'" *Politico,* April 22, 2009. The article is available at: http://dyn.politico.com/printstory.cfm?uuid=D05A3346-18FE-70B2-A8BC4C0B6AC3D747.

[22] [Department of the Treasury.] *Report to Congress on Financial Implications of U.S. Participation in the International Monetary Fund.* Available at: http://www.ustreas.gov/press/releases/reports/imfreportq1q42007.pdf.

[23] "Budget Implications of U.S. Contributions to the International Monetary Fund," *Congressional Budget Office Director's Blog,* May 19, 2009, from http://cboblog.cbo.gov/?p=270.

[24] The Secretary needed to certify that (a) no changes had been made in the NAB agreement that would extend its current term beyond five years or would prevent the United States from withdrawing after five years if it so chose; (b) the IMF would borrow resources from the NAB only when it needed extra resources to deal with an impairment of the international monetary system or an exceptional situation that posed a threat to the stability of the system; and (c) that the IMF has fully explored other means of supplementing its resources before it draws on NAB resources. The NAB agreement approved by the G-20 already included these provisions or requirements.

[25] P.L. 91-599 and P.L. 91-619, enacted in December 1970, added Sec. 22 to the BWAA and appropriated necessary funds. The Administration had requested that funds for the quota increase be both authorized and appropriated. U.S. Bureau of the Budget. *The Budget of the United States Government, Fiscal Year 1971,* Appendix, p. 105.

[26] P.L. 94-564, enacted in October 1976, added Sec. 25 to the BWAA, saying that "the U.S. Governor of the Bank (*sic*) is authorized to consent to an increase in the quota of the United States in the Fund equivalent to 1,705 million Special Drawing Rights." The next year, P.L. 95-435, enacted in October 1977, added Sec. 28 to the BWAA, saying that "The Secretary of the Treasury is authorized to make resources available as provided in decision 5509-(77/127) of the Fund, in amounts not to exceed the equivalent of 1,450 million Special Drawing Rights." In neither case were appropriations required. See also Treasury Secretary William E. Simon's paper, "The Exchange of Assets Concept," reprinted in U.S. Congress. Committee on Banking, Currency and Housing. Subcommittee on International Trade, Investment and Monetary Policy. *Hearings on H.R. 13955, June 1 and 3, 1976.* USGPO, 1976, p. 31.

[27] Congressional Budget Office. *U.S. Participation in the Witteveen Facility: The Need for a New Source of International Finance*. March 1978. This paper is available at http://www.cbo.gov/ftpdocs/67xx/doc6727/78-CBO027.pdf.

[28] P.L. 96-389, enacted in October 1980, added Sec. 32 to the BWAA. This says the Secretary of the Treasury "is authorized to consent to an increase in the quota of the United States in the Fund equivalent to 4,202.5 million Special Drawing Rights, limited to such amounts as are appropriated in advance in appropriation Acts." Congress substituted the latter language for the original text, which approved participation in the quota increase "to such extent or in such amounts [as] are provided in appropriation Acts." The latter language would have required action by the appropriations committees but would not have required formal appropriations to effect the U.S. increase in the IMF.

[29] P.L. 97-35, enacted August 1981, adding Sec. 39 to the Bretton Woods Agreement Act. This authorized U.S. participation in a new capital increase for the World Bank, providing that 'any subscription to such additional shares shall be effective only to such extent or in such amounts as are provided in advance in appropriations acts." This is the same language Congress had chosen not to enact the previous year in connection with U.S. payments to the IMF.

[30] Statement of Douglas Holtz-Eakin, Director. Congressional Budget Office. *The Costs and Budgetary Treatment of Multilateral Financial Institutions' Activity*. Testimony before the Senate Committee on Banking, Housing and Urban Affairs, May 19, 2004. A copy of this testimony is available at http://www.cbo.gov/ftpdocs/54xx/doc5458/05-19- MFIs.pdf. CBO's last scored IMF legislation in 1998 when it considered H.R. 3114, the International Monetary Fund Reform and Authorization Act of 1998, a bill that was reported by committee but not considered by the House. A copy of the CBO cost estimate is available http://www.cbo.gov/ftpdocs/3xx/doc385/H.R.3114.pdf.

In: The International Monetary Fund (IMF) Financial Crisis and... ISBN: 978-1-61728-499-1
Editor: Rachel E. Layton

Chapter 2

THE GLOBAL FINANCIAL CRISIS: THE ROLE OF THE INTERNATIONAL MONETARY FUND (IMF)

Martin A. Weiss

SUMMARY

This chapter discusses two potential roles the International Monetary Fund (IMF) may have in helping to resolve the current global financial crisis: (1) immediate crisis control through balance of payments lending to emerging market and less-developed countries and (2) increased surveillance of the global economy through better coordination with the international financial regulatory agencies.

The current global financial crisis, which began with the downturn of the U.S. subprime housing market in 2007, is testing the ability of the International Monetary Fund (IMF), in its role as the central international institution for oversight of the global monetary system. Though the IMF is unlikely to lend to the developed countries most affected by the crisis and must compete with other international financial institutions[1] as a source of ideas and global macroeconomic policy coordination, the spillover effects of the crisis on emerging and less-developed economies gives the IMF an opportunity to reassert its role in the international economy on two key dimensions of the global financial crisis: (1) immediate crisis management and (2) long-term systemic reform of the international financial system.

The role of the IMF has changed significantly since its founding in July 1944. Late in World War II, delegates from 44 nations gathered in Bretton Woods, New Hampshire to discuss the postwar recovery of Europe and create a set of international institutions to resolve many of the economic issues—such as protectionist trade policies and unstable exchange rates—that had ravaged the international economy between the two world wars. As the global financial system has evolved over the decades, so has the IMF. From 1946 to 1973, the main purpose of the IMF was to manage the fixed system of international exchange rates agreed on at Bretton Woods. The U.S. dollar was fixed to gold at $35 per ounce and all other member countries' currencies were fixed to the dollar at different rates. The IMF monitored the macroeconomic and exchange rate policies of member countries and helped countries overcome balance of payments crises with short-term loans that helped bring currencies back in line with their determined value. This system came to an abrupt end in 1973 when the United States floated its currency and subsequently introduced the modern system of floating exchange rates. Over the past three decades, floating exchange rates and financial globalization have contributed to, in addition to substantial wealth and high levels of growth for many countries, an international economy marred by exchange rate volatility and semi-frequent financial crises. The IMF adapted to the end of the fixed-exchange rate system by becoming the lender of last resort for countries afflicted by such crises.

Current IMF operations and responsibilities can be grouped into three areas: surveillance, lending, and technical assistance. Surveillance involves monitoring economic and financial developments and providing policy advice to member countries. Lending entails the provision of financial resources under specified conditions to assist a country experiencing balance of payments difficulties. Technical assistance includes help on designing or improving the quality and effectiveness of domestic policy-making.

WHITHER THE IMF?

The current financial crisis represents a major challenge for the IMF since the institution is not in financial position to be able to lend to the United States or other Western countries affected by the crisis (with the possible exception of Iceland). The IMF's total financial resources as of August 2008 were $352 billion, of which $257 billion were usable resources.[2] The most the IMF ever lent in any one year period (the four quarters through September 1998 at the height of the Asian financial crisis) was $30 billion. The most lent during any two-year period was $40 billion between June 2001-2003 during the financial crises in Argentina, Brazil, Uruguay, and Turkey.[3] The IMF is wholly unequipped to provide by itself the necessary liquidity to the United States and affected industrialized countries. In addition, the United States and other Western countries, along with some Middle Eastern oil states, are the primary contributors to IMF resources, and it is unlikely that these countries would seek IMF assistance. The last time that developed countries borrowed from the IMF was between1976 and1978, when the United Kingdom, Italy, and Spain borrowed from the IMF to deal with the aftershocks of the 1973 increase in oil prices.[4]

Since the financial crises of a decade ago, many emerging market economies, largely in response to their criticism of the policy conditions that the IMF required of countries receiving IMF loans, have built up extensive foreign reserve positions in order to avoid having to return to the IMF should such a crisis occur again.[5] From a level of around $1.2 trillion in 1995, global foreign exchange reserves now exceed $7 trillion. The IMF tabulates that by the second quarter of 2008, developing countries' foreign reserves were $5.47 trillion compared to $1.43 trillion in the industrialized countries.[6] This reserve accumulation was driven by increasing commodity prices (such as oil and minerals) and large current account surpluses combined with high savings rates in emerging Asian countries.[7]

Emerging market foreign reserve accumulation fueled by rising commodity prices and large emerging market trade surpluses, and net foreign direct investment flows has led to a decrease in demand for IMF lending and a weakening in the IMF's budget position. IMF lending peaked in 2003 with IMF credit outstanding totaling $110.29 billion. By September

30, 2008, outstanding IMF loans had decreased by $92.6 billion to $17.72 billion (see also Figure 1).[8]

Since the IMF earns income on the interest paid on its loans, the decrease in demand for IMF's lending led to a budget shortfall in 2007. The IMF is in the process of seeking authorization from national legislatures to sell a portion of gold that the IMF holds in reserve to create an investment fund whose profits can be used to finance IMF operations and delink IMF operations (such as its global surveillance programs) from profit earned on IMF lending. Congress is expected to face a vote in FY2009 on whether or not to authorize this proposal.

The rise of emerging market countries over the past decade, has created new challenges for the IMF. Many emerging market economies argue that their current stake in the IMF does not represent their role in the world economy. Several countries, particularly in East Asia and South America, believe that their new economic weight and status should afford them a larger quota and a greater voice at the institution. In addition, many poor countries believe that the IMF's quota system is prejudiced against them, giving them little voice even though they are the majority of the IMF's borrowers. In response to these concerns, the IMF embarked in 2006 on a reform process to increase the quota and voice of its emerging market country members.[9]

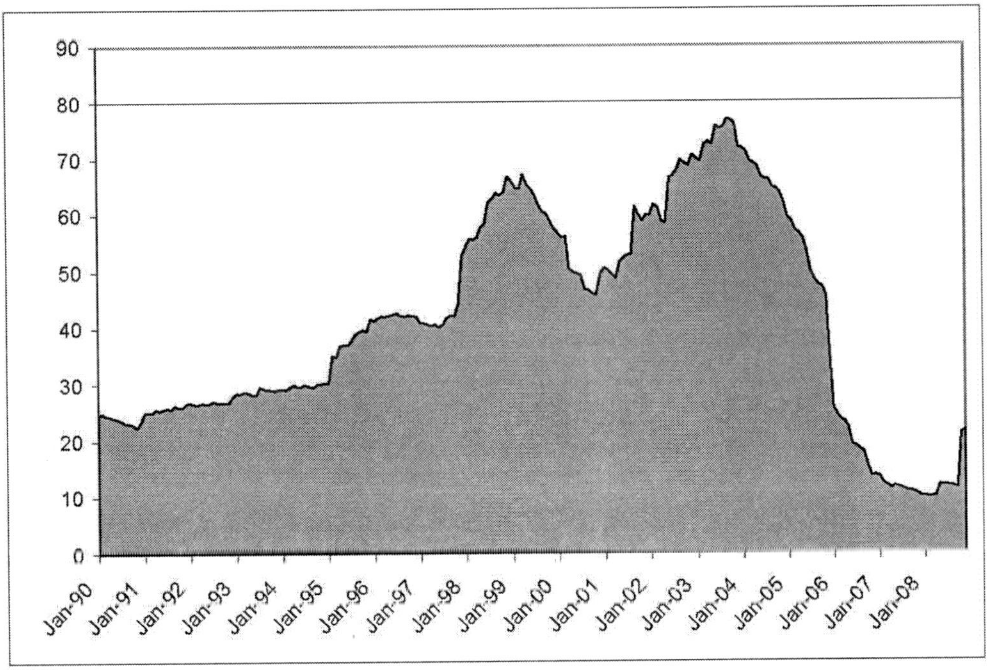

Source: International Monetary Fund

Notes: The Special Drawing Right (SDR) is an international reserve asset, created by the IMF in 1969. SDRs are allocated to member countries in proportion to their IMF quotas. The SDR also serves as the unit of account of the IMF and some other international organizations. Its value is based on a basket of key international currencies (the U.S. dollar, Euro, Japanese yen, and pound sterling). The SDR currency value is calculated daily and the; valuation basket is reviewed and adjusted every five years.

Figure 1. Outstanding IMF Credit (1990-2008, SDR)

While the IMF has struggled to define its role in the global economy, the global financial crisis has created an opportunity for the IMF to reinvigorate itself and possibly play a constructive role in resolving, or at the least mitigating, the effects of the global downturn, on two fronts: (1) through immediate crisis management, primarily balance of payments support to emerging-market and less-developed countries, and (2) contributing to long-term systemic reform of the international financial system.

Immediate Crisis Management

IMF rules stipulate that countries are allowed to borrow up to three times their quota over a three-year period, although this requirement has been breached on several occasions where the IMF has lent at much higher multiples of quota.[10] While many emerging market countries, such as Brazil, India, Indonesia, and Mexico, have stronger macroeconomic fundamentals than they did a decade ago, a sustained decrease in U.S. imports resulting from an economic slowdown could have recessionary effects overseas. Emerging markets with less robust financial structures have been more dramatically affected, especially those dependent on exports to the United States. Increased emerging market default risk can be seen in the dramatic rise of credit default swap (CDS) prices for emerging market sovereign bonds. Financial markets are currently pricing the risk that Pakistan, Argentina, Ukraine, and Iceland will default on their sovereign debt at above 80%.[11] On October 26, the IMF announced a $16.5 billion agreement with Ukraine. On October 27, the IMF announced a $15.7 billion loan to Hungary. On November 19, the IMF announced a $2.1 billion loan to Iceland. On November 24, the IMF announced a $7.6 billion loan to Pakistan.[12] On December 23, 2008, the IMF announced a $2.35 billion dollar loan for Latvia. Other potential candidates for IMF loans are Serbia, Kazakhstan, Lithuania, and Estonia.[13]

IMF Managing Director Dominique Strauss-Kahn has stressed that the IMF is able and poised to assist with crisis loans. At the IMF annual meetings in October 2008, Managing Director Strauss-Kahn announced that the IMF had activated its Emergency Financing Mechanism (EFM) to speed the normal process for loans to crisis-afflicted countries.[14] The emergency mechanism enables rapid approval (usually within 48-72 hours) of IMF lending once an agreement has been reached between the IMF and the national government. As noted before, while normal IMF rules are that countries can only borrow three times the size of their respective quotas over three years, the Fund has shown the willingness in the past to lend higher amounts should the crisis require extraordinary amounts of assistance.

A second instrument that the IMF could use to provide financial assistance is its Exogenous Shock Facility (ESF). The ESF provides policy support and financial assistance to low-income countries facing *exogenous shocks*, events that are completely out of the national government's control. These could include commodity price changes (including oil and food), natural disasters, and conflicts and crises in neighboring countries that disrupt trade. The ESF was modified in 2008 to further increase the speed and flexibility of the IMF's response. Through the ESF, a country can immediately access up to 25 % of its quota for each exogenous shock and an additional 75% of quota in phased disbursements over one to two years.

On October 29, 2008, the IMF announced that it plans on creating a new three month short-term lending facility aimed at middle income countries such as Mexico, South Korea, and Brazil. The IMF plans to set aside $100 billion for the new Short-Term Liquidity Facility (SLF). In a unprecedented departure from other IMF programs, SLF loans will have no policy conditionality.[15] Under the SLF, countries with track records of sound policies, access to capital markets and sustainable debt burden can draw up to five times their IMF quota for three months and up to two additional three-month periods. To date, no country has drawn on the SLF. For many middle-income countries this is likely due to the associated stigma of accepting IMF assistance. Concerns have also been raised that by creating a new lending mechanism the IMF is dividing potential borrowers into those that qualify for the SLF and those that would be forced to accept regular IMF lending with its associated policy conditionality.[16] To counter this stigma, some analysts have proposed coordinating an SLF package for several countries at the same time. Another option may be to coordinate an SLF loan with the newly created Federal Reserve swap arrangements for developing countries. On the same day that the IMF announced the SLF, the U.S. Federal Reserve approved $30 billion in reciprocal swap arrangements with four emerging-market countries: Brazil, Korea, Mexico, and Singapore.

At the 2009 Davos World Economic Forum, John Lipsky, the IMF's First Deputy Managing Director, said that to be able to effectively lend to all the potential countries affected by the crisis, the IMF should double its lending resources to around $500 billion.[17] In addition to potential resources freed up by the sale of IMF gold reserves, two additional financing options for the IMF are seeking additional capital from its member countries and selling bonds. The government of Japan has agreed to lend the IMF $100 billion dollars and it is reported that the agreement is almost finalized.[18] According to Mr. Lipsky, the Japanese loan would be structured in a way that is similar to two IMF programs: the General Arrangements to Borrow (GAB) and the New Arrangements to Borrow (NAB), which provide up to $50 billion in additional funding if the IMF were to exceed that amount available in its core resources. The second option would be for the IMF to issue bonds, which it has never done in its 60 year history. According to Mr. Lipsky, the IMF bonds would be sold to central banks and government agencies. According to economist and former IMF chief economist Michael Mussa, the United States and Europe blocked attempts by the IMF to issue bonds since it could potentially make the IMF less dependent on them for financial resources and thus less willing to take policy direction from them.[19] However, several other multilateral institutions such as the World Bank and the regional development banks routinely issue bonds to help finance their lending.

The IMF is not alone in making available financial assistance to crisis-afflicted countries. The International Finance Corporation (IFC), the private-sector lending arm of the World Bank, has announced that it will launch a $3 billion fund to capitalize small banks in poor countries that are battered by the financial crisis. The Inter-American Development Bank (IDB) announced on October 10, 2008 that it will offer a new $6 billion credit line to member governments, as well as increase its more traditional lending for specific projects.[20] In addition to the IDB, the Andean Development Corporation (CAF) announced a liquidity facility of $1.5 billion and the Latin American Fund of Reserves (FLAR) has offered to make available $4.5 billion in contingency lines. While these amounts may be insufficient should Brazil, Argentina, or any other large Latin American country need a rescue package, they could be very helpful for smaller countries such as those in the Caribbean and Central America that are heavily dependent on tourism and property investments.[21]

In Asia, where countries were left no choice but to accept IMF rescue packages a decade ago, efforts are under way to promote regional financial cooperation, so that governments can avoid having to borrow from the IMF in a financial crisis. One result of these efforts is the Chiang Mai Initiative, a network of bilateral swap arrangements among east and Southeast Asian countries. In addition, Japan, South Korea, and China have backed the creation of a $10 billion crisis fund. Contributions are expected from bilateral donors, the Asian Development Bank (ADB), and the World Bank.[22]

Lastly, economic conditions over the past decade have created a new class of bilateral creditors who could challenge the IMF's role as the lender of last resort. The rise of oil prices has created vast wealth among Middle Eastern countries and persistent trade surpluses in Asia have created a new class of emerging creditors. These countries either have the foreign reserves to support their own currencies in a financial crisis, or they are a potential source of loans for other countries.

Reforming Global Macroeconomic Surveillance

In addition to revising its emergency lending assistance guidelines to make the IMF's financial assistance more attractive to potential borrowers, there is a role for the IMF to play in the broader reform of the global financial system. Efforts are underway to expand the IMF's ability to conduct effective multilateral surveillance of the international economy. In addition, there are efforts to increase cooperation with the international financial standard setters as the Financial Stability Forum (FSF), the Bank for International Settlements (BIS), as well as in various international working groups such as the Basel Committee on Banking Supervision and the Joint Forum on Risk Assessment and Capital. The deepening interconnectedness of the international economy may call for such increased cooperation between the IMF, which performs global macroeconomic surveillance, and the individual global financial regulatory bodies.

The IMF Articles of Agreement require (Article IV) that the IMF "oversee the international monetary system in order to ensure its effective operation" and to "oversee the compliance of each member with its obligations" to the Fund. In particular, "the Fund shall exercise firm surveillance over the exchange rate policies of member countries and shall adopt specific principles for the guidance of all members with respect to those policies." Countries are required to provide the IMF with information and to consult with the IMF upon its request. The IMF staff generally meets each year with each member country for "Article IV consultations" regarding the country's current fiscal and monetary policies, the state of its economy, its exchange rate situation, and other relevant concerns. The IMF's reports on its annual Article IV consultations with each country are presented to the IMF executive board along with the staff's observations and recommendations about possible improvements in the country's economic policies and practices.

As the global financial system has become increasingly interconnected, the IMF has conducted multilateral surveillance beyond two bi-annual reports it produces, the *World Economic Outlook* and the *Global Financial Stability Report,* four regional reports, and regular IMF contributions to intergovernmental fora and committees, including the Group of Seven and Group of Twenty, and the Financial Stability Forum. These efforts at multilateral surveillance, however, have been criticized as being less than fully effective, too focused on bilateral issues, and not fully accounting for the risks of contagion that have been seen in the current crisis. A 2006 report by the IMF's internal watchdog agency, the Independent Evaluation Office (IEO) found that, "multilateral surveillance has not sufficiently explored options to deal with policy spillovers in a global context; the language of multilateral advice is no more based on explicit consideration of economic linkages and policy spillovers than that of bilateral advice."[23] Participants at an October 2008 IMF panel on the future of the IMF reiterated these concerns, adding that many developed countries have impeded the IMF's efforts at multilateral surveillance by largely ignoring IMF's bilateral surveillance of their own economies and not fully embracing the IMF's first attempt at multilateral consultations on global imbalances in 2006. According to Trevor Manuel, South Africa's Finance Minister, "one has to start from the fundamental view that if you accept public policy and you accept the interconnectedness of the global economy, then you need an institution appropriate to its regulation."[24] Analysts argue, however, that developed countries have long ignored IMF advice on their economic policy, while at the same time pressuring the IMF to use its role in patrolling the exchange rate system to support their own foreign economic goals.

End Notes

1 Such as the Bank for International Settlements, Financial Stability Forum (FSF), and the Organization for Economic Cooperation and Development (OECD).

2 IMF resources that are considered non-usable to finance IMF operations are (1) its gold holdings, (2) the currencies of members that are using IMF resources and are therefore, by definition, in a weak balance of payments or reserve position, (3) the currencies of other members with relatively weak external positions, and (4) other non-liquid IMF assets.

3 Brad Setser, "Extraordinary Times," Council on Foreign Relations, September 29, 2008. It is worth noting that thefinal rescue packages during the Asian crisis totaled many times $30 billion once bilateral assistance was included.

4 Oxford Analytica, "IMF reaffirms role in global economy." October 15, 2008.

5 Many analysts believe that the tight monetary and fiscal policies that the IMF required of countries accepting IMFloans accentuated the immediate economic impact of the crisis while having marginal impact on the countries' long-term structural reform.

6 IMF Currency Composition of Official Foreign Exchange Reserves (COFER) available at http://www.imf.org/external/np/sta/cofer/eng/index.htm.

7 Georges Pineau and Ettore Dorrucci, "The Accumulation of Foreign Reserves," *European Central Bank*, March 2006.

8 Total IMF Credit Outstanding for all members from 1984-2008, available athttp://www.imf.org/external/np/fin/tad/extcred1.aspx.

9 For background, see CRS Report RL33626, *International Monetary Fund: Reforming Country Representation*, by Martin A. Weiss.

10 The 1997 package for South Korea was 19 times as large as their quota at the IMF.

11 David Oakley, "Emerging Nations hit by growing debt fears," *Financial Times*, October 14, 2008.

12 Information on ongoing IMF negotiations is available at http://www.imf.org.

13 Oxford Analytica, "IMF reaffirms role in the global economy." October 15, 2008.

14 The EFM was set up in 1995 and has been used on six occasions—in 1997 for the Philippines, Thailand, Indonesia, and Korea; in 2001 for Turkey; and in 2008 for Georgia.

15 "IMF to Launch New Facility for Emerging Markets Hit by Crisis," *IMF Survey Online*, October 29, 2008.

16 Edwin Truman, On What Terms is the IMF Worth Funding, *Peterson Institute for International Economics*, December 2008.

17 "As Contingency, IMF Aims to Double its Lendable Resources," *IMF Survey Magazine: Policy*, February 2, 2008.

[18] "IMF talks to borrow $100 billion from Japan almost completed," *Japan Times*, February 4, 2009.
[19] Bob Davis, "IMF Considers Issuing Bonds to Raise Money," *Wall Street Journal*, February 1, 2009.
[20] Bob Davis, "International Groups Offer Latin America More Loans," *Wall Street Journal*, October 14, 2008.
[21] "Q&A: Central American "Exports, Production, Employment" Hit by Crisis" *Inter Press Service News Agency*, October 14, 2008.
[22] Malcolm Moore, "Asia Mounts its own Bank Bailout," *The Daily Telegraph*, October 15, 2008.
[23] Independent Evaluation Office (IEO) of the IMF, *An Evaluation of the IMF's Multilateral Surveillance*, September 1, 2006.
[24] Camilla Anderson, "Future Role of IMF Debated As Financial Crisis Takes Toll," *IMF Survey Online*, October 16, 2008.

In: The International Monetary Fund (IMF) Financial Crisis and… ISBN: 978-1-61728-499-1
Editor: Rachel E. Layton

Chapter 3

INTERNATIONAL MONETARY FUND (IMF): FINANCIAL REFORM AND THE POSSIBLE SALE OF IMF GOLD

Martin A. Weiss and Jonathan E. Sanford

SUMMARY

The International Monetary Fund faces a unique set of challenges in the current economic environment. With the continuing growth in the emerging market economies, the demand for IMF assistance has shrunk dramatically. In order to prevent a future need for an IMF-bailout, many emerging market countries are accumulating vast amounts of foreign exchange reserves. In 2006, IMF Managing Director Rodrigo de Rato created a panel of "eminent persons" to advise the IMF about reform of its income model, given the lower demand for IMF lending. The panel proposed the creation of an endowment that would be funded either with quota resources or through the sale of gold from the IMF reserves. This has raised questions among Members of Congress about the benefits of selling IMF gold and the presumed need for reform of the IMF 's income model.

DECREASING IMF FINANCES

As the IMF enters its seventh decade, it faces a broad range of challenges—most pressing of which is its deteriorating balance sheet. Outstanding IMF credit has decreased from a peak of $82 billion in 1999 to $20.4 billion in 2006, over half of which is lent to Turkey.[1] These are the lowest loan levels the IMF has seen in 25 years.[2] Many of the IMF's middle-income and developing country borrowers, including Thailand, Russia, Argentina, and Brazil, have been repaying their IMF loans early. These early payments may also signal that, with the emergence of a new class of creditor nations including China and many Persian Gulf countries, developing country borrowers no longer view IMF loans as attractive. Furthermore, some prefer not to put themselves in a position where they must take the IMF's policy advice as a condition for access to IMF loans.

Total IMF resources at the end of May 2007 were $340 billion, of which $248 billion were usable resources. However, the IMF possesses only a small portion of this total. Therefore, it cannot invest money from its quota resources in order to raise money to fund its operations.[3] With a decline in lending has come a decline in operating revenue, with the IMF reporting a small shortfall in its FY2007 budget.

Compounding the IMF's fiscal challenges, many emerging market economies are rapidly accumulating central bank reserves in order to avoid having to borrow from the IMF in the future (Table 1). Additionally, were a major financial crisis to occur, it is unclear how effective the IMF would be in shoring up the financial markets. Every day, over $2 trillion changes hands in world currency markets. In the 1970s and earlier, the IMF could loan countries enough money to defend their currencies against short-term speculative pressure. Most experts agree that the IMF could no longer do this today and, if it were to lend $30 billion to a medium size country to help it defend its currency against widespread perceptions that it was overvalued, the money from the IMF loan would be lost very quickly and the country would be forced to devalue anyway.[4] Experts generally agree that the IMF must now work with market forces rather than against them if it wishes to help countries deal with currency or balance of payments crises.

Table 1. Ratio of Reserves to Imports of Goods and Services

	1999	2000	2001	2002	2003	2004	2005	2006	2007
Emerging Markets and Developing Countries	46.3	44.7	49.5	55.3	60.5	62.7	66.4	71.4	75.1
Regional Groups	31.2	39.1	45.5	46.9	48.3	53.6	57.2	63.6	67.4
Sub-Sahara	28.7	33.6	33.2	31.2	28.0	34.7	38.0	42.1	45.5
Excluding Nigeria and South Africa	30.2	33.2	31.0	35.3	34.4	34.0	31.1	34.8	35.4
Central and Eastern Europe	38.8	34.6	34.8	41.1	39.3	34.8	35.2	31.9	29.3
Commonwealth of Independent States	17.6	30.5	34.4	41.0	52.1	64.3	75.7	96.0	109.1
Russia	17.2	40.6	44.6	52.9	71.5	92.7	107.2	135.2	152.7
Developing Asia	58.6	49.2	58.4	68.1	74.6	79.6	81.9	87.9	93.9
China	83.3	67.4	79.7	89.0	91.1	101.5	115.5	124.3	132.2
India	52.9	52.6	65.0	90.0	107.1	97.0	72.5	70.4	68.6
Middle East	64.0	75.5	78.7	74.3	78.5	77.9	90.5	98.3	97.9
Western Hemisphere	38.0	35.9	37.3	40.5	47.6	44.8	43.8	44.0	46.2
Brazil	37.6	43.5	49.2	61.1	77.2	65.9	54.8	71.3	86.2
Mexico	20.4	18.6	24.2	27.3	31.4	29.8	30.5	26.2	25.9

Source: Barry Eichengreen, "A Blueprint for IMF Reform: More than just a Lender," International Finance, Fall 2007.

IMF REFORM

To stimulate discussion on possible reform options, former IMF Managing Director Rodrigo Rato convened a committee of eminent persons to examine the IMF's income model. Headed by Andrew Crockett, former head of the Bank for International Settlements, the committee also included former Federal Reserve Chairman Alan Greenspan and former European Central Bank President, Jean Claude Trichet. Current IMF Managing Director Dominique Strauss Kahn is expected to introduce reform proposals during 2008.

As the Crockett Report illustrates, the IMF's income derives largely from a single source—the difference between the rate the IMF charges when it lends and the rate the IMF pays countries for use of their quota resources. This creates a perverse situation, where, according to Mr. Crockett: "when the world economy is not doing well and the Fund has to lend in crisis situations, it is well furnished with resources. When the Fund is successful in stabilizing the global economy, then it is short of resources."[5]

The Crockett Report Recommendations

The Committee released its report on January 31, 2007.[6] The report made several recommendations to provide sufficient financing for the IMF's three major functions: (1) providing a source of short-term finance for countries suffering from balance of payments crises; (2) providing a public good of surveillance of the international economy; and (3) providing bilateral technical assistance to countries as they pursue market-oriented economic reform.

To meet these goals, the Committee recommends (1) revising the IMF's investment operations; (2) creating an endowment fund; (3) charging separately for IMF services; and (4) eliminating the IMF's waiver on reimbursement of the administrative charges for the IMF's concessional lending facilitates. The Committee rejected the option of financing the IMF's oversight and research functions through a periodic levy on member nations due to fear that this would overly politicize the IMF's activities. According to the Committee: "subjecting the Fund's administrative expenditure to national budgetary procedures might indirectly threaten the independence of the Fund's policy advice."[7]

The Committee made two recommendations regarding the IMF's existing investment options: (1) broaden the IMF's investment mandate for existing reserves by extending portfolio duration beyond the current 1-3 year benchmark index and expand the types of financial instruments that the IMF is allowed to invest, and (2) use quota resources subscribed by member countries to invest in marketable securities. The Committee also recommended that the IMF create an endowment fund through the sale of 12.9 million ounces of gold held in its reserves. Gold sales have been used in the past to generate income. In 1957, for example, gold was sold to create a Special Reserve to cover Fund losses incurred early in its existence. Between 1976 and 1980, 50 million ounces were sold by public auction to fund special loans to low-income countries.

IMF Gold

The IMF holds 103.4 million ounces of gold in reserves, valued at around $95.01 billion at current market prices.[8] The IMF acquired virtually all of this gold through four types of transactions. First, before they were revised in 1978, the IMF Articles of Agreement required that 25 percent of a country's quota subscriptions was to be paid in gold. This was the largest source of IMF gold. Second, all payments of charges (i.e. interest on members' use of IMF credit) were originally made in gold. Third, a member wanting to obtain the currency of another member could do so by selling gold to the IMF. (South African gold sales between 1970 and 1971, for example, were the main such source of gold.) Fourth, members could use gold to repay the IMF for previously extended IMF credit.

In 1978, IMF members adopted an amendment to the Articles of Agreement allowing each country to determine its own exchange rate system. The amendment officially severed the link between currency and gold. IMF member countries were prohibited from defining the value of their currency in terms of gold and the IMF was prohibited from lending gold or defining its assets in terms of gold. Countries could use any exchange rate system (other than using gold as a base) for defining the value of their currencies. Prior IMF approval of exchange rate changes would no longer be required. Since the 1978 amendment, the use of gold in the IMF's operations has been severely limited. If an 85 percent majority approves, the IMF may sell gold outright on the basis of prevailing market prices. It may also accept gold in the discharge of a member's obligations, using the market price at the time of acceptance. All other transactions, such as gold purchases, loans, leases, swaps, or use of gold as collateral, are prohibited.

In 1995, the IMF Executive Board undertook a review of the role of gold in the IMF in a post- gold standard international economy. Following this review, there was broad agreement from members of the IMF Executive Board that the IMF 's policy on gold should be governed by several principles including:

- As an undervalued asset held by the IMF, gold provides fundamental strength to its balance sheet. Any mobilization of IMF gold should avoid weakening its overall financial position; and
- The IMF should continue to hold a relatively large amount of gold among its assets, not only for prudential reasons, but also to meet unforeseen[9] contingencies.

Issues for Congress

In the past, proposals to sell IMF gold reserves have been unpopular among some Members of Congress. Some have argued that there is a potential lack of IMF transparency. Some claim that the gold held by the IMF belongs to the member nations and it is not the IMF 's place to propose gold sales to fund current operating expenses. Some also claim that gold sales have the potential to weaken the global price of gold and the effect on the IMF balance sheet is unclear.

In the late 1990s, limited gold-sales were proposed to finance the IMF's initial contribution to the Heavily Indebted Poor Countries (HIPC) initiative. Due to the concerns raised above, the Clinton Administration and several members of Congress strongly objected to these plans, and a compromise was reached at the September 1999 IMF annual meetings, which authorized off- market transactions in gold of up to 14 million ounces to help finance IMF participation in the HIPC program. Between December 1999 and April 2000, transactions involving a total of 12.9 million ounces of gold were carried out between the IMF and two members, Brazil and Mexico, that had financial obligations to the IMF. Gold was sold at the market price and profits were placed in a special IMF HIPC account. At the same time, the IMF accepted back the gold sold to Brazil and Mexico in settlement of their financial obligations to the Bank. The result was that the balance of the IMF 's holdings of physical gold remained unchanged, although its usable resources shrank.[10]

Under Article V, Sec. 12 of the IMF 's Articles of Agreement, approval of gold sales by the IMF requires an 85 percent IMF voting majority. The United States has almost a 17 percent vote and could thus block any sale of IMF gold. Understanding this "virtual" veto, Congress, in 1999, enacted legislation in the *FY 2000 Consolidated Appropriations Act* that authorized the United States to vote at the IMF in favor of a limited sale of IMF gold to fund the IMF's participation in HIPC debt cancellation. However, the act requires the explicit consent of Congress before the Executive Branch can support any future gold sales.[11]

Prior to the adoption of this law, the requirement for congressional agreement was less clear. In 1976, Congress approved legislation, section 3 of P.L. 94-564, which prohibited the Administration from supporting any sale of IMF gold that would be used to create a trust fund "for the special benefit of a single member, or of a particular segment of the membership, of the Fund."[12] Subsequently, Congress approved section 4(a)(1) of P.L. 95-147 which stated, in part, that the United States could not support the sale of IMF gold for "the establishment of any additional trust fund whereby resources of the International Monetary Fund would be used for the special benefit of a single member, or of a particular segment of the membership, of the Fund."[13] Were these provisions of law still in effect, the Secretary of the Treasury might arguably be able to support a sale of IMF gold for the purpose of establishing a trust fund if the proceeds would benefit the whole membership of the Fund, as might be the case with the present proposal for a sale that would help offset IMF operating expenses. With the passage of the 1999 law, however, that option is not possible and an act of Congress is required before the Administration can support any sale of IMF gold.

The Crockett panel also proposed, in addition to gold sales, that the IMF should augment its income through a more aggressive investment program. The IMF would borrow money from its member countries by drawing on their quota resources to fund these investments. The sale of gold and the use of quota resources were not posed as alternatives. Nevertheless, it could be argued that if gold is not sold to fund the proposed endowment plan, more quota resources will be needed to fund the investment program.

Questions might be raised about this use of quota resources. First, the IMF 's quota resources were originally intended to finance the IMF's loan operations, not to subsidize its administrative costs. Their use for the latter purpose deserves careful consideration. Second, only the countries with strong currencies are likely to be asked to provide permanent low-cost loans to the IMF for this purpose.

As the IMF deliberates on the Crockett Report recommendations, Congress may wish to consider the following questions in anticipation of a potential request to authorize the sale of a portion of IMF gold reserves: (1) Are gold sales desirable compared to the other alternatives for raising revenue? (2) If gold sales are not authorized, should the IMF fund its new investment plan by borrowing quota resources from the United States and other countries with strong currencies without also asking other countries to bear some of the costs? (3) How should the United States raise the money—be it on-budget or off-budget—to finance its share of the investment plan? (4) Will the IMF be more effective if it is autonomously financed rather than being dependent solely on income from its loan operations to fund in its administrative budget? In particular, will the IMF be more effective in the exercise of its surveillance and its other economic oversight functions if these activities are funded autonomously through an endowment or investment plan?

Alternatively, some in Congress might wish to reconsider the raison d'etre of the IMF in an international economy marked by rapidly growing emerging market reserves and capital flows from the emerging to the developed countries. The Fund's three current functions—crisis lending, technical assistance and surveillance of the international monetary system—might be reoriented within the IMF or allocated to other institutions to better reflect the new reality. For example, the IMF's function as lender of last resort could be performed by regional reserve-pooling arrangements such as that developed in Asia under the Chiang Mai Initiative, or through enhanced functions of the Bank for International Settlement. The Fund's technical assistance functions could be provided by the multilateral development banks. A renewed IMF could focus on its member countries' economic policies and on surveillance of the international exchange rate and monetary systems. Such reforms will likely be on the IMF's agenda over the next several years.

End Notes

[1] International Monetary Fund, "IMF Financial Activities—Update January 18, 2007."

[2] Oxford Analytica Daily Brief, "IMF could cut spending to cover losses," November 30, 2006.

[3] Quotas are, in effect, a line of credit. When the IMF makes a loan, it borrows from its member countries and it relends that money to its own borrower countries. Repayments from IMF borrowers are used to repay countries for quota resources used. Countries pay the IMF interest for their loans and the IMF pays interest to the countries whose quotas are used. The difference in these interest rates produces the income the IMF currently uses to fund its operations.

[4] See, for example, testimony by Dr. Adam Lerrick before the Senate Banking Committee's Subcommittee on Security and International Trade and Finance, August 2, 2007.

[5] Transcript of a Press Briefing on the Final Report by the Committee to Study Sustainable Long-term Financing of the IMF (Crockett Report), January 31, 2007. Available at http://www.imf.org/external/np/tr/2007/tr070131.htm.

[6] Committee to Study Sustainable Long-term financing of the IMF, The International Monetary Fund, January 2007. Document is available at http://imf.org/external/np/oth/2007/013107.pdf.

[7] Ibid, p. 8.

[8] The price of gold on January 28, 2008 was $918.88 per ounce. See http://goldprice.org/.

[9] See "Gold in the IMF: a Factsheet," International Monetary Fund, http://www.imf.org/external/np/exr/facts/gold.htm.

[10] The IMF may hold gold as an asset, but it cannot lend gold nor can it use gold as security for borrowing funds. The transactions in 1999 shifted money out of the IMF's general resources account into a special fund for HIPC debt cancellation. To offset this deduction, the IMF revalued some of its gold by an equal amount. See Jonathan E. Sanford, "IMF Gold and the World Bank's Unfunded HIPC Mandate," *Development Policy Review*, January 2004.

[11] P.L. 106-113, *Consolidated Appropriations Act*, 2000, Sec. 504(d).

[12] P.L. 94-564, *A Bill to Provide for Amendment of the Bretton Woods Agreement.*

[13] P.L. 95-147, *A Bill to Authorize the Secretary of the Treasury to Invest Public Moneys.*

In: The International Monetary Fund (IMF) Financial Crisis and... ISBN: 978-1-61728-499-1
Editor: Rachel E. Layton

Chapter 4

INTERNATIONAL MONETARY FUND: REFORMING COUNTRY REPRESENTATION

Martin A. Weiss

SUMMARY

Many developing countries have long argued that they deserve an increase in the influence that they wield at the International Monetary Fund (IMF). They point out that after years of sustained economic growth, their representation does not reflect their current economic position in the world economy. Proposed changes would give these emerging economies as well as poor borrowers and countries that do not significantly contribute to funding IMFoperations greater say in order to enhance the perceived legitimacy and effectiveness of the institution.

At the spring 2006 IMF meetings, IMF Managing Director Rodrigo de Rato presented a loosely fleshed out proposal that would provide for a two-step process. In the first step, there would be a so-called ad hoc quota increase that would immediately raise the representation of a few select countries who it is commonly agreed are under-represented at the Fund and follow with fundamental reform of the IMF quota system.

De Rato's reform agenda was approved by IMF members at the fall 2006 IMF meetings in Singapore. At the meetings, IMF members granted four countries quota increases: China, South Korea, Turkey, and Mexico. These ad-hoc increases are to be followed by additional reforms during the next two years. Fundamental reform can take several forms. Four options are: (1) closer alignment between actual and existing quotas; (2) revising the quota formulas; (3) reorganizing the Executive Board; and (4) increasing the number of basic votes.

These reform options are not mutually exclusive. It is likely that any eventual reform may comprise aspects of several of the options discussed. Any potential reform, however, must enhance both the IMF's relevance and credibility. There is often tension between these two goals. The IMF is relevant precisely because it caters to the financial needs of the world's neediest countries. However, it is credible only to the extent that it is financially sound and is able to fulfill its mission. Increasing the representation of developing countries may only be successful if it can be accomplished without damaging the credibility of the institution and sacrificing the IMF's financial stability.

The Bush Administration has supported this proposal. In testimony and speeches since 2006, Administration officials explained that they are willing to support an ad-hoc increase for a few countries, but only if it is tied to fundamental reform of the IMF governance system. Depending on which course of action IMF members choose, action may be required by the 110th Congress. Congress must give its consent by law before the United States may agree to participate in any new IMF funding agreements that change the U.S. quota, require additional contributions from the United States, amend the IMF Articles of Agreement, or dispose of any gold currently held by the IMF.

International Monetary Fund: Reforming Country Representation

INTRODUCTION

Representation at the International Monetary Fund (IMF) is linked roughly to the degree of financial support countries provide to the institution and their relative share of the world economy. Many developing countries have long argued that they deserve an increase in their representation, on the grounds that after years of sustained economic growth, their participation does not reflect their current economic position in the world economy. Proposed changes would give these emerging economies as well as borrowers and countries that do not contribute to funding IMF operations greatersay in order to enhance the perceived legitimacy and effectiveness of the institution. This in turn may enhance the ability of the Fund to carry out its mission of international monetary cooperation and exchange rate stability.[1]

The IMF has introduced a two-step reform process beginning with an ad hoc quota increase for a few under-represented emerging market countries: China, Mexico, South Korea, and Turkey. These increases are to be followed withinthe next two years by fundamental reform of the quota system. Quota reform is at the heart of the IMF reform debate as quotas largely determine representation and voting rights, as well as financial contributions. However, since quotas are fundamental to so many aspects of a country's representation at the IMF, any change is difficult politically. Some fast-growing economies will gain voting power while others will lose. An overwhelming consensus of all IMF member nations is required for any quota reform to take effect.

The Bush Administration has expressed support for the two-step IMF proposal. Fundamental reform of the IMF quota and voting system could take a variety of forms and several options are being considered. Congressional action may or may not be required depending upon which fundamental reform option (if any) is implemented. The United States is the largest contributor to the IMF and has the largest vote in the institution. Congress is responsible for authorizing and appropriating U.S. contributions to the IMF and must give its consent to any change in the size of the U.S. quota. Although there are potential scenarios where the Bush Administration would not need to seek Congress's approval, and there is no current legislation addressing IMF reform, many of the IMF reform proposals may likely require congressional authorization and/or appropriations.

This chapter explains how countries are represented at the IMF, discusses the reform agenda, analyzes various options to reform the quota system, and evaluates the role of Congress.

COUNTRY REPRESENTATION AT THE IMF

Broad policy is set and determinations on lending for specific countries are made by three levels of decision-making bodies in the IMF (**Box 1**). Unlike the United Nations General Assembly, which relies on a one-country, one-vote governance system, the IMF uses a weighted voting system based on a country's quota. The United States, with 17.08% of the total vote, has the largest single vote in the institution.

BOX 1. DECISION MAKING AT THE IMF

The Board of Governors is the highest authority in the IMF. All countries are represented on the Board of Governors, usually at the Finance Minister or Central Bank governor level. Although the Board of Governors has ultimate authority for running the IMF, it has delegated nearly all its powers to the Executive Board. The Board of Governors meets annually at the fall IMF-World Bank meetings.

The Executive Board handles day-to-day authority over operational policy, lending, and other matters. It is the main decision-making body at the IMF. The board has 24 members each representing from 1 to 24 countries (see Box 2) who usually meet three or more times a week to oversee and supervise the activities of the IMF. Funds cannot be raised and loans and policies cannot be approved without Executive Board agreement.

Other Groups: In addition to the official representation of the Board of Governors and the Executive Board, there are several other cross-cutting groups of countries that are actively involved with the IMF. These include the G-15 and the G-24. The G-15 was established at the Ninth Non-Aligned Summit Meeting in Belgrade, Yugoslavia in September 1989. Comprised of countries from Latin America, Africa, and Asia, the G-15 focuses on cooperation among developing countries in investment, trade, and technology. The membership of the G-15 has expanded to 17 countries, but the name has remained unchanged. The G-24 was established in 1971 and coordinates the positions of developing countries on international monetary and development finance issues and to ensure that their interests were adequately represented. The G-24 has been very active on governance reforms and has promoted several particular policies. Members meet at the IMF/World Bank spring and fall meetings and release an official communiqué.

Quotas

Quotas are the foundation of country representation at the IMF. Based loosely on each country's global economic standing, quotas specify: (1) the amount of financial resources each member is required to contribute to the Fund; (2) the amount of financing a member may receive from the Fund;[2] and (3) the amount of voting power each country has at the IMF.

Quotas are expressed as "Special Drawing Rights" (SDR).[3] Total quotas at end-September 2007 were SDR 217.3 billion (about $338.3 billion). Countries contribute to the IMF mainly in local currency. Since the currencies of many emerging market and developing countries are weak and not used by the IMF to fund its operations, only about 69% of the IMF's total quota resources are deemed usable by the IMF.[4]

Since the IMF's founding, it has been the stated intention of the IMF to base quotas on various formulas that technically deduce a country's ability to contribute to the IMF and its likelihood of drawing IMF resources. The IMF periodically calculates country quotas based on these formulas. In practice, quotas have only been loosely guided by the calculated quotas and actual quotas are determined more by political negotiations among the member countries.[5]

A 2000 study of the history and relevance of the IMF quota formula found that the formula had only an indirect influence on actual quotas.[6] The study also found that the gap between actual and calculated quotas has persisted and thus actual IMF quotas (and subsequent voting power) do not accurately reflect the current world economy. Since 1945, there have been 12 general quota reviews. Of these, seven have led to an increase in the financial resources of the institution. Of the total quota increase since 1945, less than one-third has been based on the quota formula. The remaining increase was general or "equi-proportional," each country receiving an increase proportional to their existing share. Since quota reviews have maintained the status quo, Western Europe, the United States, and the other dominant countries when the IMF was created have benefitted while emerging countries, specifically Asia, and other developing countries have quotas and voting power disproportionately low relative to their growing global economic weight.

Voting

Unlike the United Nations General Assembly, which relies on a one-person, one-vote governance system, the IMF uses a weighted voted system. The IMF's founders agreed that the voting system should combine elements of the one-country, one-vote principle with proportional voting depending on contribution levels. The voting system adopted at Bretton Woods give 250 votes automatically to every country (basic votes) and one additional vote for each $100,000 of quota. Over time, as the size of the IMF's quota increased while the number of basic votes stayed the same, basic votes have become a marginal component of the total number of votes, down to 2.1% from 11.3% initially. Many analysts agree that any fundamental reform would require an increase in the number of basic votes.[7]

Constituencies

The IMF uses a voting system where the Executive Directors (EDs) can represent either a single country or several countries grouped in mixed-state constituencies (**Box 2**). A result of this constituency system is a significant power asymmetry among members on the Board. Moreover, the distribution of voting strength among EDs has become more unequal over time. The minimum voting power that the IMF allows each ED to hold dropped to 4.0% in 2005. In practice, however, this rule is waived and 15 EDs each have fewer than 4.0% of the institution's votes. The two EDs that represent 43 African countries wield 3.0% and 1.4% of the IMF's votes respectively. By contrast, the U.S. ED holds 17% of the vote, and the four other largest contributors having voting power ranging between 5% and 6%.

BOX 2. THE EXECUTIVE BOARD AND MIXED-STATE CONSTITUENCIES

There are currently 24 members on the IMF Executive Board representing in varying degrees every IMF member country. Of the 24 Board members, eight represent individual countries, and 16 individuals represent the remaining members. According to Section 3 of the IMF's Articles of Agreement, the five countries having the largest quotas appoint their own executive director. This means that the United States, Japan, Germany, Britain, and France are allowed to appoint their own representatives on the Board. In addition to the five largest shareholders, China, Russia, and Saudi Arabia have enough votes to elect their own Executive Directors. All other countries have gravitated into mixed-state groupings or constituencies. These constituencies range in size from 4 countries (a South Asian constituency led by India) to 24 (an African constituency led by Equatorial Guinea). The mixed-state constituencies are flexible in their membership. Countries have periodically switched constituencies, often to a new group that will allow them to have a bigger vote or leadership role.

Unlike the eight countries that have their own ED, the influence of countries in mixed-state constituencies is not equivalent to their quota-determined votingweight. Since they vote in constituencies, very small countries can easily be sidestepped by the larger countries in the constituency.[8] For many countries at the IMF they "can at best express a divergent opinion orally but cannot bring it to bear in the form of a vote."[9] Executive Directors must cast their votes as single unit even though some of the countries they represent may disagree with their position. Of the 16 mixed-state constituencies, five have a country with a majority of the total votes, and three have countries that control over 40% of the total vote. Appendix 1 ranks the largest member of each constituency and their percentage of the total votes within their constituency.

The IMF's Articles of Agreement set the various thresholds required for IMF decisions. The majority of IMF decisions require a 50% majority vote. However, some special matters (changes in the Articles of Agreement or approval of new quota increases, for example) require an 85% affirmative vote. Since the U.S. vote exceeds 15%, no quota increases, amendments or other major actions can go into effect without U.S. consent. The same can be said for other major blocks of IMF member countries, principally European countries.[10]

An important issue regarding voting, however, is that within the Executive Board there is a very strong institutional aversion to formal voting. Executive Board Rule C-10 states that "the Chairman [Managing Director] shall ordinarily ascertain the sense of the meeting in lieu of a formal vote."[11] Since the United States or a combination of European countries could block most policy issues if they were to actually come up to a vote, it is difficult to determine how true an Executive Board consensus often is. Thus if it appears that the United States (or other large quota holders) does not support a policy issue requiring 70% or 85% approval, it will never come to a vote, and there will be no formal record of U.S. dissent. This may have the effect of stifling debate on the Executive Board.

IMF and U.S. Policy on IMF Governance Reform

Context

The world has changed dramatically since the IMF was founded. Established in 1946 with a membership of 46 countries, the IMF now includes 185 countries and oversees a vastly different world economy with a new distribution of economic power. Unlike in 1946, emerging market economies, primarily in Asia and Latin America, play a vibrant and crucial role in the world economy. However, the distribution of quota and voting power at the IMF has changed very little to reflect these changes.

The IMF's response to the Asian Financial Crisis of the late 1990s highlighted the lack of representation of many key emerging market economies in IMF decision-making. Many countries believe that the IMF's response was heavy-handed and exacerbated the crisis.[12]

Discontent with the IMF has had tangible effects on the Fund's operations and spurred reform efforts. Several major borrowers have taken advantage of the benign economic conditions beginning in 2003 to prepay their IMF loans. In 2003, Thailand paid off its IMF debts two years early. In 2004, Russia prepaid $3.3 billion to the IMF. In 2005, Argentina and Brazil both paid their remaining IMF debt early. These early payments significantly reduce the IMF's lending activities to middle-income countries, a primary source of income for the IMF.

In addition to removing themselves from IMF lending, some member countries are also creating alternative institutions to the IMF. Under the Chiang Mai Initiative, several Asian countries are seeking to insulate themselves from the IMF by accumulating large foreign exchange reserves to remove any potential need to seek IMF lending if they run into difficulties with their international financial relations.[13] The Chiang Mai Initiative is in direct response to the perceived mishandling by the IMF of the East Asian financial crisis in the late 1990s. If developing countries continue to withdraw from IMF lending and its sphere of influence, the financial future of the institution may be in doubt.[14] Therefore, these countries' actions have heightened the pressure on the IMF to seek reform.

The IMF's Reform Effort

Responding to this pressure, IMF Managing Director Rodrigo de Rato included the need for governance reform in his 2005 Mid-Term Strategic Review, presented to IMF members at the fall 2005 annual meetings.[15] In the report, de Rato wrote, "fair weight and voice are crucial to the legitimacy of a universal institution. The current allocation puts this legitimacy at risk in many regions, for example, in Africa, where the Fund is heavily engaged, and in Asia, whose place in the world economy has grown far more than its role in the Fund."[16]

At the spring 2006 meetings, de Rato presented a loosely fleshed out reform proposal that would consist of a two-step process. In the first step, there would be a so-called ad hoc increase that would immediately raise the representation of a few select countries that are commonly viewed as under-represented at the Fund. This ad-hoc increase would be followed in the next two years by more fundamental reforms of the IMF governance framework.

IMF member countries endorsed the de Rato proposal at the spring meetings. The Communiqué released at the meetings by the IMF's International Monetary and Finance Committee (IMFC)[17] reiterated the theme raised by Managing Director de Rato: "the IMF's effectiveness and credibility as a cooperative institution must be safeguarded and its governance further enhanced, emphasizing the importance of fair voice and representation for all members."[18] The Communiqué went on to call upon the IMF to work with the IMFC and the IMF's Executive Board to come up with concrete proposals for "fundamental reform" of the system by which countries are represented at the IMF.[19]

At the fall 2006 meetings, the IMF won approval for a more detailed reform proposal beginning with small quota increases for China, Mexico, Turkey, and South Korea. Following this increase, the IMF will work during the next two years to adjust IMF quotas through a new quota formula, a second round of ad hoc increases, and increases in the number of basic votes available to all countries. There was some resistance to the proposal at the meetings from other emerging economies including Brazil, India, and Argentina. These countries, among others, opposed the initial ad hoc increase arguing that reforms should be adopted for all developing countries simultaneously.[20]

Dominique Strauss Kahn, de Rato's successor as IMF managing director, has vowed to continue with the reform proposal. Since the beginning of his tenure in November 2007, he has invigorated the reform effort, building on the decision bythe IMFC at the October 2007 Annual Meeting that, "the reform should enhance the representation of dynamic economies, many of which are emerging market economies, whose weight and role in the global economy have increased."[21]

U.S. Policy

The Bush Administration has expressed support for the IMF reform agenda. For many years, it has been the policy of the U.S. government to further integrate developing countries into the global economy and its main international institutions. In his statement at the spring 2006 IMF meetings, then-U.S. Treasury Secretary John Snow told fellow IMF members that, "[t]he United States strongly supports the efforts to realign quotas and Board representation at the IMF in order to reflect changes in the global economy."[22] The Administration hopes that this ad hoc quota increase will act as a spur for broader IMF governance reform within the next two years. Moreover, the Administration would like to give China a greater say at the IMF as an incentive for them to revalue its currency, the yuan.[23] Timothy Adams is quoted as saying, "If we're going to give China or any other country ... greater weight in the IMF, then they need to take their responsibilities in that institution seriously, and they need to play by the rules as they're laid out."[24] However, giving China a substantial increase in quota may upset several Members of Congress who wish to see China appreciate the value of its currency prior to their gaining any additional representation at the IMF.[25]

Finally, the Bush Administration wants to see the IMF Executive Board better reflect the IMF's full membership. A broad consensus appears to be emerging that European countries are over-represented at the IMF compared to their share of global GDP. European countries have three full seats on the IMF Executive Board (Germany, France, and the United Kingdom), and currently chair or co-chair seven of the group constituencies. The 25 EU members appoint or play a predominant role in appointing 10 of the 24 members of the Executive Board (42%), even though as a group they have only 29.8% of the vote.[26] Among other things, this gives them a disproportionate voice in IMF discussions.

The Bush administration has expressed support for rationalization of European shares in the institution. In a speech at the Institute for International Economics laying out the Bush Administration's vision for IMF reform, Timothy Adams noted, "Consolidation of European chairs [seats on the Executive Board] would help to increase the voice of emerging market and developing country members."[27] It is unclear, however, how willing European countries are to relinquish quota or consolidate their votes.

FUNDAMENTAL REFORM ISSUES

As the recent reform discussion illustrates, it appears that IMF management, the Bush Administration, and most developing countries would like to see reform of the IMF governance system. However, three broad issues may need to be addressed before any potential reform proposals can proceed.

Should Reform Involve Amending the Articles of Agreement?

Any reform that does not involve amending the Articles of Agreement will likely be easier to gain a consensus among IMF members and easier to implement. Revising the Articles is a cumbersome process, since doing so requires the consent of the United States Congress and many other national governments and legislatures.

Will Anyone Lose Quota?

The Bush Administration has said on several occasions that it would consider a decrease in the total U.S. quota share. It is unlikely, however, that it would propose dropping the U.S. share to below 15%, that needed to block the most important votes (those requiring an 85%

majority).[28] The U.S. share could be reduced without any requirement for action by Congress so long as the numerical size of the U.S. quota is unchanged.[29]

The Bush Administration has also indicated that it would like to see a voluntary rebalancing of quotas within the existingtotal from overweight countries to the most underweight emerging economies.[30] However, this would involve other countries, likely European, taking a more forward leaning position on reducing their quota and vote at the IMF than they have to date.

Ad Hoc Quota Increase Only

The U.S. Administration has stated that it will only support an ad hoc increase in quotas if it is tied to broader reform. In testimony to the House Financial Services Committee on May 17, 2006, Secretary Snow explained the U.S. position. "We [the Bush Administration] have agreed that a first step could consist of a limited ad hoc increase for the most under-represented members. But we have emphasized that an ad hoc quota increase by itself is inadequate to resolve the quota and representation issues that are steadily eroding the IMF's legitimacy and effectiveness. *We are only willing to support a limited ad hoc quota increase at the IMF Annual Meetings in Singapore if it is credibly linked to a second step that delivers fundamental reform.*" (emphasis added)[31]

As noted earlier, IMF members agreed to an ad hoc quota increase for China, Mexico, South Korea, and Turkey at the fall 2006 IMF meetings. This ad hoc increase does not require amending the IMF Articles of Agreement and does not lead to European countries, or any other country, losing any quota though it marginally reduces their quota share.

However, an ad hoc increase does not address the broader concerns affecting the majority of developing countries at the IMF. Anne Krueger, IMF first deputy director, speaking in Tokyo on June 6, 2006, argued that such an ad hoc increase by itself would be insufficient to meet the reform goals expressed by IMF members, especially the Asian countries that appear to be turning away from the IMF. In her remarks, Deputy Director Krueger argued that to ensure that Asia's emerging economies engage further with the IMF,and support a stronger IMF role in the global economy, a new system needs to be devised that better allocates quota, representation of the Executive Board, and overall votes based on some measure of a country's economic size.[32]

Fundamental Reform Options

At the fall 2006 meetings, IMF members agreed to pursue fundamental reform of the IMF quota system within the next two years. This can take several forms. Four options are (1) closer alignment between actual and calculated quotas; (2) revising the quota formulas; (3) reorganizing the Executive Board; and (4) increasing the number of basic votes.

Closer Alignment between Actual and Calculated Quotas

One option to boost the quota for emerging countries could be to move towards closer alignment between calculated and actual quotas. The IMF periodically calculates quotas based on a set of formulas to determine a country's economic weight and likelihood of needing IMF assistance.[33] These calculated quotas are supposed to guide IMF quota determinations. In practice, these quota formulas have only loosely guided actual quotas, which have been decided more through political negotiations. A large gap exists between the calculated and actual quotas and thus one proposal has been to move closer toward the calculated quotas.

Such a realignment could occur during a general quota review. The IMF will conclude its 13th general quota review in 2008 and could use a general increase to closer align quotas with their calculated rates (if approved by all national governments and the necessary national legislatures). This would succeed in boosting the quota share of many emerging countries. However, the increased quota would come at the expense of other developing countries in Africa, the Middle East, and Latin America. Moreover, the total quota (and vote) of developing countries would decrease while the advanced economies shares would increase (Table 1).[34]

Within these categories, there would also be broad shifts between countries. For the industrialized countries, the U.S. share would decrease slightly from 17.4% to 17.2%, the German share would increase from 6.1% to 7.0%, the French would decrease from 5.0 to 4.3%, and Japan's share would rise from 6.2% to 7.2%. Russia and Saudi Arabia, both countries which have their own seat on the Executive Board, would see major declines in quota. Russia's share would decline from 2.8% to 1.3%, and Saudi Arabia's would decline from 3.3% to 1.0%. These changes would lead to an overall increase in the share of quota held bythe advanced economies from 61.6% to 67.6% if the current calculated quota formulas are used.

More dramatic changes are seen in the quota shares of developing countries. China, most notably, would see an increase from 3.0% to 5.1%. India, on the other hand, would lose quota with their share dropping from 1.9% to 1.0%. Argentina's share would decrease from 1.0% to 0.4%, Korea's would increase from 0.8% to 2.3%, and Mexico's would increase from 1.2% to 1.9%.

Table 1. Actual and Calculated IMF Quotas

	Current Quota	Calculated Quota based on Existing Formulas (2005)
Advanced Economies	61.6%	67.6%
Major Advanced Economies	46.0%	47.9%
Of which: United States	17.4%	17.2%
Other Advanced Economies	15.6%	19.6%
Developing Countries	30.9%	27.7%
Africa	5.5%	2.3%
Asia	10.3%	15.8%
Middle East (including Malta and Turkey)	7.6%	4.5%
Western Hemisphere	7.5%	5.1%
Transition Economies	7.5%	4.7%

Source: International Monetary Fund

The poorest countries, mostly located in Sub-Saharan Africa, would see a large quota decrease, from 5.5% to 2.3%. Since the objective of the IMF management and the Executive Board is to boost the representation of all developing countries, not just those in emerging economies, it is unlikely that IMF members would agree to move closer to the calculated quotas based on the existing five formulas.

Revising the Calculated Quota Formulas

U.S.officials have repeatedly stated their desire for a new set of formulas that closely links a country's IMF quota and vote with their GDP. Secretary Snow reiterated this point in his House testimony: "[fundamental reform] must include revising the IMF's quota formulas with GDP as the predominant variable." Administration officials note however that quotas of the poorest countries should not be decreased, a likely result if there is a greater reliance on GDP for determining quotas. The Bush Administration and most other developed countries agree that it is appropriate to "over-represent" the very poorest countries by giving them a larger quota and vote than what would be inferred from their GDP.

In the current set of quota formulas, GDP has a low percentage of weighting, while economic openness is highly weighted. A result of this is to give small, economically open European countries (such as Belgium and the Netherlands) a large quota. These formulas have guided IMF quota allocations since 1983 and have not been significantly changed since.

In 1999, the IMF convened an independent working group to discuss options to simplify the IMF quota formulas. Chaired by Harvard economics professor Robert Cooper, the Quota Formula Review Group (QFRG) evaluated the history of IMF quotas. After analyzing various options, the group recommended a single formula with two variables: a measure of the ability to contribute to the IMF (GDP) and a measure of external economic vulnerability (variability of current receipts and long-term capital flow).[35] Following the review, IMF Executive Board members agreed with the need to simplify the IMF formula, but were concerned that the QFRG formula would lead to an even greater concentration of IMF quotas among the large industrialized countries.[36] No significant action was taken.

An alternative proposal has been put forward by the G24 group of countries. Currently, the GDP figures used by the IMF for the quota calculations are calculated at market rates averaged over several years. The G24, however, proposes that the IMF move to a purchasing power parity (PPP) based GDP measure. In the G24's view, market-based exchange rates do not equalize prices across countries and thus understate developing countries' GDPs.[37] On the other hand, others, including the IMF, believe that market based exchange rates represent the actual cost of transferring goods between countries, and that using PPP-based calculations, which equate the relative prices of goods regardless of location to calculate GDP, would inaccurately estimate a country's abilityto contribute to the IMF as well as its relative role in the world economy and possible need for IMF assistance. Prices of goods are often lower in developing countries which may allow nominal exchange rates to underestimate the size of their economy. However, in many cases prices in these emerging economies, China for example, are significantly distorted by government subsidies and price controls.

Shifting to a PPP-based GDP measure would imply major differences if the GDP measure became the dominant determinant of IMF quota shares. **Table 2** shows GDP measures for several countries in PPP and market-based figures. Moving to a PPP-based measure would significantly increase emerging market countries' quota share.

Table 2. IMF Quotas and Selected Countries GDP (Current Dollar and PPP Measures)

	Current Quota %	Percentage of World GDP, 2004 (current $)	Percent of World GDP, 2004 (PPP, constant 2000 $)
United States	17.4%	28.4%	20.5%
Euro Area	25.2%	23.0%	15.3%
Japan	6.2%	11.2%	6.6%
China	2.3%	4.7%	13.5%
India	1.9%	1.7%	6.0%
Brazil	1.4%	1.7%	2.7%

Source: International Monetary Fund

As Table 2 highlights, moving to a PPP-based GDP measure would suggest a much higher quota for several emerging economies, such as China, India, and Brazil. The Quota Reform Working Group discussed whether to measure GDP at current dollar rates or based on PPP and their debate highlighted the issues raised by moving to a PPP-based measure. A minority of the QFRG members supported moving to a PPP-based rate, arguing that market exchange rates do not necessarily equalize prices of tradable goods across countries, even after allowing for quality and transport costs.

The majority of the group, however, favored the continued use of market-based rates. This is also the prevailing view among the IMF's industrialized countries. The majority members of the QFRG noted that there are significant data problems with PPP-based rates. PPP-based rates are not available for all IMF members, and many of those available are based on fragmentary data. The QFRG minority also reiterated that it is necessary to consider the cost of actually moving goods from one place to another. Market prices properly reflect these costs while PPP-based equate prices of goods regardless of the transportation costs. Although these costs are decreasing, using PPP-based measures gives, according to the QFRG, "a seriously misleading indicator of ability to contribute to international undertakings."

There is no current agreement on what a "proper" quota formula would be. Leo Van Houtvan, long-term Secretary of the IMF and Counselor to the Managing Director, wrote in 2002, "there is no quota formula that is sensible from a financial perspective and that would also solve the governance issue."[38] Although the suggestion of the QFRG to use a formula comprised of GDP, variability of current receipts, and long-term capital flow was not acted on by the Executive Board, IMF members agreed with the QFRG that a simpler, more transparent formula would be beneficial for successfully guiding quota allocations. Other possible variables that could be included in such a formula are official reserves, current payments, ratio of exports to GDP, per capita income or population, external debt, share of food and energy in imports, access to capital markets, and variability of exchange rates.

Reorganizing the Executive Board

Arguably the most controversial, and perhaps most significant proposal for improving developing countries' representation at the IMF is reorganizing the Executive Board. Quota reform is important from a fundamental framework sinceit determines the voting share of each member country. However, for the vast majority of IMF members, since the IMF operates on the basis of consensus among the 24 EDs, Executive Board realignment may likely be the more effective reform for boosting developing countries' representation and participation.

Currently, the power asymmetry on the Executive Board is vast. In its current configuration, eight countries hold single seats on the Board and control 48% of the vote. The remaining 164 countries are grouped into 16 mixed-state constituencies. The most powerful of these has 5.13% of the IMF vote and the weakest has 1.41%. The latter represents 24 poor African countries, many of whom have programs with the IMF. In addition to having a marginal vote in greater IMF discussions, this situation raises capability issues. Many analysts have raised concerns that it is difficult for one Executive Director tosuccessfullyrepresent the diverse interests and needs of 24 often IMF-dependent countries. In this situation, where many countries are spoken for by a few Executive Directors, the "voice" of many countries likely suffers.

Reshaping the Executive Board may prove difficult. Since European countries have the largest and most widely dispersed representation, any reform will likely be impossible without strong European support. In March 2006, the European Parliament released a resolution on the strategic review of the IMF. The resolution supported the idea of moving toward a single voting constituency for the EU, but no practical guidelines were offered. Originally, the document was to propose increasing the basic votes of all members, and devising some form of mechanism to increase the shares for the poorest developing countries.[39] However, both of these suggestions were removed from the final text.[40]

It is unclear to what extent European countries are willing to consolidate their representation. Although the ad-hoc increased was achieved with only a small decrease in European representation, fundamental second-stage reform would likely require much more sustained coordination among Europeans to rationalize their representation. It has been argued that the legal, political, and institutional climate in Europe may not facilitate moving toward a single EU seat.[41] EU governments have no mechanism for coordinating their policies on a real-time basis without relinquishing authority to the European Commission or some other function of the EU bureaucracy. The legislatures of the EU countries that provide funds to the IMF may not wish to cede their policy choices from national control.

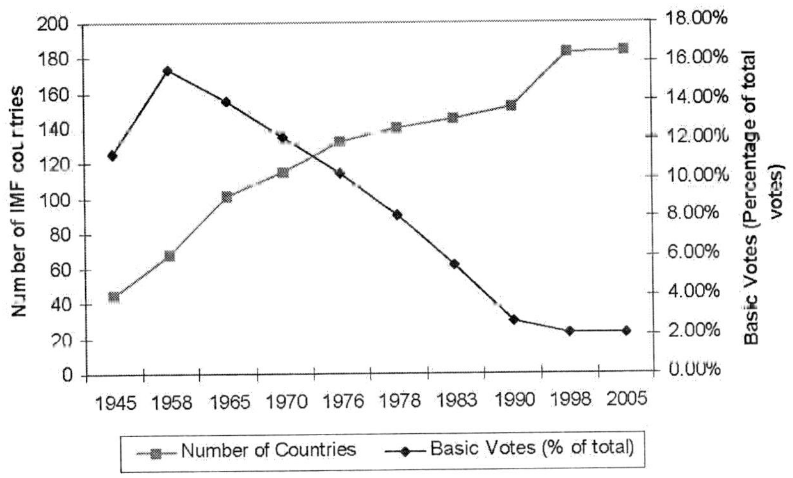

Source: International Monetary Fund

Figure 1. IMF Basic Votes.

Depending on how Executive Board reform occurs, congressional action may or may not be required. If IMF members agree on a voluntary shuffling of countries between the existing constituencies, no formal authorization from the U.S. Congress would be needed. Were this to occur and European countries were less dispersed among the multiple Executive Board constituencies than they currently are, EU countries may have a vote on the IMF Executive Board much larger than the U.S. vote. Further reform by consolidating several EU countries into a single IMF Executive Board seat, however, would likely involve congressional authorization as it would involve fundamentally revising the Executive Board system and would probably involve amending the IMF Articles of Agreement.

Increasing Basic Votes

At a speech to the Center for Global Development on July 31, 2006, Managing Director de Rato said that to protect the voice and vote of the poorest countries, he would like to see an increase in the number of basic votes allocated to all countries regardless of quota size.[42] The U.S. government has stated that it could consider such an increase in basic votes as part of the overall IMF reform package.[43] As Figure 1 illustrates, basic votes as a percentage of total votes has decreased substantially since the IMF was created, even as the number of IMF member countries (each receiving basic votes) has increased.

An increase in basic votes may not be as politically difficult as consolidation of EU chairs because no one country will gain votes at another's expense. However, any change would require amending the IMF Articles of Agreement, a difficult process requiring a broad level of support in the institution and approval by legislators.

Increasing the number of basic votes has been discussed during the past several quota reviews. One possible way to increase basic votes would be a fixed increase, giving the same amount of votes to each country. Basic votes could be reset at the original level of 11.3% of the total votes or potentially increased. Some analysts have suggested setting basic votes at 20% of the total votes. Another option would be to give only poor countries an increase in basic votes. While an increase in basic votes would raise the number of votes available to poor countries, their relative voting power would remain unchanged unless they were given a larger increase than industrialized countries.

CONGRESSIONAL ROLE

Depending on which reform approach IMF members choose, action may be required during the second session of the 110th Congress. The U.S. Congress has an active and vital role in creating U.S. policy at the IMF. Congress must give its consent by law before the United States may agree to participate in any new IMF fundingagreements that change the U.S. quota, require additional contributions from the United States, amend the IMF Articles of Agreement, or dispose of any gold currently held by the IMF.[44] Congress has also actively used its oversight role to shape U.S. policy at the institution. On many occasions, Congress has enacted legislation specifying what U.S. policy shall be in the international financial institutions (IFIs) and how the U.S. Executive Directors at these institutions shall vote and the objectives they shall pursue.[45]

Congress has also used increases in U.S. funding for the IMF (and the multilateral development banks (MDBs)) as a way to require various reforms in U.S. policy. One example is the 1998 IMF quota increase which sought numerous reforms including the increased transparency of IMF operations. Another example is various provisions in recent funding for the World Bank that tied part of the U.S. contributions to the World Bank's concessional lending facility, the International Development Association (IDA), on reforms to stem corruption in World Bank programs.

For quota and voting issues, Congress plays a crucial role. IMF governance issues are among the most important policy issues dealt with at the institution and, when voted on, require an 85% majority of members. Since the United States is the largest single shareholder, with a 17% voting share, it has a de facto veto on any possible reform proposals which involve amendments to the IMF charter.[46]

Furthermore, any change in the U.S. quota size must be approved by the U.S. Congress. The Bretton Woods Agreements Act specifies that unless Congress by law authorizes such action, neither the President nor any person or agency on his behalf can "request or consent to any change in the quota of the United States."[47] No general increase in the quota of the IMF has ever been approved without Congress consenting to the U.S. share of the increase.[48]

The proposed quota reform may likely coincide with the thirteenth general review of IMF resources. The IMF's Articles of Agreement require that the IMF review its financial resources at least every five years. Although it is not required that the IMF seek to raise additional capital from its members every five years (the last quota increase was in 1998), quota increases have been a way for countries to adjust quotas and votes among IMF members. Like the 1998 quota increase, which sparked a vibrant discussion within Congress on the role and value of the IMF, if the Administration proposes a quota increase for the United States or puts forward a reform proposal that requires congressional consent, even if the U.S. quota does not change, such a discussion may reoccur. If the Administration sidesteps Congress, Congress could use its oversight role and *Sense of Congress* legislation to express its view of IMF governance reform.

Table 3. Congressional Action Needed for Various Reforms

Option	Congressional Action
Ad Hoc Increase for selected countries	None required.
Full quota Increase	Requires congressional authorization, and appropriation if the amount of U.S. quota increases.
Revise quota formula	Does not require amending the IMF's Articles of Agreement and thus only requires congressional authorization if the amount of U.S. quota increases.
Reorganize Executive Board	Does not require congressional authorization for countries to move among the constituencies. If there is reform of the total size of the board or its operations, congressional authorization is required since the Articles of Amendment would need to be amended.
Increase Basic Votes	Requires amending the IMF's Articles of Agreement and thus requires congressional authorization.

Source: International Monetary Fund

To summarize, the actual role that Congress may need to take as the IMF pursues its reform agenda is not clear. The Bush administration has made periodic statements suggesting its preferred approach of either a voluntary exchange of quota to several emerging economies or a selective increase as a first-step toward reform. These options would not require congressional approval. Further reform, however, may likely require congressional action. Table 3 lays out the required steps for the various proposals.

Conclusion

The reform options discussed in this chapter are not mutually exclusive. It is likely that any eventual fundamental reform may comprise aspects of several of the options discussed. Any potential reform mustmaintain both the IMF's relevanceand credibility. As the reform discussion has highlighted, there is often tension between these two goals. The IMF is relevant precisely because it caters to the financial needs of the world's neediest countries. However, it is credible only to the extent that it is financially sound and is able to fulfill its mission. Increasing the representation of developing countries may only be successful if it can be accomplished without damaging the credibility of the institution and sacrificing the IMF's financial stability.

For the Fund to maintain its credibility as the primary international financial institution, the industrialized creditor countries will likely need to maintain their dominance in the institution. Moreover, to increase the vote of the poorest developing countries would require increasing their quota. It is not clear whether many of these countries can afford and are willing to increase their financial contributions or to take steps that would make their national currencies usable in IMF operations. Any resolution of the governance issue will thus be a political compromise that balances the financial needs of the institution with a distribution of votes and representation that is acceptable to most members.

Appendix A. Voting Power within Constituencies

Chair (or largest member)	Rank	Percentage of total votes within constituency
India	1	80%
Canada	2	79%
Italy	3	77%
Brazil	4	57%
Switzerland	5	56%
Chile	6	49%
Netherlands	7	49%
Belgium	8	41%
Spain	9	33%
Sweden	10	32%
Indonesia	12	30%
South Africa	13	29%
Iran	14	28%
Kuwait	15	28%
Congo	16	18%

Source: International Monetary Fund

End Notes

[1] See CRS Report RL32364: *The International Monetary Fund: Organization, Functions, and Role in the International Economy*, by Jonathan Sanford and Martin A. Weiss.

[2] Over time, this linkage has weakened and several countries have been granted special access, allowing them to borrow several times their IMF quota. Argentina, for example borrowed over five times its quota in 2002. In addition, the poorest countries borrow from the IMF under the Fund's concessional facility, the Poverty Reduction and Growth Facility (PRGF). The resources for the PRGF do not come from quotas and are not restricted by any limits.

[3] Special Drawing Rights (SDR) are the IMF's unit of account. Initially defined as equivalent to 0.888671 grams of fine gold, the value of the SDR was switched to a basket of international currencies following the collapse of the Bretton Woods system of fixed parity exchange rates in 1973. The current basket includes the euro, Japanese Yen, the British pound sterling, and the U.S. dollar.

[4] See "IMF's Financial Resources and Liquidity Position, 2004 — June 2006," *The International Monetary Fund*, 2006.

[5] When the IMF was created at the Bretton Woods conference, there was debate between the United States (represented by Harry Dexter White) and the United Kingdom (represented by John Maynard Keynes) over many aspects of the proposed institution. Both the White and Keynes plans proposed fixing quotas on some type of formula that would determine a country's relative global economic standing and allocate an appropriate quota. Such a formula could include consideration of a country's reserves of gold and foreign currencies, magnitude of its balance of payments, national income, population, or any other of a host of economic indicators. Very quickly into the negotiations, it was clear that no formula would determine a quota system that would please all of the 44 new IMF member nations. Moreover, by the time of the Bretton Woods conference, the United States, Great Britain, and the other major donors had reached agreement on the total capitalization of the new institution and their contributions. Thus the United States and the other contributor nations determined the final quota structure through negotiations and then backed into a formula to give the desired result. Explaining how he came up with the quota formula, Raymond Mikesell, an advisor to the U.S. delegation at Bretton Woods, recalled, "I had anticipated this request and gave a rambling twenty-minute seminar on the factors taken in calculating the quotas, but I did not reveal the formula. I tried to make the process appear as scientific as possible, but the delegates were intelligent enough to know that the process was more political than scientific." Since then, the quota formula has been formalized and expanded several times to include additional variables; however the quota formulas are only used as a guide for quota reviews. See Raymond F. Mikesell, "The Bretton Woods Debates: A Memoir," Princeton University Essays in International Finance, No. 192, March 1994, pp. 35-39.

[6] "External Review of Quota Formulas," *International Monetary Fund*, 2000.

[7] At the Bretton Woods Conference, the British proposed a simple voting structure where each country would have a direct vote in proportion to their quota. Mr. White however was concerned that such a system would give the United States and Great Britain too much control over the institution. On the other hand, he noted that to give all countries equal representation would be equally problematic, since the resources were not contributed equally. Mr. White proposed a mixed system that combined elements of the one-country, one-vote system and a proportional system. Mr. White proposed that each country be given 100 basic votes plus an additional vote for each million dollars of quota. Mr. White and Lord Keynes agreed on the mixed-voting system, however they compromised on a system that gave significantly less voting power to small countries than Mr. White's original proposal since countries receive one vote for each $100,000 of quota rather than Mr. White's original proposal of one vote for each $1 million of quota.

[8] For example, Guatemala has an 0.11% voting share at the IMF based on its quota. However, Guatemala never actually independently votes at the IMF on this percentage. As part of a constituency led by Mexico and also including Costa Rica, El Salvador, Honduras, Nicaragua, Spain, and Venezuela, Guatemala shares one executive director on the Executive Board who currently wields 92,989 votes or 4.3%. Within its constituency, Guatemala has 2.5% of the total votes. Spain has 33.1% of the intra-constituency votes, Venezuela has 28.9% and Mexico has 28.1%. Within this constituency, no other country has more than 3.0% of the constituency vote.

[9] Richard Gerster, Proposals for Voting Reform Within the International Monetary Fund, *Journal of World Trade*, June 1993, quoted in David Rapkin and Jonathan Strand, "Reforming the IMF's Weighted Voting System," *The World Economy*, 2006.

[10] With a combined vote of 15.89%, Germany (5.99%), France (4.95%), and the United Kingdom (4.95%) could also block any governance reforms if they voted together.

[11] See Miles Kahler, *Leadership Selection in the Major Multilaterals*, Institute for International Economics, 2001, p. 23.

[12] See CRS Report RL30517, *Asian Financial Crisis and Recovery: Status and Implications for U.S. Interests*, by Richard Cronin.

[13] See C. Randall Henning, *East Asian Financial Cooperation, Institute for International Economics*, October 2002.

[14] See Devesh Kapur and Richard Webb, "Beyond the IMF," Paper for the G-24 Technical Meeting, March 2006 and James Boughton, "Does the World Need a Universal Financial Institution," IMF Working Paper 05/116, June 2005.

[15] The Managing Director's Report on the Fund's Mid-Term Strategy, *International Monetary Fund*, September 15, 2006.

[16] Ibid., p. 12.

[17] The IMFC is the primary advisory board for the full IMF Board of Governors. The IMFC has 24 members who are Governors of the IMF. The membership reflects the composition of the IMF's Executive Board: each member country that appoints, and each group of member countries that elects, an Executive Director appoints a member of the IMFC.

[18] Communiqué of the International Monetary and Financial Committee of the Board of Governors of the International Monetary Fund, April 22, 2006, available at [http://www.imf.org/external/np/cm/2006/042206.htm].

[19] The IMFC meets twice annually (in the springand the fall) to consider major policy issues affecting the international monetary system and make recommendations to the IMF's Board of Governors.

[20] Gary Duncan, "China Wins Bigger Vote Share in Wide Overhaul of IMF," *The Times (London)*, September 17, 2006.

[21] International Monetary Fund, Communiqué of the International Monetary and Financial Committee of the Board of Governors of the International Monetary Fund, October 20, 2007.

[22] John Snow, IMFC statement, April 24, 2006.

[23] Paul Blustein, "U.S. to Support More IMF Votes for China," *The Washington Post*, August 24, 2006.

[24] Michael M. Phillips, "Politics & Economics: U.S. Plots Deal Over Yuan Valuation — China Is Quietly Offered Help On Getting Bigger IMF Role If It Eases Currency Stance," *Wall Street Journal*, July 24, 2006.

[25] See CRS Report RL33762, *Congress, the IMF, and Exchange Rate Reform: Legislative Proposals*, and CRS Report RL33322, *China, the United States and the IMF: Negotiating Exchange Rate Adjustment*, both by Jonathan E. Sanford. See also CRS Report RL32165, *China's Currency: Economic Issues and Options for U.S. Trade Policy*, by Wayne M. Morrison and Marc Labonte.

[26] Edwin Truman, "Rearranging IMF Chairs and Shares: The Sine Qua Non of IMF Reform," in Edwin Truman, ed. *Reforming the IMF for the 21st Century*, Institute for International Economics, 2006, p. 203.

[27] Timothy Adams, "The IMF: Back to Basics," in Edwin Truman, ed. *Reforming the IMF for the 21st Century*, Institute for International Economics, 2006, p. 135.

[28] Originally, the special majority for major IMF votes was 80%. This was later raised to 85%.

[29] For example, an ad hoc quota increase would increase the total amount of IMF quota. If the U.S. quota does not change, an increase in total IMF quota would lead to a decrease in the relative U.S. quota share.

[30] Adams, p. 134.

[31] John Snow Testimony before the House Financial Services Committee, May 17, 2006.

[32] "Making the IMF relevant for Asia A revitalized Fund would help tackle global imbalances" [ASIA EDITION], *Financial Times*, June 8, 2006.

[33] Currently, the formula consists of five equations containing variables for: the overall size of the economy (GDP), capacity to contribute to the IMF (international reserves), two indicators of financial openness (current account transactions and variability of current receipts), and a measure of the potential need to borrow IMF resources (the ratio of current receipts to GDP).

[34] This and the following data are from "Quotas and Voice — Further Considerations," *International Monetary Fund*, September 2, 2005.

[35] "External Review of Quota Formulas," *International Monetary Fund*, 2000.

[36] "Quotas and Voice — Further Considerations," *International Monetary Fund*, 2005.

[37] John B. McLenaghan, "Purchasing Power Parities and Comparisons of GDP in IMF Quota Calculations," Paper presented to the G24 Technical Group Meeting, Manila, Philippines, March 17-18, 2005.

[38] Leo Van Houtvan, "Governance of the IMF: Decision Making, Institutional Oversight, Transparency, and Accountability." *International Monetary Fund*, 2002, p. 8.

[39] This could be in the form of a trust fund set up to help finance the purchase of quota shares for poor countries.

[40] Both documents are available at [http://www.globalpolicy.org/socecon/bwi-wto/imf/ 2006/0323euapproved.htm].

[41] Lauren M. Phillips, Lead, "Follow or Get out of the Way" *Overseas Development Institute*.

[42] Rodrigo de Rato, *Renewing the IMF's Commitment to Low-Income Countries Speech*, The Center for Global Development, Washington, D.C., July 31, 2006.

[43] Snow, IMFC statement.

[44] The Bretton Woods Act Agreement, 22 USC 286c

[45] For example, the Anti-Terrorism and Effective Death Penalty Act of 1996 (P.L. 104-132) instructs the Treasury Department to oppose any loan or other use of IFI funds to or for any country for which the Secretary of State has determined is a state-sponsor of terrorism. A list of all Congressional mandates for the IMF is included in:

Government Accountability Office, *Treasury Has Sustained Its Formal Process to Promote U.S. Policies at the International Monetary Fund GAO-06-876R*, June 29, 2006.

[46] There have been numerous instances of selective quota increases for IMF member countries that did not require congressional authorization or appropriations since the actual value of the U.S. quota was unchanged. However, such increases did reduce the relative U.S. quota share in the institution but since they were all very small increases, the U.S. percentage share remained relatively unchanged.

[47] 22 USC 286c

[48] J. Lawrence Broz and Michael Brewster Hawes, "US Domestic Politics and International Monetary Fund Policy, in *Delegation and Agency in International Organizations*. Edited by Darren Hawkins, David A. Lake, Daniel Nielson, and Michael J. Tierney. *Forthcoming*, Cambridge University Press, 2006.

In: The International Monetary Fund (IMF) Financial Crisis and... ISBN: 978-1-61728-499-1
Editor: Rachel E. Layton

Chapter 5

CURRENCY MANIPULATION: THE IMF AND WTO

Jonathan E. Sanford

SUMMARY

The International Monetary Fund (IMF) and World Trade Organization (WTO) approach the issue of "currency manipulation" differently. The IMF Articles of Agreement prohibit countries from manipulating their currency for the purpose of gaining unfair trade advantage, but the IMF cannot force a country to change its exchange rate policies. The WTO has rules against subsidies, but these are very narrow and specific and do not seem to encompass currency manipulation. Several options might be considered for addressing this matter in the future, if policymakers deem this a wise course of action.

This chapter describes how the International Monetary Fund (IMF) and World Trade Organization (WTO) deal with the issue of currency manipulation. It also discusses apparent discrepancies in their charters and ways those differences might be addressed.

INTERNATIONAL MONETARY FUND

The IMF is the leading international organization in the area of monetary policy. With the end of the cold war, its membership is now nearly universal. Only North Korea, the Vatican, and four other mini-countries in Europe—none having its own currency—are not members of the Fund. The IMF makes loans to countries undergoing financial or balance of payments crises; provides technical assistance to governments on monetary, banking and exchange rate questions; does research and analysis on monetary and economic issues; and it provides a forum where countries can discuss international finance issues and seek common ground on which they can address common problems.

Although the IMF is a monetary institution, the promotion of world growth and balanced international trade are also among its basic goals. Article I of its Articles of Agreement says, among other things, that the IMF was created in order to "facilitate the expansion and balanced growth of international trade, and to contribute thereby to the promotion and maintenance of high levels of employment and real income and to the development of the productive resources of all members as primary objectives of economic policy." It was also created to "assist in the establishment of a multilateral system of payments in respect to current transactions between members and in the elimination of foreign exchange restrictions which hamper the growth of world trade."

Between 1946 and 1971, the IMF supervised a fixed parity exchange rate system, in which the value of all currencies was defined in terms of the U.S. dollar and the dollar was defined in terms of a set quantity of gold. Countries could not change their exchange rates from the level recognized by the IMF by more than 10% without the Fund's consent. Moreover, said the original language of the IMF Articles, "A member shall not propose a change in the par value of its currency except to correct fundamental disequilibrium."[1] This system broke down in 1971 when the United States devalued the dollar twice without any consultation with the IMF. After a period of turmoil in world currency markets, an amendment to the IMF Articles was adopted in 1978. It said that countries could use whatever exchange rate system they wished—fixed or floating—so long as they followed certain guidelines and they did not use gold as the basis for their currencies.

The new language of Article IV, which went into effect in 1978, said that countries should seek, in their foreign exchange and monetary policies, to promote orderly economic growth and financial stability and they should avoid manipulation of exchange rates or the international monetary system *to prevent effective balance of payments adjustment or to gain unfair competitive advantage over other members.* Some countries claim that their exchange rate policies are not in violation of Article IV because they are not seeking to gain competitive advantage (though this may be the result of their actions) but rather *to stabilize the value of their currency in order to prevent disruption to their domestic economic system.* To date, the IMF has not publicly challenged this statement of their objective.

The Fund was required to "exercise firm surveillance over the exchange rate policies of all members and [to] adopt specific principles for the guidance of all members with respect to those policies." The IMF adopted the requisite standards in 1977 (before the Amendment went into effect) and it updated them in 2007. The 1977 agreement said that, among other things, "protracted large-scale intervention in one direction in exchange markets" might be evidence that a country was inappropriately manipulating the value of its currency. The 2007 agreement added a requirement that "A member should avoid exchange rate policies that result in external instability." When a country's current account (balance of payments) is not in equilibrium, the IMF said in its explanation of the new provision, the exchange rate is "fundamentally misaligned" and should be corrected.[2]

The IMF can exercise "firm surveillance" but it cannot compel a country to change its exchange rate. Nor can it order commercial foreign exchange dealers to change the prices at which they trade currencies. It can offer economic advice and discuss how changes in countries' exchange rates might be in their own interest. It can also provide a forum, such as its new multilateral consultation mechanism or discussion on the IMF executive board, where other countries can urge a country to change its exchange rate procedures. However, in the end, the authority to make the change resides with the country alone.

WORLD TRADE ORGANIZATION

The WTO is the central organization in the world trade system. When the WTO was created in 1995, countries were required to accept as a condition of WTO membership the existing trade rules embodied in the General Agreement on Tariffs and Trade (GATT). They also had to accept new rules governing other areas of international commerce, such as services and trade-related international property rights. The agreement establishing the WTO says that the members recognize "that their relations in the field of trade and economic endeavor should be conducted with a view to raising standards of living, ensuring full employment and a steady growing volume of real income and effective demand, and expanding the production of and trade in goods and services" and to do this in a manner "consistent with their respective needs and concerns at different levels of economic development."[3]

Unique among the major international trade and finance organizations, the WTO has a mechanism for enforcing its rules. If a country believes another country has violated WTO rules, to its detriment, it may request the appointment of a dispute settlement panel to hear its complaint. The other country cannot veto the establishment of a panel or adoption of a WTO decision by WTO members. The panel reviews the arguments in the case and renders judgment based on the facts and WTO rules. If the losing party does not comply with the ruling within a reasonable period of time, the WTO may, if requested by the complaining party, authorize it to impose retaliatory measures (usually increased customs duties) against the offending country or to take other appropriate retaliatory measures against that country's trade.

Whether currency disputes fall under the WTO's jurisdiction is a debatable issue. The WTO rules specify that countries may not provide subsidies to help promote their national exports. Most analysts agree that an undervalued currency lowers a firm's cost of production relative to world prices and therefore helps to encourage exports. It is questionable, however, where currency undervaluation is an export subsidy under the WTO's current definition of the term.[4]

The term "subsidy" has a precise definition in the WTO. It requires that there must be a financial contribution by a government to the exporter or some other form of income or price support. Government financial support can take a variety of forms, such as direct payments to the exporter, the waiver of tax payments or special government purchases or the provision of low-cost goods or services (other than general infrastructure) that lowers the cost of production. Currency manipulation would not appear to qualify under the WTO definitions.

In addition, an export subsidy is a subsidy that is "contingent on export performance." In the case of an undervalued currency, everyone who exchanges money will be affected by the current exchange rate no matter whether they are buying or selling and no matter whether or not they are involved in international trade. While subsidies must be "specific to an industry" to be actionable in the WTO, a prohibited subsidy, such as an export subsidy, is considered to be specific *per se*.

Until the world financial system frayed in the 1970s, the IMF exercised strict control over exchange rates. It was inconceivable that a country could persistently value its currency at a level below that approved by the IMF. When the IMF's rules were changed in 1978, so that it no longer governed world exchange rates, the GATT rules were not adjusted to reflect the new reality of international finance. When the WTO was created in 1995, it adopted the existing GATT rules as its own without fundamental change.

Policy Options in the Multilateral Sphere

A number of countries have been suspected or accused in recent years of manipulating the value of their currency for the purpose of gaining unfair trade advantage. The George W. Bush Administration had numerous conversations with China about exchange rate issues. Nonetheless, Bush Administration officials were careful never to say publicly that China was manipulating its currency in violation of IMF rules. During his confirmation hearing on January 23, 2009, by contrast, then Treasury Secretary-designate Timothy Geithner reported that "President Obama, backed by the conclusions of a broad range of economists, believes that China is manipulating its currency." The Administration has not pursued this line of thought, however, in its subsequent discussions with the Chinese government.

If the Treasury Department were to find, in its semi-annual reports to Congress on the topic, that China or any other country were manipulating its currency in order to gain unfair trade advantage, certain provisions of the 1988 trade act would be triggered. To date, neither the prior Clinton or Bush or the current Obama Administrations have made such a finding. If such a finding were made, the U.S. Government would be to press the government of the offending country to revalue its currency. This would likely involved renewed efforts through the IMF to mobilize international support on this issue. It is less clear, though, whether the new Administration would also take this complaint about currency manipulation to the WTO in order to seek remedies through its procedures.

As noted before, the IMF Articles of Agreement prohibit this currency manipulation for the purpose of gaining unfair trade advantage, but the Fund has no capacity to enforce that prohibition. By contrast, the WTO has the capacity to adjudicate trade disputes, but to date it has done nothing to suggest that trade issues linked to currency manipulation are within its zone of responsibility. If policymakers want to address this situation, several options might be considered.

Amend the Articles of the IMF

One option might be changes in the IMF's Articles of Agreement that would give the Fund more authority over international exchange rates and more authority to require that countries comply with its rules. This would restore, to some degree, the power the IMF exercised over exchange rates from 1946 to 1971. Two objections might be raised, however.

First, an 85% majority vote of the IMF member countries is necessary if any change in the IMF Articles is to become effective. Most countries seem to believe that the present system of floating and fixed exchange rates is working reasonably well and there seems to be little desire, on the part of the members, to amend the IMF's current rules.

Second, few countries want the IMF to have the kinds of power over their economies that it would need to compel violators comply with its rules. For example, if the IMF had the power to declare that China's currency was undervalued and to require adjustments, it would also have the power to declare the U.S. dollar or the Euro were overvalued and to require the United States or the Euro zone countries to make changes in their domestic policies in ways that would correct the situation.

Amend the WTO Agreements

Another possibility might be a formal change in the WTO agreements that would define currency manipulation as a prohibited form of export subsidy. It is not easy to amend WTO agreements, however, since the process basically requires the unanimous consent of all Members. Countries that manipulate their currencies could easily block the approval of the amendment. However, they would have to argue that currency manipulation is an acceptable trade practice notwithstanding the language of the IMF's Article IV. It seems more likely that any such change in the WTO rules will be the result of discussions during multilateral trade negotiations, in which restrictions on currency manipulation will be balanced by other changes desired by the countries that believe currency manipulation is an acceptable trade practice.

Seek Adjudication

Alternatively, the United States might consider taking its complaint against countries that manipulate their currency to a formal WTO dispute settlement panel. While in the past, currency issues have not been seen as being encompassed by the WTO dispute settlement process, the United States could argue that changed conditions in the world economy now require adjudication of such disputes.

Article XV of the GATT agreement says that, when disputes between signatory countries involve questions about balances of payments, foreign exchange reserves or exchange arrangements, GATT countries shall "consult fully with the International Monetary Fund" and shall accept the IMF's determination as to matters of fact and as to whether a country's exchange arrangements are consistent its obligations under the IMF Articles of Agreement. GATT Article XV also says that countries "shall not, by exchange action, frustrate the provisions of this agreement nor, by trade action, the intent of the provisions" of the IMF Articles of Agreement.

Traditionally, these references to exchange arrangements have been seen as referring (as they did when the GATT was created in 1947) to currency controls, exchange licenses, transaction taxes and other official actions that limit a potential purchaser's ability to get the foreign exchange needed to purchase goods from abroad.[5] The GATT allows countries to impose temporary import restrictions when they face balance of payments difficulties (Article XII) or when they are at risk for a serious decline in their foreign exchange reserves (Article XVIII).

In recent decades, however, the term "exchange arrangements" has expanded to reflect new developments in the world economy. The language of Article IV, adopted by the IMF in 1978, says (section 2) that each member country shall notify the IMF of the exchange arrangements it intends to apply, in other words, whether its currency will float in value or be pegged to another currency. It says the IMF shall oversee the international monetary system to ensure that each country's exchange arrangements are compatible with its obligations under Article IV. IMF Article IV also says that, in its oversight of countries' exchange arrangements, the Fund shall exercise firm surveillance over the exchange rate policies of its member countries. In effect, a case can be made that the term "exchange arrangements" arguably has become synonymous with the concept "exchange rate regime" and "exchange rate policies."

As it is used in GATT Article XV, the term "exchange arrangement" refers to issues that are the sole province of the IMF. Thus, one could argue that the meaning of the term in the GATT should reflect its current meaning at the IMF and not the meaning prevalent in 1947. An undervalued currency encourages exports by reducing their cost and it discourages imports by making them more expensive than they might be otherwise. Consequently, one might argue that countries with this type of exchange arrangement are engaging in "exchange action" that may have the effect of frustrating "the provisions of the [GATT] agreement."

There has never been a definitive ruling by the GATT or WTO on the meaning of Article XV, including how provisions of the GATT agreement might be frustrated by exchange action. Some might argue that currency undervaluation raises the price of imports in a way that unilaterally rescinds tariff concessions approved during multilateral trade talks.

Accordingly, a case could be made that the WTO should use the broader meaning of the term "exchange arrangements" and take currency valuation arrangements into account in its dispute settlement process. There has also been increased interest, in recent years, in the issue of currency manipulation and its impact on world trade and financial relationships. It could be argued, therefore, that this might be an appropriate and perhaps auspicious moment for issues relating to the trade impact of currency manipulation to be raised in the WTO dispute adjudication process.

Improve the IMF-WTO Agreement

Another option is to strengthen the current interagency agreement between the WTO and the IMF. The present agreement was signed in 1996 and updated in mid-2006. Among other things, it says (paragraph 1) that the two organizations "shall cooperate in the discharge of their respective mandates."[6] It says (paragraph 2) the two agencies "shall consult with each other with a view to achieving greater coherence in global economic policymaking." It also says (paragraph 8) that the two agencies shall communicate with each other about "matters of mutual interest."

Article XV of the GATT agreement says that the GATT (now WTO) shall cooperate with the IMF in order to "pursue a coordinated policy with regards to exchange questions that are within the jurisdiction of the Fund." It is unreasonable to expect that the WTO should be expected to enforce the rules of the IMF. Nevertheless, one might expect that conversations about the ways the activities of one organization might be hindering the other "in the discharge of" its assigned duties could transpire. Their different policies towards the question of exchange rate manipulation do not seem to encourage "greater coherence in global economic policymaking."

Changes in the existing inter-agency agreement can be effected by a majority vote in each institution. No such agreement can change their basic rules. However, it might provide that their disparate treatment of currency manipulation is inconsistent with their promise to "cooperate in the discharge of their respective mandates" and to promote "greater coherence in global economic policymaking." The IMF and WTO could also work with each other to identify and mitigate situations where their rules and procedures were not consistent or not mutually supportive and areas where changes in policy or institutional arrangements might be recommended to their member countries.

End Notes

[1] This language is quoted from Section 5 of the original language of Article IV as approved by the 1944 Bretton Woods conference and confirmed by all member countries when the IMF officially came into existence in 1946.

[2] IMF. *IMF Surveillance—the 2007 Decision on Bilateral Surveillance*. Factsheet, June 2007.

[3] *Agreement Establishing the World Trade Organization*, 1995, preamble.

[4] *Agreement on Subsidies and Countervailing Measures*, Articles 1 to 3.

[5] See, for example, John H. Jackson, *World Trade and the Law of GATT*. New York: The Bobbs-Merrill Company, 1969, pp. 479-495.

[6] *Agreement Between the International Monetary Fund and the World Trade Organization*, updated June 30, 2006.

In: The International Monetary Fund (IMF) Financial Crisis and... ISBN: 978-1-61728-499-1
Editor: Rachel E. Layton

Chapter 6

THE G-20 AND INTERNATIONAL ECONOMIC COOPERATION: BACKGROUND AND IMPLICATIONS FOR CONGRESS

Rebecca M. Nelson

SUMMARY

Governments discuss and coordinate economic policies using a mix of formal institutions, such as the World Trade Organization (WTO) and International Monetary Fund (IMF), and more informal economic forums, like the Group of Seven, or G-7, and the Group of 20, or G-20. This chapter focuses on informal economic forums, and, specifically, the role of the G-20 in coordinating governments' responses to the current economic crisis. The members of the G-7 are Canada, France, Germany, Italy, Japan, the United Kingdom, and the United States. The G-20 includes the G-7 members plus Argentina, Australia, Brazil, China, India, Indonesia, Mexico, Russia, Saudi Arabia, South Africa, South Korea, Turkey, and the European Union (EU).

Since the mid-1970s, leaders from the G-7, a small group of developed countries, have gathered annually to discuss and coordinate financial and economic policies. Large emerging-market economies such as China started to have more sway in financial markets in the 1990s, and the Asian Financial Crisis in 1997-1998 showed that emerging markets were too important to exclude from international economic discussions. The G-20 was formed in 1999 as an opportunity for finance ministers and central bank governors from both developed and emerging-market countries to discuss financial issues. The G-20 remained a less prominent forum than the G-7, as it involved meetings among finance ministers while the G-7 sessions also involved summit meetings among heads of governments or heads of state.

With the onset of the current financial crisis, the G-7 leaders decided to convene the G-20 leaders for a meeting, or "summit," to discuss and coordinate policy responses to the crisis. To date, the G-20 leaders have held three summits to coordinate policy responses to the crisis: November 2008 in Washington, DC; April 2009 in London; and September 2009 in Pittsburgh. At the Pittsburgh summit, the G-20 leaders announced that the G-20 would henceforth be the premier forum for international economic coordination, supplanting the G-7's role as such.

The G-20 leaders have made commitments on a variety of issue areas. Implementation of some of these commitments by the United States would require legislation. Issues that are likely to influence future policy debates and/or the legislative agenda include: financial regulatory reform, a new international framework to monitor and coordinate economic policies, voting reform at the IMF and World Bank, increased funding of multilateral development banks (MDBs), elimination of fossil fuel subsidies, concluding a new international agreement to reduce greenhouse gas emissions, concluding the WTO Doha multilateral trade negotiations, and meeting previous commitments on foreign aid.

The shift from the G-7 to the G-20 as the premier forum for international economic coordination may raise issues for international economic coordination in the future. Some suggest the shift will foster cooperation, by increasing the legitimacy of the decisions reached and including countries that are big players in the global economy. Others argue that the shift will hinder efforts at cooperation, because such a large, heterogeneous group of countries will have trouble reaching agreements on key issues. Some say the G-20 meetings should be even larger and more comprehensive, to include poor and small nations in their deliberations. Others say that the existing G-20 is already sufficiently diverse and increasing the size would make it too cumbersome and less effective.

INTRODUCTION

The Group of Twenty, or G-20, is a forum for advancing international economic cooperation among developed and emerging-market countries.[1] Since the G-20 was established in 1999, the G-20 finance ministers and central bank governors have met annually to discuss economic and financial issues. In the wake of the current global financial crisis, the leaders of the developed countries decided to convene the G-20 heads of government or heads of state for a meeting, or "summit," to discuss and coordinate policy responses to the crisis.[2] The summit, held in Washington, DC in November 2008, was the first time this particular group of leaders had gathered to coordinate economic policies. For the past 30 years, economic discussions among advanced economies at the leader level occurred among the Group of Seven (G-7) nations, a much smaller group of developed countries as shown in Figure 1.[3]

The G-20 leaders convened for two additional summits, in London in April 2009 and in Pittsburgh in September 2009, to continue discussions on policy responses to the crisis. In each of the three G-20 summits, the G-20 leaders made several policy commitments, and the depth and scope of these commitments have increased over time. In Washington, DC, the commitments were focused on short- and medium-term responses to the crisis, including regulatory reform, expansionary macroeconomic policies, and commitments to free trade. In London, the G-20 leaders reached more substantial agreements on crisis management, including increasing the resources of the International Monetary Fund (IMF) and multilateral development banks (MDBs) by $1.1 trillion. At the Pittsburgh summit, the G-20 pledged commitments on a diverse set of issue areas, including changes in the relative voting power of member countries at the IMF and World Bank, creating a new framework to correct global imbalances, taking new steps to address food security issues, and eliminating fossil fuel subsidies.

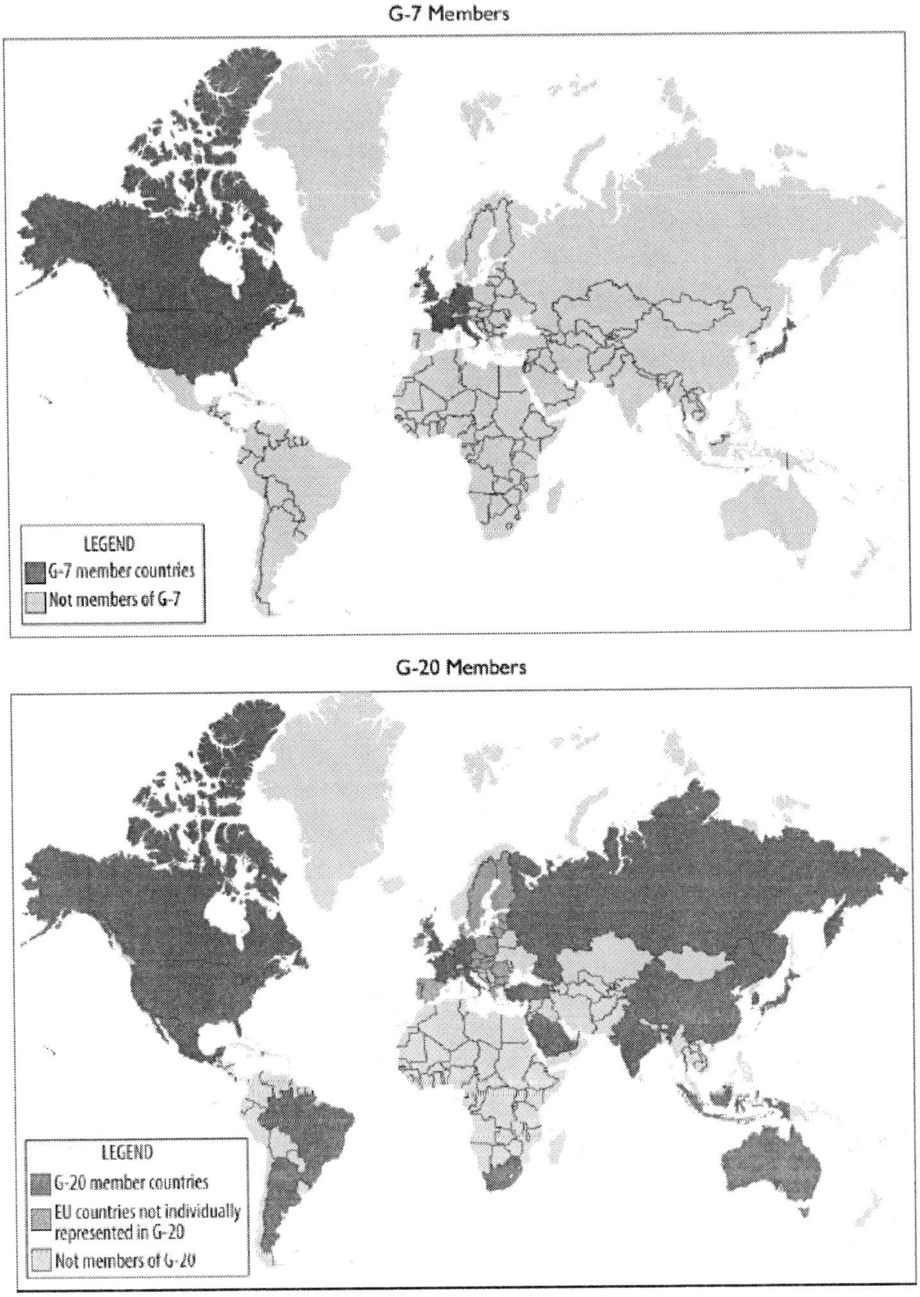

Source: G-20 website, http://www.g20.org

Notes: The European Union (EU) is a member of the G-20. Pink (for color copies) or medium gray (for blackand-white copies) indicate members of the European Union (EU) that are not individually represented in the G-20.

Figure 1. Expansion of the G-7 to the G-20

Additionally, the G-20 leaders announced at the Pittsburgh summit that, henceforth, the G-20 would be the premier forum for international economic cooperation, displacing the G-7's long-standing status as the primary forum for coordinating international economic policies. G-20 discussions are not to cover international relations and foreign policy issues, though this may change in future years. For these issues, the Group of Eight, or G-8 (the G-7 members plus Russia) will likely continue to be the principal forum, though more consultation with other countries is also likely. The transition from the G-7 to the G-20 for economic issues may have a substantial impact on international economic coordination in the future. Some argue that the transition will foster greater cooperation, while others contend these goals could be hindered.

Congressional interest in the G-20 is, at the least, two-fold. First, implementing many of the commitments made by the Administration at the G-20 summits to date would require reform of U.S. laws and regulations. As a consequence, the agreements reached by the G-20 leaders may influence policy debates and the legislative agenda. Second, the transition from the G-7 to the G-20 may impact U.S. coordination with other countries on international economic issues in the future. To provide oversight of U.S. participation in international economic forums, it is important to highlight the issues raised by the shift from the G-7 to the G-20.

This chapter addresses the following key issues:

- Context on the emergence of the G-20 as the premier forum for internationaleconomic coordination;
- Background on how the G-20 operates, including where and when the G-20 meets and how the G-20 reaches decisions;
- An overview of the three G-20 summits and analysis of how they have evolved;
- Major G-20 commitments that are likely to shape the policy agenda moving forward; and
- Broader issues raised by the shift from the G-7 to the G-20.

THE RISE OF THE G-20 AS THE PREMIER FORUM FOR INTERNATIONAL ECONOMIC COOPERATION

Economic Coordination in Formal Institutions and Informal Forums

Since World War II, governments have created and used formal international institutions and more informal forums to discuss economic policies. As economic integration has increased over the past 30 years, however, international economic policy coordination has become even more active and significant. Globalization may bring economic benefits, but it also means that a country's economy is increasingly affected by the economic policy decisions of other governments. These effects are not always positive. For example, a country's exports may decline should another country devalue its currency or restrict imports to attempt to reverse a trade deficit or protect domestic industries. Instead of countries unilaterally implementing these "beggar-thy-neighbor" policies, some say they may be better off coordinating to refrain from such negative outcomes. Another reason countries may want to coordinate policies is that some economic policies, like fiscal stimulus, are more effective in open economies when countries implement them together.

Governments use a mix of formal international institutions and international economic forums to coordinate economic policies. Formal institutions, such as the International Monetary Fund (IMF), the Organization for Economic Co-operation and Development (OECD), the World Bank, and the World Trade Organization (WTO), are typically formed by an official international agreement and have a permanent office with staff performing ongoing tasks. Governments have also relied on more informal forums for economic discussions, such as the G-7 and the Paris Club.[4] These economic forums do not have formal rules or a permanent staff. This chapter focuses on informal forums, particularly the G-20.[5]

1970s – 1990s: Developed Countries Dominate Financial Discussions

Prior to the current global financial crisis, international economic discussions at the top leadership level primarily took place among a small group of developed industrialized countries. Beginning in the mid-1970s, leaders from a group of five developed countries—France, Germany, Japan, the United Kingdom, and the United States—began to meet annually to discuss international economic challenges, including the oil shocks and the collapse of the Bretton Woods system of fixed exchange rates. This group, called the Group of Five, or G-5, was broadened to include Canada and Italy, and the Group of Seven, or G-7, formally superseded the G-5 in the mid-1980s. In 1998, Russia also joined, creating the G-8.[6] Russia does not usually participate in discussions on international economic policy, which continued to occur mainly at the G-7 level. Meetings among finance ministers and central bank governors typically precede the summit meetings.

Macroeconomic policies discussed in the G-7 context include exchange rates, balance of payments, globalization, trade, and economic relations with developing countries. One of the most significant agreements reached by the G-7 was at the first summit in Rambouillet, France, in 1975. The G-7 leaders agreed to a new monetary system to replace the system of fixed exchange rates that unraveled in the early 1970s and set the stage for amending the IMF Articles of Agreement to allow floating exchange rates.[7] Examples of other significant agreements reached by the G-7 are the Plaza Agreement in 1985 and the Louvre Accord in 1987. The Plaza Agreement aimed to depreciate the U.S. dollar in relation to German Deutsche mark and the Japanese yen, and the Louvre Accord aimed to halt the continued decline of the U.S. dollar. Over time, the G-7's and, subsequently the G-8's, focus on macroeconomic policy coordination expanded to include a variety of other global and transnational issues, such as the environment, crime, drugs, AIDS, and terrorism.

1990s – 2008: Emerging Markets Gain Greater Influence

Expanding the G-7 to the G-20 is a significant shift in how international economic coordination has been organized for the past three decades. At the same time, the impetus for this shift has been building as emerging-market countries have become more active in the international economy.

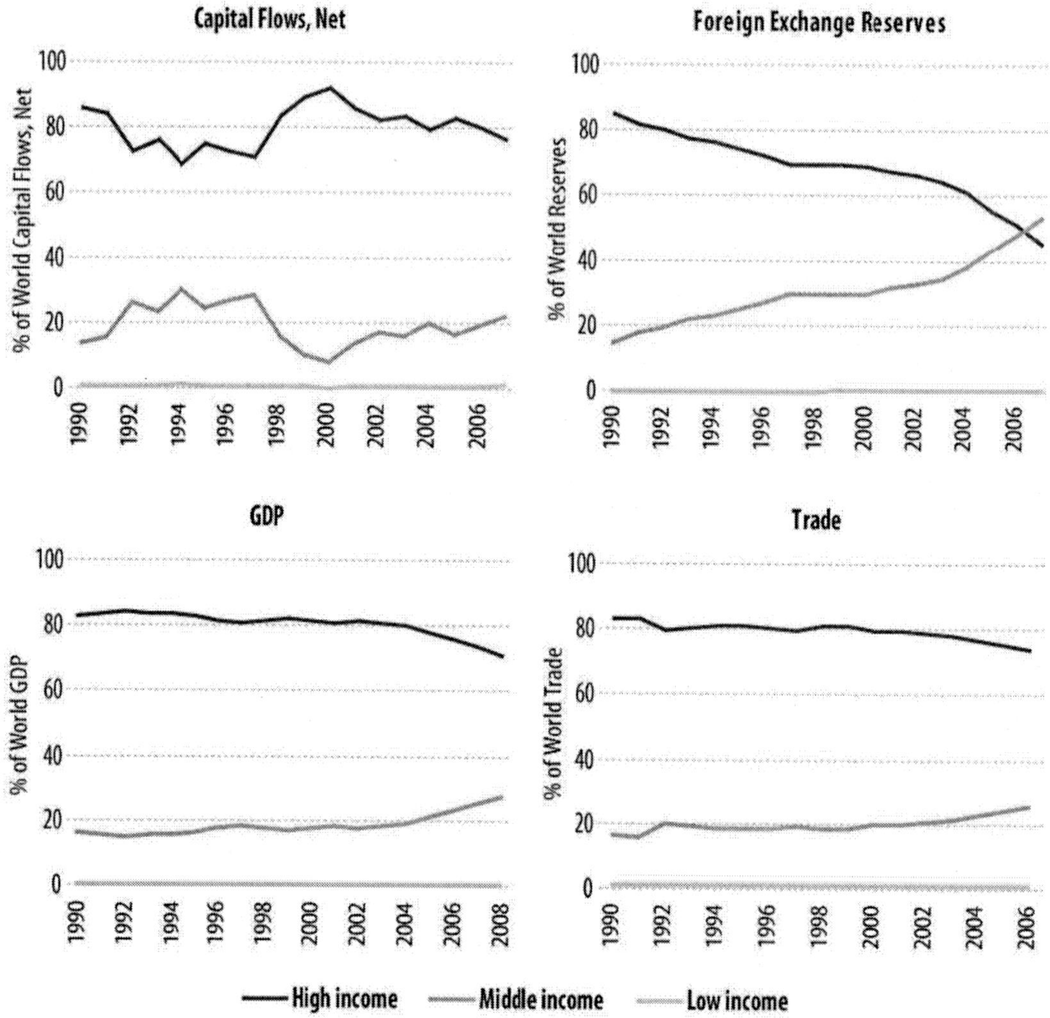

Source: World Bank World Development Indicators. Capital includes portfolio investment and foreign direct investment.

Figure 2. Increasing Role of Emerging-Market Countries in the International Economy

Consider **Figure 2**, which examines the proportion of world capital flows (net), foreign exchange reserves, GDP, and trade held by high-, middle-, and low-income countries. In the early 1990s, middle income countries (roughly equivalent to emerging-market countries) started receiving a much larger proportion of the world's capital flows, including portfolio investment and foreign direct investment. Their share dropped during the Asian financial crisis in the late 1990s, but has slowly been rising since 2000. Likewise, middle-income countries' share of world foreign exchange reserves has been steadily on the rise since the 1990s. In recent years, the reserve holdings of middle-income countries has become larger than the reserve holdings of high-income countries. Middle-income countries' share of world GDP and world trade was largely stagnant in the 1990s but has started to increase over the past decade.

Although middle-income countries, or emerging-market countries, have become more active in the international economy, particularly in financial markets starting in 1990, this was not reflected in the international financial architecture until the Asian financial crisis in 1997-1998. The Asian financial crisis in 1997-1998 demonstrated that problems in the financial markets of emerging-market countries can have serious spillover effects on financial markets in developed countries, making emerging markets too important to exclude from discussions on economic and financial issues. The Group of 22, or G-22, was established as a temporary forum for finance ministers and central bank governors from both advanced industrialized and emerging-market countries to discuss the Asian Financial Crisis.[8] The G-22 met twice in 1998, and was superseded by the Group of 33, or G-33, to discuss international financial stability and the international financial stability forum.[9] The G-33 was also a temporary forum that met twice in 1999.

Including emerging-market countries in economic discussions proved to be fruitful, and the G-20 was established in late 1999 as a permanent international economic forum for developed and emerging-market countries. However, the G-20 was a secondary forum to the G-7 and G-8; the G-20 convened finance ministers and central bank governors, while the G-8 also convened leaders in addition to finance ministers.

Emerging markets were also granted more sway in international economic discussions when the G-8 partly opened its door to them in 2005.[10] The United Kingdom's Prime Minister Tony Blair invited five emerging economies–China, Brazil, India, Mexico, and South Africa– to participate in its discussions but not as full participants (the "G-8 +5"). The presence of emerging-market countries gave them some input in the meetings but they were clearly not treated as full G-8 members. Brazil's finance minister is reported to have complained that developing nations were invited to G-8 meetings "only to take part in the coffee breaks."[11]

2008 – Present: Emerging Markets Get a Seat at the Table

It is only with the outbreak of the current financial crisis in fall 2008 that emerging markets have been invited as full participants to international economic discussions at the highest level. There are different explanations for why the shift from the G-7 to the G-20 occurred. Some emphasize a recognition by the leaders of developed countries that emerging markets have become sizable players in the international economy and are simply "too important to bar from the room."[12]

Others suggest that the transition from the G-7 to the G-20 was driven by the negotiating strategies of European and U.S. leaders. It is reported that that France's president, Nicolas Sarkozy, and Britain's prime minister, Gordon Brown, pushed for a G-20 summit, rather than a G8 summit, to discuss the economic crisis in order to dilute perceived U.S. dominance over the forum, as well as to "show up America and strut their stuff on the international stage."[13] Likewise, it is reported that President George W. Bush also preferred a G-20 summit in order to balance the strong European presence in the G-8 meetings.[14] Some attribute the G-20's staying power to the political difficulties of reverting back to the G-7 after having convened the G-20.

How the G-20 Operates

Frequency of Meetings

The G-8 and G-20 heads-of-state meetings, or summits, are the focal points of the G-8 and G-20 discussions and where the forums' key decisions are announced. However, various lower-level officials meet frequently before the summits to begin negotiations and after the summits to discuss the logistical and technical details of implementing the agreements announced at the summits.

Prior to the current global financial crisis, the G-20 finance ministers and central bank governors have met once a year since the G-20 was established in 1999. The annual meeting of G-20 finance ministers and central bank governors has been preceded by extensive preparation to provide them with up-to-date analysis and insights and to better inform their consideration of policy challenges and options. This includes two deputies meetings each year as well as extensive technical work, including an array of workshops, reports, and case studies on specific subjects.

As economic discussions at the leader level transition from the G-7 to the G-20, it is expected that the G-20 schedule will mimic the G-7's schedule in the past. The G-7 leaders, and Russia, have met annually, and the G-7 finance ministers and central bank governors have met at least semiannually, and as frequently as four times a year, to monitor developments in the world economy and assess economic policies. The G-20 leaders are scheduled to meet twice in 2010, June 2010 in Canada and November 2010 in South Korea. Starting in 2011, the G-20 expects to hold summits on an annual basis.

At various points in time, usually at the request of the G-8 leaders, the G-7 or G-8 ministers of development, education, employment and labor, energy, ministers, global information and society, health, justice, science, and trade have also occasionally convened to discuss pertinent issues. The G-20 has already, for example, called on the G-20 employment and labor ministers to meet in 2010 to discuss the problem of unemployment.

In addition to the summits and various ministerial meetings, there are also meetings among the leaders' personal representatives, known as "sherpas."[15] Sherpas meet several times a year to prepare for the forthcoming summit, attend the formal summit meetings with the leaders, and hold several follow-up meetings. The sherpa team for each country typically includes a lead sherpa and two "sous-sherpas": a finance sous-sherpa and a foreign affairs sous-sherpa.[16] The foreign affairs sous-sherpa covers issues outside the purview of finance, such as trade and the environment.

Finally, a variety of task forces, working groups, and expert groups have been established by the G-8 leaders or G-7 finance ministers over the years as well to support the work of the G-8 and the G-7. Examples include the Financial Action Task Force (FATF), the Financial Stability Forum (FSF), the Counter-Terrorism Action Group, and the Global Fund to Fight AIDS, Tuberculosis, and Malaria, and the G-8 Renewable Energy Task Force.

U.S. Representation

Because the G-20 began as a forum for finance ministers and central bank governors, the Treasury Department and the Federal Reserve have traditionally been the primary U.S. agencies involved in the G-20 meetings. As the G-20 has replaced the G-7 on finance issues, the Treasury Department has taken the lead on the G-20 meetings. However, the Treasury Department works closely with other agencies throughout the G-20 process. In addition to the Federal Reserve, the Treasury Department also coordinates with the State Department, the U.S. Agency for International Development, and, increasingly, the Department of Energy to coordinate G-20 issues. The White House, particularly through the National Security Council and the U.S. Trade Representative, is also heavily involved in the G-20 planning process.

The U.S. sherpa for the G-20 is the Deputy National Security Advisor for International Economic Affairs, a position currently held by Mike Froman. The U.S. sous-sherpa for finance issues is the Under Secretary of International Affairs at the Treasury Department, who also represents the U.S. at G-20 meetings at the level of deputy finance minister. Lael Brainard has been designated for this position subject to confirmation by the Senate. The Senate Finance Committee held her confirmation hearing in November 2009 and while a vote on her confirmation has not yet been scheduled, it is anticipated that it will occur soon. Finally, the U.S. sous-sherpa for foreign affairs issues is the Under Secretary for Economic, Energy, and Agricultural Affairs at the State Department. Robert D. Hormats currently holds this position.

Location of Meetings and Attendees

Unlike formal international institutions, such as the United Nations and the World Bank, the G-20 does not have a permanent headquarters or staff. Instead, each year, a G-20 member country serves as the chair of the G-20. The chair hosts the highest level meetings, which before the crisis was among finance ministers but moving forward will be the leaders' summit meetings. The chair also establishes a temporary office that is responsible for the group's secretarial, clerical, and administrative affairs, known as the temporary "secretariat." The secretariat also coordinates the G-20's various meetings for the duration of its term as chair and typically posts details of the G20's meetings and work program on the G-20's website.[17]

The chair rotates among members and is selected from a different region each year. Table 1 lists the previous and current chairs of the G-20, as well as the member country slotted to chair in 2010 (South Korea) and 2011 (France). The United States has never officially chaired the G-20, although the United States has hosted two of the three G-20 summits held to date.

In addition to the G-20 members, Spain and the Netherlands have also attended, as observers, the three G-20 summits to date. Several regional organizations and international organizations have also attended the G-20 summits. For example, official participants at the London summit included the leaders of the G-20 member countries as well as representatives from the following organizations:

- the European Commission
- the European Council

Table 1. Chairs of the G-20, 1999-2011

Year	Country
1999-2001	Canada
2002	India
2003	Mexico
2004	Germany
2005	China
2006	Australia
2007	South Africa
2008	Brazil
2009	United Kingdom
2010	South Korea
2011	France

Source: G-20 website, http://www.g20.org.

- the Association of Southeast Asian Nations (ASEAN)
- the Financial Stability Board (FSB, formerly the Financial Stability Forum, FSF)
- the International Monetary Fund (IMF)
- the New Partnership for Africa's Development (NEPAD)
- the United Nations
- the World Bank
- the World Trade Organization[18]

Agreements

All agreements, comments, recommendations, and policy reforms reached by the G-20 finance ministers and central bankers, as well as by G-20 leaders, are done so by consensus. There is no formal voting system as in some formal international economic institutions, like the IMF. Participation in the G-20 meetings is restricted to members and not open to the public. After each meeting, however, the G-20 publishes online the agreements reached among members, typically as communiqués or declarations.[19] The G-20 does not have a way to enforce implementation of the agreements reached by the G-20 at the national level; the G-20 has no formal enforcement mechanism and the commitments are non-binding. This contrasts with, for example, the World Trade Organization (WTO), which does have formal enforcement mechanisms in place.[20] However, according to the participants, each G-20 meeting reviews the agreements and commitments reached at prior meetings.

Overview of the G-20 Summits

The G-20 has been at the forefront of coordinating responses to the economic crisis. As mentioned previously, the G-20 has held three summits since the onset of the financial crisis: Washington, DC in November 2008, London in April 2009, and Pittsburgh in September

2009. These summits are generally preceded by meetings of finance ministers and other chief economic officials. The G-20 has two summits scheduled for 2010: Canada in June 2010 and South Korea in November 2010. Starting in 2011, the G-20 leaders are expected to convene on an annual basis, though meetings at a financial minister level are likely to occur more often.

After each summit, the G-20 leaders issue a declaration or communiqué detailing the agreements reached among the members.[21] The types of agreements reached at the G-20 summits have evolved as the crisis has transitioned from economic free-fall to signs of recovery and as the G-20 has solidified as a forum for international economic cooperation at the leader level. With each subsequent summit, the G-20's commitments have become more specific, extended over longer time horizons, covered more issue areas, and emphasized greater participation of emerging-market countries in the international financial architecture.

Washington, DC, November 2008

The Washington, DC summit focused on immediate crisis management. The G-20 pledged to pursue extensive regulatory reforms, including the creation of new international regulatory standards and national level reforms. The G-20 also pledged to use expansionary macroeconomic policies, both fiscal and monetary, to stimulate aggregate demand and encourage economic growth, or at least keep things from getting worse. Finally, the G-20 committed to refrain from protectionist trade policies.

London, April 2009

The London summit occurred several months after the Washington, DC summit, but the G-20 leaders were still in crisis management mode. The G-20 leaders reiterated many of the commitments from the Washington, DC summit and also reached agreement on more specific and far-reaching policy responses to the crisis. One of the biggest commitments from the London summit was the pledge to increase funding for the IMF and the MDBs by $1.1 trillion, including a tripling of the IMF's lending capacity.[22] The G-20 leaders also pledged $5 trillion in fiscal stimulus spending over the next two years and to create the Financial Stability Board (FSB) as the successor to the Financial Stability Forum (FSF) to coordinate and monitor progress on regulatory reforms. The G-20 also emphasized their commitment to concluding the World Trade Organization (WTO) Doha Round of multilateral trade negotiations, which have stalled since 2001, and honoring their foreign aid commitments. Reforming the international financial institutions (IFIs) to increase the representation of emerging-market countries was discussed, but no real specific commitments were put forth.

Pittsburgh, September 2009

The Pittsburgh summit occurred as the global recession was bottoming out, although unemployment was generally still rising in developed countries. The tone of the Pittsburgh communiqué reflects a sense of accomplishment with the G-20's response to address the crisis, while recognizing more work was needed. The G-20 leaders announced the creation of a new framework to coordinate and monitor national economic policies in order to correct the current global imbalances and prevent such imbalances from occurring in the future. The G-20 also announced more specific plans to increase the representation of emerging-market countries at the IMF and World Bank, as well as specific commitments on a host of new policy areas, including economic development and the environment.

Protests at G-20 Summits

Each of the three G-20 summits have attracted protesters. The protesters tend to come from a mix of broad movements, including environmentalists, trade unions, socialist organizations, faith-based groups, anti-war camps, and anarchists.[23] At the Pittsburgh summit, for example, thousands of protestors gathered in the streets, holding signs with slogans such as "We Say No To Corporate Greed" and "G20=Death By Capitalism."[24] The protests have primarily been peaceful, although at times tensions between the police and protesters have escalated. In Pittsburgh, protestors began throwing rocks,[25] police used pepper gas against a group of students,[26] and several protestors were arrested.[27]

Issues on the Horizon

The major G-20 commitments that are likely to influence the policy agenda in the near future are described and analyzed in greater detail below.

Regulatory Reform

Some argue that a major cause of the current global financial crisis was the failure of policymakers to adequately regulate financial markets both domestically and globally. Consequently, proposals for regulatory reform have been central components of each of the three G-20 summits to date. The proposals have generally emphasized the need for new international regulatory standards and the implementation of regulatory reforms at the national level. Examples of the reforms proposed include:

- Creating new global accounting standards,
- Expanding the transparency of complex financial instruments,
- Strengthening and harmonizing capital standards,
- Reassessing banker compensation,
- Regulating all systemically important financial institutions,
- Regulating credit rating agencies, and
- Fighting illicit financial activity.

At the G-20 summit held in Pittsburgh, the G-20 leaders announced several deadlines for some key regulatory reforms. These include:

- Developing new standards for bank capital by end-2010,
- Implementing new capital standards by end-2012,
- Strengthened regulation of over-the-counter derivatives markets by end-2012,
- Addressing cross-border resolutions and systemically important financial institutions by end-2010,
- Converging on new global accounting standards by June 2011,
- Implementing countermeasures against tax havens from March 2010, and
- Initiating a peer review process of non-cooperative jurisdictions (NCJs) byFebruary 2010.

As noted earlier, the G-20 leaders also announced the creation of the FSB as a successor to the FSF. The FSF was founded in 1999, the wake of the Asian financial crisis, to promote international financial stability. The new FSB has a larger membership, including the major emerging-market countries, and a stronger mandate to coordinate and monitor progress in strengthening financial regulation. Secretary of Treasury Tim Geithner considers that, in effect, the FSB will be the fourth pillar in the architecture of international cooperation along with the IMF, the World Bank, and the WTO.[28]

The FSB is currently undertaking a project to compare national implementation of regulatory reforms and identify cross-country differences and any need for policy actions to address them. As the FSB itself acknowledges, the FSB can develop coherent policy proposals and monitor progress on implementation, but "only national authorities can assure implementation that is effective and consistent across borders."[29] In the FSB's analysis to date, the FSB finds that while regulatory reforms are well underway, they are far from complete.[30] Given the G-20's commitments on regulatory reform in the Pittsburgh summit and the FSB's project to assess the status of national implementation of regulatory reforms, regulatory reform is likely to be a key issue moving ahead and major legislation has been introduced by key committees.

A New Framework to Coordinate and Monitor Economic Policies

Some believe that the United States' external deficit and China's external surplus contributed to an unstable imbalance in the world financial system. In order to correct this imbalance, and promote compatible national economic policies in the future, the G-20 announced a new "Framework for Strong, Sustainable and Balanced Growth."[31] The Framework would operate in three stages. First, the G-20 members would agree on shared policy objectives, updated as economic conditions evolve. Second, each G 20 member would agree to establish national, medium-term policy frameworks, and the G-20 members would work in conjunction with the IMF to assess the collective implications of national policy frameworks for global growth and financial stability. Third, the G-20 members would, based on the results of the peer review process, consider and agree to actions that are necessary to meet the common objectives.

If the peer review process, or "cooperative process of mutual assessment," reveals policies that are not consistent with the G-20's shared policy objectives, the only mechanism currently available for inducing policy change is the threat of "naming and shaming." This has worked to some extent for the G-7 economic process, but it has worked less well in international organizations. Some question, then, whether the new G-20 Framework will be different than IMF surveillance.[32] The IMF has the responsibility to monitor the international monetary system and the economic and financial policies of individual IMF member countries. In recent years, it has also monitored broader global and regional trends. Under its surveillance programs, the IMF can point to weaknesses in an economy but does not have authority to enforce policy changes to address those weaknesses. Countries that do not need to borrow from the IMF have often shrugged off its advice. It is not clear under the current framework for the G-20 how the mutual assessments will translate into policy actions by participating countries on particular key issues such as correcting global imbalances that may require increasing savings in the United States or increasing spending in China.

That said, even if the G-20 Framework is in practice similar to IMF surveillance, the G-20 Framework would raise the profile of monitoring economic policies to the leader level and would emphasize the importance of multilateral surveillance. It is also worth noting that "naming and shaming" has at times been an effective strategy for inducing reform. For example, the Financial Action Task Force on Money Laundering (FAFT)'s blacklist of non-cooperative countries and entities was effective in bringing about reforms on anti-money-laundering efforts.

Developing countries are publicly supportive of the Framework, but *The Economist* reports that they are uneasy about formalizing a realignment of global imbalances.[33] *The Economist* speculates that developing countries' public support for the Framework is driven by suspicions that the policy reforms suggested by the mutual assessments will be difficult to enforce.[34] Moreover, some worry that efforts to address the problem of international financial imbalances without simultaneous efforts to address the conditions which caused the imbalances to occur might have unsatisfactory results.

Increasing the Representation of Emerging Markets in International Financial Institutions (IFIs)

There has been frustration among emerging-market countries that the IMF and the World Bank have not been reformed to reflect their increased weight in the world economy. The G-20 pledged a shift of at least 5% of the IMF quota share (which impacts voting power) from over-represented countries to under-represented countries by January 2011.[35] The G-20 leaders also committed to increase at least 3% of the voting power for developing and transition countries at the World Bank. Although the G-20 leaders agreed to this voting reform in the abstract, it has yet to be decided exactly which countries would lose or gain voting rights. Taking voting power away from countries is politically sensitive, and negotiations over the specifics of voting reform are expected to be difficult, particularly with European countries who are likely to lose voting shares in the reforms.[36] The United States, by contrast, is unlikely to lose voting power in the negotiations, as the United States is actually an under-represented country at the IMF. The United States chose to allow its proportional share to decline in recent decades, partly to make room for new members and partly to lower its financial obligation.

To date, voting reform at the IMF has garnered more attention than the World Bank. Which countries, more specifically, are over- and under-represented at the IMF? There is general agreement that each IMF member's quota should broadly reflect its relative size in the world economy.[37] One way to gauge which countries are over- and under-represented at the IMF is to compare a country's share of world GDP with its IMF quota share.[38] By this metric, countries with quota shares that are larger than their share of world GDP may be considered to be overrepresented at the IMF. For example, because Saudi Arabia's quota share in the IMF is 2.93% but its share of world GDP is only 0.71%, Saudi Arabia may be considered to be over-represented. Another example is Belgium, whose quota share is 1.93% even though its share of world GDP is only 0.59%.

By contrast, countries may be considered to be under-represented at the IMF when their quota share is smaller than their share of world GDP. The United States is generally considered to be under-represented at the IMF, with a quota share of 17.67% but 21.82% of world GDP. Figure 3 shows examples of countries that are over- and under-represented at the IMF.[39]

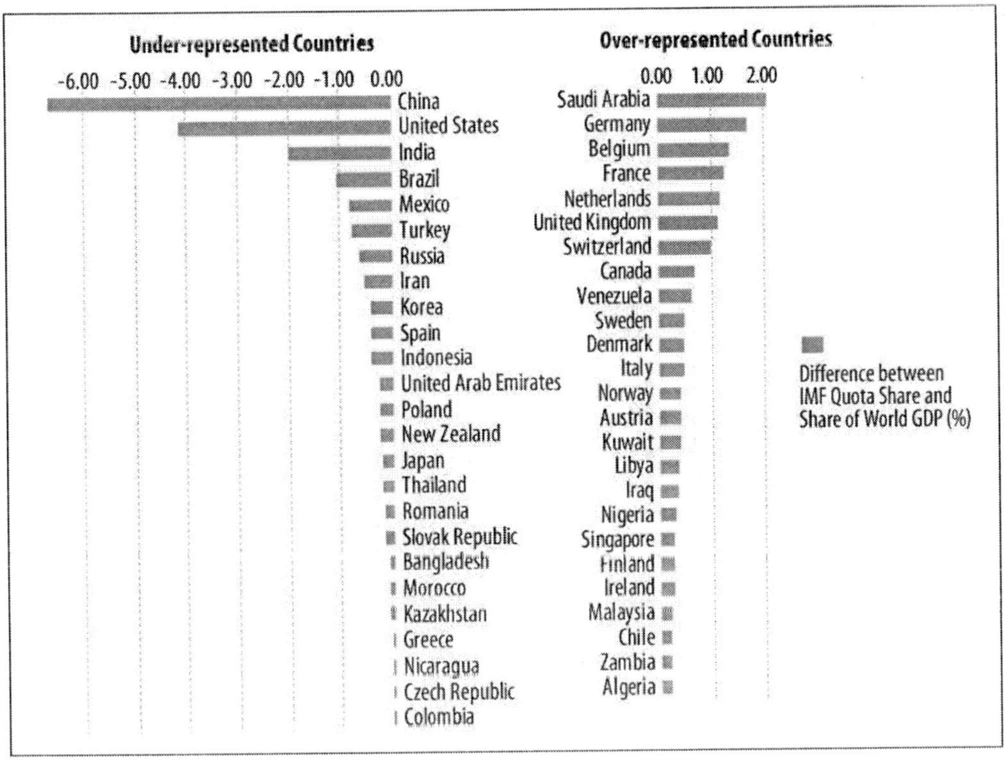

Source: Data used in calculations from "Updated IMF Quota Day – September 2009," International Monetary Fund, September 23, 2009. Available at http://www.imf.org/external/np/fin/quotas/2009/091509.htm.

Notes: 25 IMF members with the smallest and largest differences between IMF quota share and share of world GDP. GDP is adjusted for purchasing power parity (PPP).

Figure 3. Examples of Country Representation at the IMF

The G-20 leaders also pledged that the heads and senior leadership of the international financial institutions should be appointed through an "open, transparent, and merit-based selection process." This may affect the 60-year-old unwritten convention that the Managing Director of the IMF is selected by Western European countries and the President of the World Bank is selected by the United States. However, the wording in the G-20 statement is vague and to date there is no consensus within the U.S. government or internationally on how this would be implemented in practice.

Increased Funding of the Multilateral Development Banks (MDBs)

As the current financial crisis spread internationally during 2008 and 2009, more and more countries turned to the IMF and the World Bank for loans. IMF lending almost doubled from $17.1 billion to $32.54 billion between October and December 2008. Expecting a greater demand for IMF loans in the future, the G-20 leaders agreed at the London summit to triple the Fund's lending capacity to $750 billion as part of a larger $1.1 trillion package to increase IFI funding.[40] Specifically, the leaders agreed to increase the resources of the New Arrangements to Borrow (NAB), a supplemental fund that bolsters IMF resources, by up to $500 billion. To fulfill this commitment, Congress approved the extension of a $100 billion loan to the NAB in May 2009, included in the FY2009 Spring Supplemental Appropriations for Overseas Contingency Operations (P.L. 111-32). In the end, total new commitments to the NAB are greater than $500 billion, more than originally expected.[41]

At the G-20 summit in Pittsburgh, the G-20 turned their attention to the lending capacity of the multilateral development banks (MDBs). Proposals have been made in all the MDBs in the past year suggesting that substantial increases in their capital stock are needed. There are two general reasons why the MDBs are requesting general capital increases. First, demand for loans is high. The current crisis and the resulting shrinkage in private capital flows is creating a large gap in the external financing needs for developing countries. The World Bank estimates this gap is between $350 billion and $635 billion for 2009 alone, and is expected to continue in 2010 and beyond.[42] Second, it has been noted that the Inter-American Development Bank (IDB)'s request for a general capital increase comes on the heels of a loss of nearly $1.9 billion in 2008.[43]

An overview of these MDB proposals for capital increases are provided below:

- **International Bank for Reconstruction and Development (IBRD), a facilityof the World Bank:** [44]According to a report prepared by the bank's staff, the IBRD needs a capital increase in the range of $2.8 billion and $8.7 billion.[45] The IBRD's current capital base is $190 billion.[46]

- **International Finance Corporation (IFC), a facility of the World Bank:**[47] According to a staff report, the IFC needs a capital increase of $1.8 billion to $2.4 billion.[48] The IFC's current capital base is $16 billion.[49]

- **African Development Bank (AfDB):** In June 2009, the Board of Governors of the AfDB began consideration of a proposal to triple the institution's capital baseto $100 billion.[50]

- **Asian Development Bank (AsDB):** On May 12, 2009, the Board of Governors of the AsDB agreed to triple the Bank's capital base, from $55 billion to $165 billion.[51] Under the terms of the plan, each country will be eligible to subscribeshares totaling 200% of its current subscription by the end of 2010.

- **European Bank for Reconstruction and Development (EBRD):** The Presidentof the EBRD has recommended to member countries that the institution's capitalbase be increased by 50% from €20 million to €30 million.[52] In dollars, this isapproximately an increase from $30 million to $45 million.

- **Inter-American Development Bank (IDB):** In March 2009, a commission appointed by President Luis Alberto Moreno of the IDB proposed that thefinancial base of the institution should be tripled through a new capital increaseof up to $180 billion.[53]

The proposals are in the preliminary stages, and the Treasury Department is currently analyzing the capital needs of the different MDBs to see if any capital increase is warranted, and if so, how much it should be. The G-20 leaders have called on their finance ministers to consider how mechanisms such as temporary callable and contingent capital could be used to increase MDB lending in times of crisis. The current hope is to conclude negotiations on commitments for any general capital increases by Spring 2010. If the United States agrees to participate in a capital increase for any of the MDBs, it is anticipated that this would be included in the FY2012 budget. There is also strong indication that donors would require that a capital increase of any of the MDBs would be accompanied by reforms of the MDBs.

In the view of many, the need and size of any MDB capital increases would depend on the availability of private funds. Prior to the current global financial crisis, in 2007, net capital inflows to emerging markets were at a historic peak of $1,252 billion in 2007.[54] Capital flows began slowing in 2008 and fell to $349 billion in 2009. Capital flows to emerging markets are forecasted to rebound to $672 billion in 2010. There are some important differences among regions, as shown in Figure 4. Capital has returned to emerging markets in Latin America and Asia more quickly than to emerging markets in Eastern Europe, Africa, and the Middle East.

The new lending capacity generated by new increases in the capital base of the MDBs would not be available to support expanded lending until at least 2012. It cannot be determined at this time whether private flows will have returned to the 2007 levels by that time and whether new loans or guarantees by the MDBs would be needed to attract or enhance such private flows. Also, it is not clear whether the high level of inflows seen before the crisis were sustainable or whether their size actually contributed to the severity of the crisis in some instances when the flow precipitously declined. Overall, however, the resurgence of capital flows to emerging markets raises questions about the need for permanent capital increases, and, if reform fatigue sets in, it is unclear how much momentum this issue will have going forward.

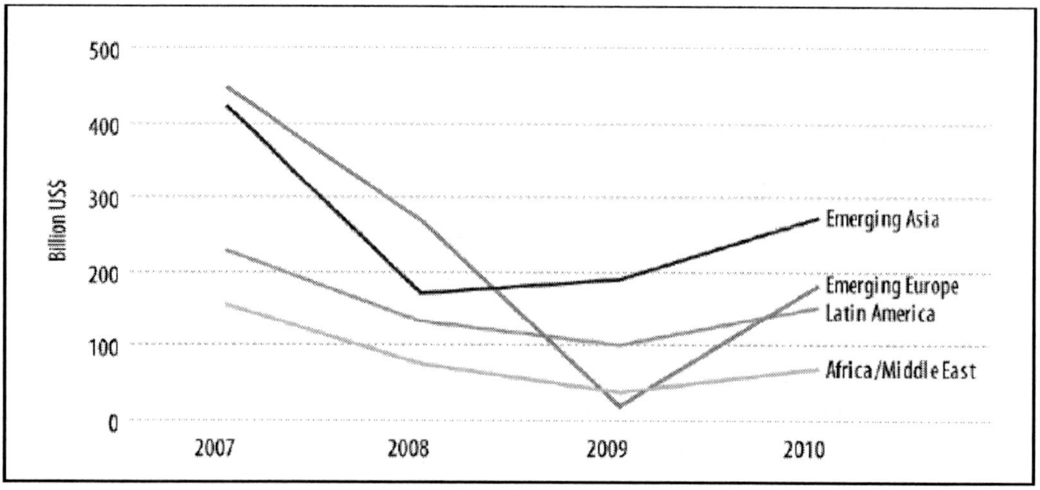

Source: "Capital Flows to Emerging Market Economies," *Institute for International Finance*, October 3, 2009.

Notes: Data for 2009 and 2010 are forecasts. Emerging Europe includes Bulgaria, Czech Republic, Hungary, Poland, Romania, Russia, Turkey, and Ukraine. Latin America emerging markets include Argentina, Brazil, Chile, Poland, Ecuador, Mexico, Peru, and Venezuela. Emerging Asia includes China, India, Indonesia, Malaysia, Philippines, South Korea, and Thailand. Africa/Middle East emerging markets include Egypt, Lebanon, Morocco, Nigeria, Saudi Arabia, South Africa, and UAE.

Figure 4. Net Capital Inflows to Emerging Market Economies, by Region

Official Development Assistance

Concern about the toll of the current global financial crisis on low-income countries has been a central feature at the G-20 summits. The G-20 leaders have reaffirmed their resolve to meet the Millennium Development Goals (MDGs) and the foreign aid commitments to Africa put forth at the 2005 G-8 summit in Gleneagles, Scotland.[55] The G-20 also pledged to take new steps to increase access to food, fuel, and finance among the world's poorest. Specifically, the G-20 leaders called on the World Bank to develop the new trust fund to support the new Food Security Initiative for low-income countries that was announced in the summer of 2009. The G-20 also pledged, on a voluntary basis, to increase funding for programs to bring clean and affordable energy to the poorest, such as by providing funding for the Scaling Up Renewable Energy Program and the Energy for the Poor Initiative. The G-20 agreed to support the safe and sound spread of new modes of financial service delivery capable of reaching the poor, building on the example of micro finance. The G-20 also pledged to launch a "G-20 SME [small and medium-sized enterprise] Finance Challenge," which is a call to the private sector to put forward its best proposals for how public finance can maximize the deployment of private finance on a sustainable basis.

There is general concern that pledges to meet existing aid commitments may fall short. The MDG Gap Task Force, created by the Secretary-General of the United Nations to monitor progress on reaching the MDGs, has expressed concern that foreign aid may fall due to the crisis at a time when aid needs to increase in order to reach the MDGs.[56] Additionally, the MDG Gap Task Force is concerned that the distribution of aid is skewed to a just a couple of countries, specifically Iraq and Afghanistan.

Whether the G-8 will meet the targets for aid to Africa, as promised in Gleneagles, is also in question. According to the organization ONE, which monitors aid commitments and disbursements to Africa, this is primarily caused by shortfalls from a few G-8 members, particularly Italy and France.[57]Other G-8 members, including Canada, Japan, and the United States, are on track to meet their G-8 Gleneagles commitments to Africa.[58]

Given the difficulty in meeting existing aid commitments, it is unclear as to what extent the G-20 members will take the steps necessary to implement the new programs aimed at increasing access to food, fuel, and finance in low-income countries. Some have pointed out that details of the new plans are sparse, contributing to questions about their implementation.[59]

A Green Recovery

As the current financial crisis has begun to seemingly bottom out, the G-20 leaders have turned to other issues, including the environment. The G-20 leaders have committed to eliminating fossil fuel subsidies over the medium-term and reach an agreement on reducing greenhouse gas emissions at the U.N. Climate Change conference in Copenhagen in December 2009.[60]

Support for the ban on fossil fuel subsidies comes from the Obama Administration, who pushed for the G-20 commitment in Pittsburgh.[61] It is estimated that the removal of fossil fuel subsidies by 2020 would reduce greenhouse gas emissions by 10% in 2050, and it is reported that the President views the elimination of fossil fuel subsidies as a "down payment" on the international goal of reducing greenhouse gas emissions by 50% from 1990 levels by 2050.[62]

In addition to the environmental benefits, eliminating fossil fuel subsidies may also even out the large price swings that have characterized the oil markets in recent years.[63] With fossil fuel subsidies, increases in the price of oil are not necessarily passed on to consumers. This means that demand for oil can continue to rise even as oil prices increase and in fact further contribute to the price increase, leading to large upswings in the price of oil. Stabilizing oil prices may prove important as the current financial crisis has led to what some see as under-investment in the energy sector, such as energy companies drilling fewer oil and gas wells. Under-investment in the energy sector may lead to higher energy prices, particularly for oil and electricity, in a few years.[64] Additionally, elimination of fossil fuel subsidies may ease the budget deficit problems of many countries.

Eliminating fossil fuel subsidies may prove difficult. Governments in low-and middle-income countries, who spend $310 billion a year on fossil fuel subsidies compared to the $20-30 billion spent annually by developed countries, may be reluctant for political reasons to eliminate these subsidies.[65] In 2008, cuts in subsidies in Egypt, India, and Indonesia resulted in street protests and political upheaval.[66] Eliminating fossil fuel subsidies in rich countries may also face obstacles. The Environmental Law Institute, a think-tank, estimates that the United States spent $72 billion on fossil-fuel subsidies between 2002 and 2008.[67] Elimination of fossil fuel subsidies would require Congressional approval, and it is expected that the oil industry would strongly oppose such legislation.[68]

Reaching an agreement on reducing greenhouse gas emissions, as a successor to the Kyoto Protocol, at the United Nations Framework Convention on Climate Change (UNFCCC) in Copenhagen in December 2009 may also face difficulties.[69] Some economists estimate that a new international agreement to reduce greenhouse gas emissions would cost $100 billion a year by 2020, and it is not clear who would foot the bill.[70] Developing countries susceptible to adverse effects of climate change have also expressed concerns that the size of the cuts in greenhouse gas emissions being discussed are not big enough. Developed countries want more concrete promises from developing countries, and even among developed countries there are disagreements about how much emissions should be cut by.

Preparatory talks held in Bangkok in October 2009 have resulted in leaders downplaying expectations, suggesting that the December 2009 summit will merely lay the groundwork for negotiations in 2010.[71] In mid-November, President Barack Obama conceded at the Asia Pacific Economic Co-operation (APEC) summit in Singapore that it was unlikely that a new agreement on greenhouse gas emissions would be reached at the December summit in Copenhagen.[72] However, it is reported that President Obama intends to tell delegates at the conference that the United States is committed to reducing its greenhouse gas emissions in the range of 17% below 2005 levels by 2020 and 83% by 2050.[73] The 17% reduction is consistent with the legislation passed by the House in June 2009 (H.R. 2454). The Senate has not passed legislation on greenhouse gas emissions; equivalent legislation is pending in the Senate.

Conclude WTO Doha Round of Multilateral Trade Negotiations

The G-20 leaders have also pledged to conclude the WTO Doha Round of multilateral trade negotiations in 2010. Doha negotiations have been stalled since 2001 due to differences among the United States, the European Union, and developing countries on major issues including agriculture, industrial tariffs, non-tariff barriers, and services.[74]

To date, there appears to be a disconnect between the pledges of the G-20 leaders and the lack of specific negotiations on the ground to meet this goal. It is not evident that WTO members have made progress in resolving the stalemate over the Doha negotiations, and the G-20 pledge to get the Doha Round back on track by next year is viewed by many as unlikely to be met.[75] Confidence might be enhanced if the G-20 discussed the basic controversies deadlocking the Doha negotiations rather than just announcing their intent to reach agreement.

This skepticism surrounding Doha is underscored by the fact that G-20 members by and large have not refrained from protectionist trade policies in the face of the current global financial crisis. Data from Global Trade Alert (GTA), an independent and privately funded organization, indicate that G-20 members have implemented a total of 139 policies that almost certainly discriminate against foreign commercial interests between November 2008 and October 2009.[76] The scope of these measures are also fairly substantial, affecting on average 12 sectors and 77 trading partners. Furthermore, there are an additional 194 policies that the G-20 countries have implemented or announced that are likely or almost certainly discriminatory against foreign commercial interests. A report by the World Bank reports similar movements toward protectionist trade policies, but notes that these measures are believed to have had only marginal effects on trade.[77] Overall, the protectionist backlash appears to have been much lower than during the Great Depression in the 1930s.

IMPLICATIONS OF THE TRANSITION FROM THE G-7 TO THE G-20

Will the Transition to the G-20 Help or Hinder Economic Cooperation?

Fundamental questions for U.S. foreign economic policy are whether the shift from the G-7 to the G-20 will help or hinder efforts at international economic cooperation, and how it might affect US interests. Some argue that the shift will foster international economic cooperation. Including a broader membership, it is argued, will give greater legitimacy to the agreements reached by the G-20, since they are not just decided by the "rich club" of countries. Likewise, emerging-market countries, especially China and India, are big players in international financial markets, and it is argued that they should be included in international financial discussions. Additionally, expanding the G-7 to the G-20 may help the G-7 gain favor with large emerging-market countries, which could facilitate cooperation in non-economic areas such as climate change.

Others argue expanding the G-7 to the G-20 will weaken or undermine efforts at international economic cooperation. The G-20 countries are a heterogeneous group of countries with different political and economic philosophies. Including such a large, heterogeneous group of countries in the same forum, some argue, will limit the scope of the agreements reached, or the ability to reach agreements at all. In the same vein, some argue that record of implementation of the agreements reached by the G-20 will be worse than the implementation record of the G-7. G-20 emerging-market countries look a lot different than G-20 developed countries on a number of factors that could impact implementation, including rule of law, government effectiveness, and control of corruption, as shown in **Figure 5**. Of course, agreement among a homogeneous group of advanced industrial democracies may not much help resolve world problems if other countries do not participate.

Still others argue that international economic coordination will be no different under the G-20 than it was under the G-7. One rationale is that emerging-market countries have been de facto participants in the G-7 for several years and their views had already been incorporated in the G-7. An alternative rationale is that, in practice, the G-7 will dominate the G-20 negotiations and emerging-markets will have less influence over the discussions.

It is worth nothing that some of these views are not necessarily mutually exclusive. It is possible to imagine, for example, a situation where the G-20 makes fewer commitments than the G-7, but the commitments that the G-20 does reach are seen as more legitimate than those reached by the G-7.

Is the G-20 the Right Group of Countries?

When the developed countries decided to include emerging markets in discussions on policy responses to the crisis, the G-20 was an expedient choice because it was a well established group that encompassed the G-7 and several large emerging-market countries.

The G-20 members were selected by the G-7 when the G-20 was formed in 1999, and the decision on which countries to include reflected a need for broad geographic representation and systemic economic importance.[78] The membership of the G-20 has not changed since its establishment.

Some argue that the G-20 was the right choice for expanding the G-7, because the G-20 represents two-thirds of the world's population, 90% of world GDP, and 80% of world trade.[79] A mix of policymakers and academics have long advocated replacing the G-7 by the G-20, or at least making the G-20 a more prominent economic forum.[80]

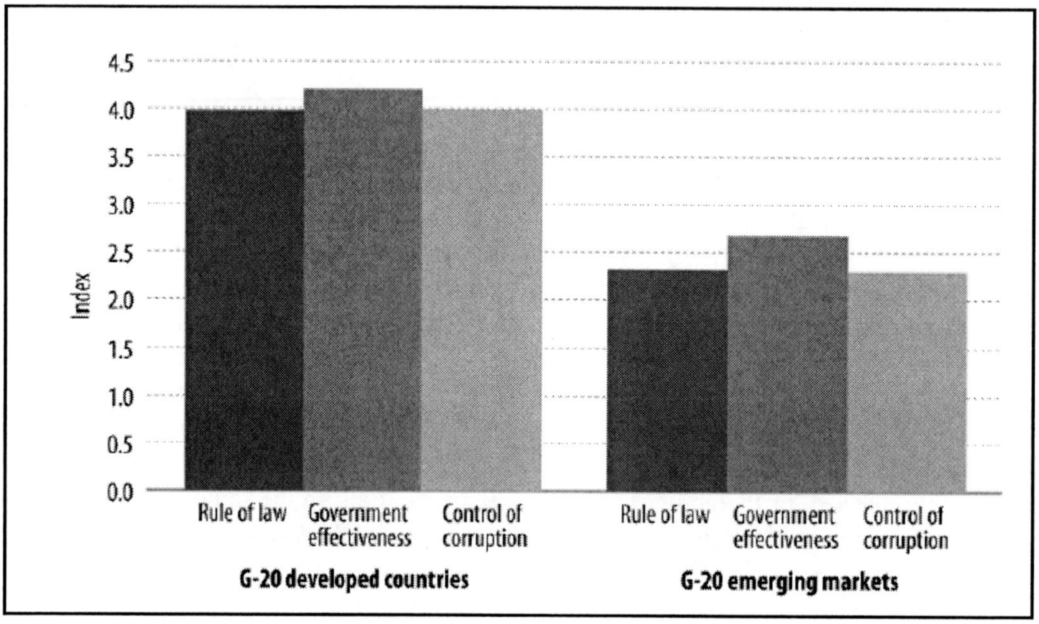

Source: Daniel Kaufmann, Aart Kraay and Massimo Mastruzzi, "Governance Matters VIII: Governance Indicators for 1996-2008," *World Bank Policy Research*, June 2009.

Notes: Data on a five point scale (re-scaled from 0 to 5), where higher scores correspond to better outcomes. G-20 developed countries include Australia, Canada, France, Germany, Italy, Japan, the United Kingdom, and the United States. G-20 emerging-market countries include Argentina, Brazil, China, India, Indonesia, Mexico, Russia, Saudi Arabia, South Africa, South Korea, and Turkey. Governance indicators are calculated by Kaufman, Kraay, and Masturzzi using a large number of individual data sources, including surveys of firms and individuals as well as the assessments of commercial risk rating agencies, non-governmental organizations, and a number of multilateral aid agencies and other public sector organizations. "Rule of law" captures perceptions of the extent to which agents have confidence in and abide by the rules of society, and in particular the quality of contract enforcement, property rights, the police, and the courts, as well as the likelihood of crime and violence. "Government effectiveness" captures perceptions of the quality of public services, the quality of the civil service and the degree of its independence from political pressures, the quality of policy formulation and implementation, and the credibility of the government's commitment to such policies. "Control of corruption" captures perceptions of the extent to which public power is exercised for private gain, including both petty and grand forms of corruption, as well as capture of the state by elites and private interests.

Figure 5. Selected Governance Indicators for the G-20 Developed and Emerging-Market Countries.

Table 2.World's Largest Countries and Entities, by GDP 2008 Data, Billions of U.S. Dollars

Rank	G-20 Members	Non G-20 Members	GDP
1.	European Union		$18,493
2.	United States		14,195
3.	Japan		4,867
4.	China		3,942
5.	Germany		3,653
6.	France		2,843
7.	United Kingdom		2,833
8.	Italy		2,330
9.	Russia		1,699
10.		Spain	1,623
11.	Brazil		1,621
12.	Canada		1,571
13.	India		1,233
14.	Australia		1,047
15.	South Korea		999
16.	Mexico		950
17.		Netherlands	863
18.	Turkey		748
19.		Belgium	507
20.		Sweden	503
21.	Indonesia		488
22.		Switzerland	473
23.	Saudi Arabia		464
24.		Norway	459
25.		Poland	451
26.		Austria	419
27.		Taiwan	409
28.		Iran	364
29.		Greece	362
30.		Denmark	349
31.		Venezuela	335
32.	Argentina		324
33.	South Africa		296

Source: IMF World Economic Outlook.

Notes: The European Union (EU) includes 27 countries.

Others have reservations with respect to whether the G-20 is the right group of developed and emerging-market countries. With the developed countries, there are concerns that European interests are still over-represented in the G-20, with Europeans taking up five of the 20 slots (Germany, France, Italy, the United Kingdom, and the European Union). This problem is exacerbated by Spain and the Netherlands, who have gained attendance to all three

G-20 summits even though they are not official members. That said, some maintain that, based on economic weight, Spain is a more justified member of the G-20 than Italy.

There are also questions about the selection of large emerging-market countries. Some argue that several emerging markets are not included in the forum, but should be based on their economic and political importance. Poland, Thailand, Egypt, and Pakistan are typically cited as examples.[81] Table 2 shows that there are 13 countries that are not members of the G-20 but whose economies are as large as other G-20 members. It is unlikely that any current members of the G-20 would resign or could be pushed out in order to allow new countries to join. One issue that may confront the G-20 in the future is how to balance, on one hand, fair representation in the forum and, on the other hand, keeping the size of the forum manageable.

Beyond the Current Crisis: What Will the G-20's Focus Be?

As the G-20 summits have progressed, the scope of discussions has broadened to include a diverse set of issues, ranging from IFI reform to food security to climate change. Some have suggested that the G-20's agenda has become too ambitious.[82] When the crisis does wind down, it is not yet clear whether the G-20's focus will return to more traditional economic policy coordination (such as exchange rates and trade) or if the new policy items on the G-20's Pittsburgh agenda will become the primary focus of the forum.

In addition, it is still to be seen how the G-20 will fit in with existing international institutions. Much of the London and Pittsburgh G-20 communiqués is devoted to reiterating commitments made in other venues, such as the WTO (for trade) and the United Nations (for climate change, for example). On one hand, the G-20's focus at the leader level on trade and climate change may provide the jolt necessary to make progress on international negotiations that have stalled for years. Likewise, the G-20 may facilitate trade-offs among major concerns that would not be possible in issue-specific forums. On the other hand, the G-20 may find it difficult to make progress on policy areas that have proven so difficult to get traction on in the past. The G-7 often made decisions which were then taken to the IFIs for implementation, and it is not clear whether the G-20 will have the same leadership capacity.

Finally, it is worth noting that it has been only in the most recent summit that global imbalances have been explicitly addressed in the G-20 communiqués. This is partly due to the fact that correcting imbalances was not an immediate way to "stop the bleeding," but it is also partly due to the fact that global imbalances are politically sensitive. For the reasons discussed above, there is some skepticism that the G-20's proposal to correct global imbalances will carry much weight.[83] China is hinting it will be strengthening its currency, the renminbi, which would help correct global imbalances,[84] although these signals have been mixed. To the extent that further action would be needed, policymakers may need to find other forums, institutions, or bilateral discussions to address these issues. The issue of imbalances has, for example, been acknowledged in bilateral discussions between the United States and China in the "U.S.-China Strategic and Economic Dialogue" (or "S&ED"), although this has not translated into concrete steps or plans of action on this issue. Other countries might be seriously affected by the consequence of bilateral deals, however, and this might complicate settlement of related issues affecting more countries in other contexts.

End Notes

[1] The G-20 includes Argentina, Australia, Brazil, Canada, China, France, Germany, India, Indonesia, Italy, Japan, Mexico, Russia, Saudi Arabia, South Africa, South Korea, Turkey, United Kingdom, and the United States, as well as the European Union (EU). Spain and the Netherlands have also been invited to participate as observers. The G-20's website is http://www.g20.org. The University of Toronto G-20 Research Group is also a good source of information; their website is http://www.g20.utoronto.ca/. The G-20 discussed in this chapter should not be confused with the coalition of developing countries in the World Trade Organization (WTO) formed in 2003, also referred to as the G-20.

[2] For more on the current global financial crisis, see: CRS Report RL34742, *The Global Financial Crisis: Analysis and Policy Implications*, coordinated by Dick K. Nanto.

[3] The G-7 includes Canada, France, Germany, Italy, Japan, the United Kingdom, and the United States. Russia has joined the G-7 meetings at the leader level (summits) as a full participant since 1998, forming the Group of Eight (G-8). With a smaller economy than the G-7 members, Russia does not usually participate in international economic discussions, however, which continued primarily at the G-7 level. For example, Russia is not included in the G-7 meetings at the finance minister level.

[4] The Paris Club is an informal group of developed countries. The group provides financial services such as debt restructuring and debt relief to indebted developing countries.

[5] For more information about formal international institutions, see, for example: CRS Report R40578, *The Global Financial Crisis: Increasing IMF Resources and the Role of Congress*, by Jonathan E. Sanford and Martin A. Weiss and CRS Report RL32060, *World Trade Organization Negotiations: The Doha Development Agenda*, by Ian F. Fergusson.

[6] While the EU is not an official member of the G-7 or G-8, the EU has participated in meetings since 1977. The EU is represented by the president of the European Commission and the president of the European Council. The EU does not hold leadership positions within the G-8 or host summits.

[7] Nicholas Bayne, "Reforming the International Financial Architecture: The G7 Summit's Successes and Shortcomings," July 2001, http://www.g8.utoronto.ca/conferences/2001/rome/bayneRev.pdf.

[8] The members of the G-22 are the G-8 members plus Argentina, Australia, Brazil, China, Hong Kong, India, Indonesia, Malaysia, Mexico, Poland, Singapore, South Africa, South Korea, and Thailand.

[9] The members of the G-33 are the G-8 members plus Argentina, Australia, Belgium, Brazil, Chile, China, Côte d'Ivoire, Egypt, Hong Kong, India, Indonesia, South Korea, Malaysia, Mexico, Morocco, the Netherlands, Poland, Saudi Arabia, Singapore, South Africa, Spain, Sweden, Switzerland, Thailand, and Turkey.

[10] Emerging markets had been sporadically invited to a few G-8 summit dinners and events as early as 1989, but their participation was very minor compared to 2005 onwards. See Peter I. Hajnal, *The G8 System and the G20* (Ashgate, 2007), pp. 47-49.

[11] Jonathan Wheatley, "G20 Calls for Expanded Role to Combat Economic Turmoil," *Financial Times*, November 10, 2009.

[12] "After the Fall," *The Economist*, November 15, 2009.

[13] "Not a Bad Weekend's Work," *The Economist*, November 16, 2008.

[14] Ibid.

[15] The term "sherpa" is a play on words. Typically, sherpas refer to local people, typically men, in Nepal who are employed as guides for mountaineering expeditions in the Himalayas. Recall that meetings held among leaders are called "summits," which also refers to the highest point of a mountain.

[16] The term "sous-sherpa" is also a play on words, referencing the French term "sous-chef" for under-chef or an assistant to a master chef.

[17] http://www.g20.org

[18] Jenilee Guebert, *Plans for the Third G20 Summit: Pittsburgh 2009*, G20 Research Group, University of Toronto, August 18, 2009, pp. 44-45, http://www.g20.utoronto.ca/g20plans/g20leaders090818.pdf.

[19] http://www.g20.org

[20] E.g., see: CRS Report RS20088, *Dispute Settlement in the World Trade Organization (WTO): An Overview*, by Jeanne J. Grimmett.

[21] The G-20 communiqués are posted online at http://www.g20.org/pub_communiques.aspx.

[22] For more on the $1.1 trillion package to increase IFI and MDB resources, and the requisite congressional authorizations, see: CRS Report R40578, *The Global Financial Crisis: Increasing IMF Resources and the Role of Congress*, by Jonathan E. Sanford and Martin A. Weiss.

[23] Carl Prine, "An Overview of Protests Expected in Pittsburgh for G-20," *Pittsburgh Tribune-Review*, September 20, 2009.

[24] Michelle Nichols, "Protesters, Police Clash After G20 in Pittsburgh," *Reuters*, September 25, 2009.

[25] Daniel Lovering and Michael Rubinkam, "G-20 March Turns Chaotic as Police, Protesters Clash on Streets of Pittsburgh," *AP Newswire (Government Feed)*, September 24, 2009.

[26] Michelle Nichols, "Protesters, Police Clash After G20 in Pittsburgh," *Reuters*, September 25, 2009.

[27] Dennis B. Roddy and Michael A. Fuoco, "Protests Lead to 19 Arrests Across City," *Pittsburgh Post-Gazette*, September 25, 2009.
[28] Treasury Department, "Press Briefing by Treasury Secretary Tim Geithner on the G20 Meeting Pittsburgh Convention Center," press release, September 24, 2009, http://www.treas.gov/press/releases/tg405.htm.
[29] Ibid., pp. 13.
[30] Financial Stability Board. Improving Financial Regulation: Report of the Financial Stability Board to the G20 Leaders. September 25, 2009.
[31] http://www.g20.org/Documents/pittsburgh_summit_leaders_statement_250909.pdf.
[32] E.g., see Chris Giles, "Three-Stage Plan for Growth," *Financial Times*, September 26, 2009 and Chris Giles, "Spot the Difference," *Financial Times*, September 23, 2009.
[33] "Regaining their Balance," *The Economist*, September 26, 2009.
[34] Ibid.
[35] IMF quotas determine a country's maximum financial commitment to the IMF and its voting power, and has bearing on its access to IMF financing.
[36] "Money, Votes and Politics," *The Economist*, October 7, 2009.
[37] E.g., see "IMF Quotas," International Monetary Fund, October 31, 2009. Available at http://www.imf.org/external/np/exr/facts/quotas.htm. Also see "Quota Reform at the G-20," Reserve Bank of Australia, February 2006. Available at http://www.treasury.gov.au/documents/1102/HTML/docshell.asp?URL=G20_Quota_Reform.htm.
[38] GDP used in this section is adjusted for purchasing power parity (PPP). GDP adjusted for PPP means that GDP is adjusted to account for differences in prices across countries. Others argue that market-based GDP, unadjusted for PPP, should be used. In the current IMF quota formula, GDP is a weighted average of market-based and PPP GDP, at 60% and 40% respectively. Using market-based GDP does produce slightly different rankings; Figures 3 and 4 are intended as examples and should not be taken as definitive rank orders of under- and over-represented countries.
[39] These are examples; see fn. 55.
[40] For more information, see: CRS Report R40578, *The Global Financial Crisis: Increasing IMF Resources and the Role of Congress*, by Jonathan E. Sanford and Martin A. Weiss.
[41] International Monetary Fund, *Bolstering the IMF's Lending Capacity*, November 5, 2009, http://www.imf.org/external/np/exr/faq/contribution.htm.
[42] World Bank, *Review of IBRD and IFC Financial Capacities: Working with Partners to Support Global Development*, October 5, 2009.
[43] Daniel Bases and Javier Mozzo, "IADB Should Increase Capital by $150-$180 Billion," *Reuters*, March 29, 2009.
[44] The International Bank for Reconstruction and Development (IBRD) is one of two World Bank facilities that lend directly to governments to finance projects and programs. The other facility is the International Development Association (IDA). The IBRD provides middle-income developing countries with loans at near-market rates using funds raised by the World Bank on the international capital markets. While many of these countries can borrow on theinternational capital markets, and are increasingly doing so, some seek loans from the World Bank to gain access to World Bank technical assistance and advisory services, as well as the prestige and legitimacy that come with World Bank-backed projects. IDA was established in 1960, 16 years after the creation of the IBRD, due to concerns that lowincome countries could not afford to borrow at the near-market rate terms offered by the IBRD. Consequently, IDA provides concessional loans and grants to poor countries funded by contributions from donors and transfers from the IBRD.
[45] World Bank, *Review of IBRD and IFC Financial Capacities: Working with Partners to Support Global Development*, September 29, 2009.
[46] Japan Credit Rating Agency, Ltd., Affirms AAA Ratings on International Bank for Reconstruction and Development; Outlook Stable, April 25, 2008, http://www.jcr.co.jp/english/top_cont/rat_info04.php?no=08i007&PHPSESSID=f809554a5fc99e428fcfd7a0cf5ec7dd.
[47] The IFC was established in 1956 and promotes sustainable private sector development by financing private sector projects and companies in the developing world, helping private companies in the developing world mobilize financing international financial markets, and providing advice and technical assistance to businesses and governments.
[48] World Bank, *Review of IBRD and IFC Financial Capacities: Working with Partners to Support Global Development*, September 29, 2009.
[49] IFC, *IFC 2009 Financials, Projects, and Portfolio*, 2009, p. 4, http://www.ifc.org/ifcext/annualreport.nsf/AttachmentsByTitle/AR2009_Volume2/$FILE/AR2009_Volume2.pdf.
[50] "African Development Bank Seeks Additional Capital-Treasurer," *Reuters Africa*, September 23, 2009.
[51] The formal proposal may be found at Asian Development Bank. *Information on Subscription for the Fifth General Capital Increase*. May 2009. See http://www.adb.org/Documents/Brochures/Fifth-General-Capital-Increase/generalcapital-increase.pdf.

[52] "EBRD Seeks 50% Increase in Capital," *Financial Times*, September 28, 2009.

[53] Joshua Goodman and Helen Murphy, " IDB Seeking Up to $180 Bln in Capital to Boost Loans (Update2)," *Bloomberg*, March 29, 2009.

[54] Data for this section is from "Capital Flows To Emerging Market Economies," *Institute for International Finance*, October 3, 2009.

[55] The Millennium Development Goals are a series of eight development goals, ranging from halving extreme poverty to halting the spread of HIV/AIDS, to be reached by 2015. The Millennium Development Goals were agreed to by world leaders at the United Nations Headquarters in New York in 2000. In order to help reach the Millennium Development Goals, leaders at the G-8 summit in Gleneagles, Scotland in 2005, committed to doubling aid to Africa by 2010. This is agreement is often referred to as the "Gleneagles commitments." Russia did not commit to raising aid to Africa, leading some to refer to the Gleneagles commitments as made by the G-7. For more on U.S. foreign aid see: CRS Report R40213, *Foreign Aid: An Introduction to U.S. Programs and Policy*, by Curt Tarnoff and Marian Leonardo Lawson.

[56] Millennium Development Goal (MDG) Gap Task Force, *Strengthening the Global Partnership for Development in a Time of Crisis*, 2009.

[57] ONE, *The Data Report 2009: Monitoring the G8 Promise to Africa*, May 19, 2009.

[58] Ibid.

[59] See e.g., "G20 asks World Bank to set up agriculture fund," *Reuters*, September 25, 2009.

[60] For more information, see: CRS Report R40910, *Status of the Copenhagen Climate Change Negotiations*, by Jane A. Leggett and Richard K. Lattanzio.

[61] Ben Geman, "White House Wants Fuel Subsidy Cuts on G-20 Agenda," *Washington Post*, September 16, 2009.

[62] "Fossilised Policy," *The Economist*, October 1, 2009.

[63] "No Free Lunch: The G-20's Case Against Fossil-Fuel Subsidies," *Wall Street Journal*, September 25, 2009.

[64] International Energy Agency, *World Energy Outlook 2009*, November 10, 2009.

[65] "Fossilised Policy," *The Economist*, October 1, 2009.

[66] Ibid.

[67] Environmental Law Institute, *Estimating U.S. Government Subsidies to Energy Sources: 2002-2008*, September 2009.

[68] "Fossilised Policy," *The Economist*, October 1, 2009.

[69] The Koyoto Protocol is a 1997 climate change agreement that set greenhouse gas emissions targets for industrialized countries. It was never ratified by the United States.

[70] "United Nations Framework Convention on Climate Change," *New York Times*, accessed October 21, 2009.

[71] "Bangkok Blues," *The Economist*, October 15, 2009.

[72] Edward Luce, Kevin Brown, and Fiona Harvey, et al., "Obama Damps Climate Hopes," *Financial Times*, November 16, 2009.

[73] John M. Broder, "Obama to Go to Copenhagen with Emissions Target ," *New York Times*, November 25, 2009.

[74] For more on the Doha negotiations, see: CRS Report RL32060, *World Trade Organization Negotiations: The Doha Development Agenda*, by Ian F. Fergusson.

[75] E.g., see "Regaining Their Balance," *The Economist*, 26 September 2009.

[76] http://www.globaltradealert.org/ Accessed October 20, 2009. GTA is coordinated by the Centre for Economic Policy Research (CEPR) and has been cited extensively in the media, including *The Economist*, *Forbes*, *The Financial Times*, and *The Wall Street Journal*.

[77] Elisa Gamberoni and Richard Newfarmer, *Trade Protection: Incipient but Worrisome Trends*, International Trade Department, World Bank, Trade Note #37, March 2, 2009. http://siteresources.worldbank.org/NEWS /Resources/Trade_Note_37.pdf.

[78] Brookings, *The G-20 (Group of 20)*, http://www.brookings.edu/reports/2009/~/media/Files/Programs/Global/backgrounders/G20_backgrounder.ashx.

[79] Arvind Panagariya, *The G-20 Summit and Global Trade: Restore Credit and Resist Protectionism*, Brookings, March 14, 2009. Trade data includes intra-EU trade.

[80] For an overview of these proposals, see Peter I. Hajnal, *The G8 System and the G20* (Ashgate, 2007), ch. 12.

[81] "G20 Gains Stature But is Overambitious," *Oxford Analytica*, September 28, 2009.

[82] Ibid.

[83] E.g., see Nouriel Roubini, "A Balanced Global Diet," *New York Times*, October 28, 2009.

[84] Geoff Dyer, "Chinese Hint at Stronger Renminbi," *Financial Times*, November 12, 2009.

In: The International Monetary Fund (IMF) Financial Crisis and... ISBN: 978-1-61728-499-1
Editor: Rachel E. Layton

Chapter 7

INTERNATIONAL MONETARY FUND: LENDING PROGRAMS ALLOW FOR NEGOTIATIONS AND ARE CONSISTENT WITH ECONOMIC LITERATURE

United States Government Accountability Office

WHY GAO DID THIS STUDY

The International Monetary Fund (IMF) has significantly increased its total committed lending to countries from about $3.5 billion in August 2008 to about $170.4 billion in August 2009, as countries have been severely affected by the global economic crisis. IMFsupported programs are intended to help countries overcome balance-of-payments problems, stabilize their economies, and restore sustainable economic growth. Critics have long-standing concerns that the IMF has an overly austere approach to macroeconomic policy that does not sufficiently heed country viewpoints. To help address these concerns, the IMF recently stated that it has changed its policies, including by increasing its flexibility.

GAO was asked to examine (1) the process for designing an IMFsupported program, (2) the IMF-supported programs in four recipient countries, and (3) the extent to which the findings of empirical economic studies are consistent with the IMF's macroeconomic policies. GAO analyzed IMF and recipient country documents; interviewed U.S., IMF, and foreign government officials, conducting fieldwork in four relatively large recipient countries; and analyzed published or widely cited empirical studies.

GAO received written comments from the Department of the Treasury, noting its concurrence with the report's conclusions.

WHAT GAO FOUND

Designing an IMF-supported lending program involves a complex, iterative process based on projections for key macroeconomic variables; discussions between IMF staff and country officials regarding program goals, policies, and trade-offs; use of economic judgment; and IMF Executive Board approval. An IMF-supported program is intended to help countries achieve their objectives in the context of macroeconomic stability. Programs in low-income countries are broadly geared toward increasing economic growth and reducing poverty, and generally strive for low inflation and sustainable levels of debt. In middle- and high-income countries, programs generally aim to stem capital outflows, restore confidence, and stabilize the exchange rate by, for example, setting targets for budget deficits and international reserves. Trade-offs among the different combinations of objectives and policies allow for negotiations between the IMF staff and country officials, reflecting what is technically feasible and politically acceptable.

IMF-supported programs in the four countries GAO reviewed—Liberia, Zambia, Hungary, and Iceland—include different sets of objectives, targets, and conditions that reflect country circumstances, based on negotiations between the IMF staff and country officials. In postconflict Liberia, the program focuses on rebuilding capacity and contains a target for maintaining a balanced budget with no borrowing. In Zambia—a country negatively affected by the recent economic crisis—the IMF-supported program is designed to increase economic growth, reduce poverty, and improve governance. Hungary, which faced a rising risk of default, has a program that focuses on restoring investor confidence while reducing debt and expenditures. A banking and currency collapse in Iceland precipitated the IMF-supported program, which contains some controversial approaches to monetary policy and banking reform. All four countries are making progress but face challenges in implementing conditions or achieving targets in their IMF-supported programs.

The macroeconomic policies in IMF-supported programs are broadly consistent with the findings of the empirical literature GAO reviewed, although this literature lacks precise guidance for setting policy targets. For low-income countries, empirical evidence generally suggests inflation is detrimental to economic growth after it exceeds a critical threshold, which is broadly consistent with the inflation targets included in the IMF-supported programs we reviewed. For middle- and high-income countries, the literature identified specific policy weaknesses in advance of crises, including high inflation, high public indebtedness, and low international reserves. These weaknesses are consistent with the policies upon which the IMF focuses in the 13 programs in middle- to high-income countries GAO reviewed.

ABBREVIATIONS

EFF	Extended Fund Facility
ESF	Exogenous Shocks Facility
FCL	Flexible Credit Line
G-20	Group of Twenty
GDP	Gross Domestic Product
HFSA	Hungarian Financial Supervisory Authority
HIPC	Heavily Indebted Poor Countries
IMF	International Monetary Fund
NGO	nongovernmental organization
NTSR	noise-to-signal ratio

PRGF	Poverty Reduction and Growth Facility
QPC	quantitative performance criteria
SBA	Stand-By Arrangement
SDR	special drawing rights
SPC	structural performance criteria
Treasury	U.S. Department of the Treasury

November 12, 2009

The Honorable Barney Frank
Chairman
Committee on Financial Services
House of Representatives

Dear Mr. Chairman:

In response to the deepening global economic crisis, the International Monetary Fund (IMF) has dramatically increased its lending to member countries—from a total commitment under IMF-supported programs of about $3.5 billion as of August 2008 to a record level of about $170.4 billion as of August 2009.[1] Much of this new lending has gone to middle- and high-income countries, facing balance-of-payments crises or risking default on their external debt payments, to address their short-term financing needs.[2] About two dozen low-income countries had longer-term IMF-supported programs focused on increasing economic growth and reducing poverty, as of August 2009. To help ensure that the IMF continues to have sufficient resources to meet the increased demand, in April 2009, the Group of Twenty (G-20) world leaders endorsed measures to make $1 trillion available through the IMF.[3] The $1 trillion includes the tripling of the IMF's lending capacity to $750 billion, and an agreement to back the IMF in effectively creating an additional $250 billion by issuing special drawing rights (SDR).[4] As part of these increased resources, Congress had appropriated, in June 2009, additional funds for the IMF, including making available up to about $117.5 billion for loans to the IMF.[5]

The IMF, after holding discussions and reaching agreement with country authorities, provides member countries with financing that they have not been able to obtain in private capital markets.[6] IMF-supported lending programs are intended to help countries overcome balance-of-payments problems, stabilize their economies, and restore sustainable economic growth. To help achieve these objectives, IMF-supported programs identify key macroeconomic targets, such as economic growth rates, using a macroeconomic framework.[7] These programs also establish conditions, the economic and financial policy requirements to which recipient countries agree to receive IMF funding. Furthermore, IMF-supported programs may involve financing from other, often larger, creditors that link their funding to recipients' performance on program conditions.

Critics have long-standing concerns that the IMF has an overly austere approach to macroeconomic policy that does not sufficiently heed country viewpoints, sacrificing potential economic growth and poverty reduction in order to lower a country's inflation rate and government deficit. For example, in October 2007, over 120 nongovernmental organizations (NGO) expressed their concerns to the IMF that its unnecessarily restrictive policies may undermine low-income countries' ability to increase social spending. During the 1997-1998 Asian financial crisis, as well as more recently, some NGOs also criticized the IMF for imposing spending reductions and tight monetary policy on middle-income countries that exacerbated already severe economic stress. To help address these concerns, the IMF stated that it has changed its policies in part to increase flexibility; however, countries in crisis often have to undertake difficult reforms and cut government spending to achieve macroeconomic stability. Researchers studied these contentious issues, including the relationship between inflation and economic growth, and between macroeconomic policy and crises.

In response to your request, we examined (1) the process for designing an IMF-supported program, (2) the IMF-supported programs in four selected recipient countries, and (3) the extent to which the findings of empirical economic studies are consistent with the IMF's macroeconomic policies.

To address these objectives, we focused our review on IMF-supported programs that provide countries with financial assistance. We reviewed and analyzed IMF documents and data, including the IMF Articles of Agreement; country requests for IMF-supported programs (letters of intent[8]); IMF consultation reports and assessments of country progress under IMF-supported programs (including IMF's Article IV consultation reports[9]); program design papers; strategy papers; policy documents; and IMF's Independent Evaluation Office reports. Using the letters of intent and consultation reports, we determined inflation goals in the 31 IMF-supported programs in low-income countries and macroeconomic policy requirements in 13 IMF-supported programs in middle- and high-income countries as of July 2009. We also met with officials representing the IMF, U.S. Departments of the Treasury (Treasury) and State, foreign governments, NGOs, and other international organizations. We conducted audit work in Washington, D.C., as well as Hungary, Iceland, Liberia, and Zambia, having selected these four countries as case studies to illustrate the IMF-supported programs in individual country programs. We selected these four countries to ensure geographic diversity and to examine how IMF-supported programs may differ in low-, middle-, and high-income countries receiving relatively large amounts of IMF financial assistance during the time of our review. Our choice of countries is meant to be illustrative, not representative. Furthermore, using published or widely cited empirical studies identified in economic research databases including EconLit and Google Scholar, we identified key relationships between macroeconomic policies and economic growth and crises and compared them with macroeconomic policies in current IMF-supported programs. Specifically, we reviewed two parts of the academic literature relevant to the macroeconomic policy decisions in IMF-supported programs, namely the literature that links inflation with economic growth and the crisis "early warning system" literature that identifies leading indicators of currency, banking, and debt crises.

We conducted our work from November 2008 to November 2009 in accordance with all sections of GAO's Quality Assurance Framework that are relevant to our objectives. The framework requires that we plan and perform the engagement to obtain sufficient and appropriate evidence to meet our stated objectives and to discuss any limitations in our work. We believe that the information and data obtained, and the analysis conducted, provide a reasonable basis for any findings and conclusions in this product. Appendix I contains a more detailed description of our scope and methodology.

RESULTS IN BRIEF

Designing an IMF-supported financial assistance program involves a complex, iterative process based on projections for key macroeconomic variables; discussions between IMF staff and country officials regarding program goals, policies, and trade-offs; use of economic judgment; and IMF Executive Board (IMF Board) approval. The IMF-supported program is intended to help countries achieve their objectives in the context of macroeconomic stability. The IMF macroeconomic framework provides the analytical basis for an IMF-supported program and is designed to ensure consistency among the projections for the various sectors of the economy while incorporating country-specific circumstances. IMF-supported programs in low-income countries are broadly geared toward increasing economic growth and reducing poverty. These programs generally strive to achieve low inflation and sustainable levels of debt by, for example, setting targets for the size of the budget deficit and growth in the money supply. In middle- and high-income countries, IMF-supported programs generally aim to stem capital outflows, restore confidence, and stabilize the exchange rate by, for example, setting targets for budget deficits and international reserves. A range of possible targets can be consistent with macroeconomic stability depending on the severity of existing macroeconomic imbalances. Trade-offs among these different combinations of objectives or policies allow for negotiations between the IMF staff and country officials, reflecting what is technically feasible and politically acceptable. Countries seeking IMF assistance are already experiencing challenging and often severe economic situations, and their available options usually require difficult choices. For example, countries often have to sacrifice priority spending to achieve macroeconomic stability, which includes a sustainable debt burden and low inflation. Ultimately, IMF staff and country officials reach agreement on the objectives and targets of IMF-supported programs, which then require the IMF Board's approval.

IMF-supported programs in each of the four countries we studied—Liberia, Zambia, Hungary, and Iceland—include different sets of objectives, targets, and conditions that reflect the various circumstances in each country, based on negotiations between IMF staff and country officials. Although IMF staff and country officials generally agreed on the areas that require reform, they sometimes disagreed on the content and timing of specific policies for achieving program goals. All four countries are making progress, but each has encountered challenges in implementing conditions or achieving targets in their IMF-supported programs. In the two low-income countries (Liberia and Zambia), IMF-supported programs focus on achieving long-term economic stability and growth.

- In *Liberia*—a country recovering from years of civil war and lacking basic infrastructure, rule of law, and budget accountability—the IMF-supported program is designed to help address the country's immediate needs. Given Liberia's dire situation, IMF and Liberian officials stated that Liberia has few options available for achieving its program objectives. For example, under the program target to maintain a cash-based, balanced budget, the government is precluded from borrowing to finance additional spending. Officials stated that the typical trade-off decisions—for example, between larger budget deficits and increased public expenditures—are not as relevant under this constraint.

- In *Zambia*—a country negatively affected by the recent economic crisis—the IMF-supported program is designed to increase economic growth, reduce poverty, and improve governance. Key elements of Zambia's negotiations with IMF staff continue to center on fiscal trade-offs, with the authorities preferring to use greater deficit spending to stimulate economic growth, while IMF staff suggest restraint and reform to guard against wasteful spending and maintain economic stability. For the middle- and high-income countries (Hungary and Iceland, respectively), the IMF responded to sovereign debt or banking crises with a goal of reestablishing economic stability.
- In *Hungary*, a rising risk of default and the central government's unsustainable debt helped fuel the need for an IMF-supported program. A key aspect of the program is to restore confidence by shrinking the amount of government debt, largely through reduced expenditures. While expenditure cuts are not expected to be popular with the general public, Hungarian officials acknowledged that the spending cuts in the IMF-supported program are necessary to stabilize the economy.
- *Iceland* is experiencing a crisis driven by the collapse of its banking system and excessive private sector borrowing. Its IMF-supported program contains controversial approaches to monetary policy and banking reform that have yet to be finalized. For example, authorities in Iceland would prefer to reduce high interest rates earlier than IMF staff suggest to provide a stimulus for struggling households and businesses. IMF staff caution against moving too quickly due to the risk of currency depreciation, which would increase the cost of the large stock of Iceland's foreign currency debt and could cripple recovery prospects. In addition, determining how to restructure failed banks, and particularly who will bear the losses, remains a contentious issue for Icelandic authorities and the country's foreign creditors.

The macroeconomic policies in IMF-supported programs are broadly consistent with the findings of the empirical literature we reviewed, although this literature lacks precise guidance for setting policy targets. Inflation targets are a prominent feature of IMF-supported programs in low-income countries, but there has been considerable debate about appropriate targets for these countries. For low-income countries, empirical evidence generally suggests inflation is detrimental to economic growth after it exceeds a critical threshold of approximately 5 to 12 percent. This threshold is broadly consistent with the inflation targets of 5 to 10 percent in the 31 IMF-supported programs we reviewed. Reducing inflation below this critical threshold produces no additional economic growth or may cause a country to sacrifice some long-term growth benefits, according to the evidence we reviewed. Although there are comparatively few systematic analyses, the findings of the literature suggest a complex relationship between inflation and growth that could vary across countries both in terms of the optimal inflation target and the impact of higher levels of inflation on economic growth. Given these findings and the differences across countries at various stages of development, a uniform inflation target applicable to all countries may not be appropriate. For middle- and high-income countries, the academic literature identifies weaknesses in macroeconomic policies that often precede economic crises that are consistent with the policies focused on in the IMF-supported programs we reviewed. We focused on this aspect of the academic literature because middle- and high-income countries have sought significant IMF financial assistance due to stress associated with the global financial crisis. Economic crises may include one or more of currency, banking, and debt crises, and can have severe negative effects on the economy. The empirical academic literature identifies a number of specific policy weaknesses in advance of crises, including high inflation, high public indebtedness, and low international reserves. These weaknesses are consistent with the policies upon which the IMF focused in the 13 programs in the middle- and high-income countries we reviewed. While informative for the development of macroeconomic policy, the crisis "early warning system" literature contains limitations, such as selections of countries in some studies that may bias estimates of policy effects. For example, the amount of international reserves necessary to guard against a crisis may be lower for countries excluded from the analysis. As a result, this literature provides qualitative rather than precise quantitative guidance.

The Department of the Treasury provided written comments on a draft of this chapter (see app. III), stating that it fully concurs with our conclusions. Treasury and the IMF also provided technical comments, which we incorporated as appropriate.

BACKGROUND

The IMF, an organization of 186 countries, provides surveillance, lending, and technical assistance to its member countries. IMF surveillance involves the monitoring of economic and financial developments and the provision of policy advice, with key aims including financial crisis prevention. The IMF also lends to countries with balance-of-payments difficulties, including medium- to high-income countries, to provide temporary financing and support policies to achieve macroeconomic stability in the medium term. Its loans to low-income countries are to assist policies designed to foster economic growth and promote poverty reduction. In addition, the IMF provides countries with technical assistance and training in its areas of expertise.

Upon request by a member country, an IMF loan is generally provided under a program that stipulates the specific policies and measures a country has agreed to implement. As part of an agreement to receive IMF financing, a member country may agree to implement policy measures, known as conditions, designed to resolve its balance-of-payments problems, overcome the problems that led it to seek financial aid, and help ensure that it can repay the IMF. The IMF also conducts periodic program reviews to assess whether the IMF-supported program is broadly on track and the country has met established conditions, or whether modifications are necessary to achieve the program's objectives. Based on these reviews of a country's performance, including whether the country has implemented conditions according to a specific timetable, the IMF Board determines whether the country will receive subsequent installments of IMF funding.[10]

The IMF's resources are provided by member countries through quota contributions, loan provisions to the IMF, and member contributions for lending to low-income countries. When a country joins the IMF, the country pays a quota to the organization, which may increase when IMF members agree to increase the IMF's capital. Each IMF member country is assigned a quota, based broadly on its relative size in the world economy. A member's quota determines its maximum financial commitment to the IMF and its voting power and has a bearing on the amount of IMF financing a member can receive. The IMF also may enter into multilateral or bilateral borrowing arrangements to increase its resources. Moreover, resources for IMF-supported programs to low-income countries come from funding outside quota resources, including member contributions and the IMF.

In April 2009, the G-20 world leaders endorsed measures to significantly increase the IMF's available resources to $750 billion and also supported new SDR allocations of about $250 billion to increase the international reserves of member countries. An additional special SDR allocation of about $30 billion came into effect in September 2009 under the Fourth Amendment.[11] The source of IMF's increase in resources includes both increased quota contributions and a significant amount of borrowing from some member countries. Part of these additional resources includes funding from the United States. In June 2009, the U.S. Congress passed legislation that appropriated about $7.8 billion for an increase in the U.S. quota to the IMF.[12] It also made available up to about $117.5 billion for loans to the IMF.[13] Congress set some provisions for the IMF as part of the legislation, including language directing U.S. officials to oppose loans to countries that have repeatedly supported acts of international terrorism and to programs that would force developing countries to cap spending on health care and education.[14] When signing the legislation, the President issued a statement stating that certain provisions within the legislation would interfere with his constitutional authority to conduct foreign relations and that he would not treat these provisions as limiting his ability to engage in foreign diplomacy or negotiations.[15] In addition to the increase in the IMF's overall resources, the IMF Board agreed in July 2009 to measures that will boost the IMF's concessional lending capacity available to low-income countries to $17 billion through 2014.

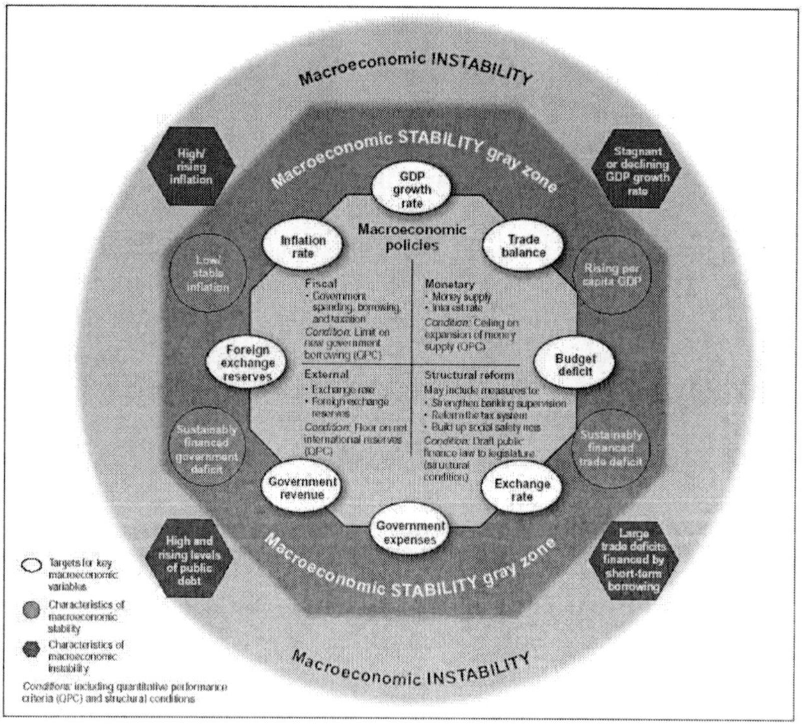

Source: GAO analysis of IMF documents.

Figure 1. Elements of an IMF-Supported Program

Table 1. Number of Countries and Total Agreed-Upon Amounts of IMF Funding by Type of IMF Lending Arrangements, as of August 2008 and August 2009

Dollars (U.S.) in billions

Type of IMF lending arrangement	Key characteristics of IMF lending arrangement	Number of countries and total agreed-upon amounts, as of August 31, 2008	Number of countries and total agreed-upon amounts, as of August 31, 2009
Poverty Reduction and Growth Facility (PRGF)	Concessional (below-market) interest loans to low-income countries eligible for PRGF assistance; eligibility based principally on the IMF's assessment of country's per capita income. Loans carry an annual interest rate of 0.5 percent; repayments made semiannually, beginning 5½ years and ending 10 years after disbursement.	22 $1.8	22 $3.2
Exogenous Shocks Facility (ESF)	Concessional financing for low-income countries that are experiencing exogenous shocks but do not have a PRGF arrangement. Interest rates and repayment terms same as those under PRGF. Length of a loan is 1 to 2 years.	0	6 $1.1
Stand-By Arrangement (SBA)	Nonconcessional loans designed to help countries address short-term balance of payments problems. Provision may be on a precautionary basis; countries may choose not to draw upon approved amounts but retain the option to do so if conditions deteriorate. Length of a loan is typically 1 to 2 years. Repayment is due within 3¼ to 5 years of disbursement.	4 $1.2	18 $84.3
Extended Fund Facility (EFF)	Use of nonconcessional resources to help countries address longer-term balance of payments problems requiring fundamental economic reforms. Interest rates and repayment terms same as those under PRGF, however, disbursements may be over a 1 to 2 year period under certain circumstances.	2 $0.6	0

Table 1. (Continued)

Type of IMF lending arrangement	Key characteristics of IMF lending arrangement	Number of countries and total agreed-upon amounts, as of August 31, 2008	Number of countries and total agreed-upon amounts, as of August 31, 2009
Flexible Credit Line (FCL) (Introduced in March 2009 to address the economic crisis)	Accelerated financing for borrower countries, useful for crisis prevention purposes. Large and up-front financing to member countries meeting preset qualification criteria. Criteria include having very strong fundamentals, policies, and track records of policy implementation. Length of a loan is 6 months or 1 year. Repayment period is 3¼ to 5 years.	Data not available because FCL did not exist	3 $81.7
Total[a]		**28 $3.5**	**49$170.4**

Source: IMF data.

Notes: Some countries may have an IMF-supported program that combines different types of arrangements. For example, Liberia had PRGF and EFF programs as of August 31, 2008. For all types of IMF lending arrangements, IMF's funding disbursements depend on performance of the recipient countries. FCL arrangements are reserved for members meeting preset qualification criteria and can be of 6 or 12 months in duration.

[a] Totals may not add up due to rounding.

Since August 2008, the IMF has dramatically increased its commitment to lend to member countries in response to the global economic crisis, as shown in table 1. The table categorizes the number of countries and amount of agreed upon IMF funding categorized by various IMF lending arrangements, which are developed and tailored to address the specific circumstances of its member countries. As shown in table 1, the number of countries with Stand-By Arrangements, typically middle- and high-income countries facing crisis and seeking to resolve their short-term balance of payments problems, have significantly increased. See appendix II for a list of the countries that have been approved to receive funding under an IMF-supported program as of August 2009.

Designing an IMF-Supported Program Is a Complex Process That Allows for Negotiated Trade-offs Among Objectives and Policies

The IMF-supported program is intended to help countries achieve macroeconomic stability and contains objectives, targets, macroeconomic policies, and conditions. The design of an IMF-supported program involves a complex process, which includes the use of a macroeconomic framework, economic judgment, and discussions between the IMF staff and country officials regarding trade-offs among different objectives and policies.

IMF-Supported Programs Are Intended to Help Countries Achieve Their Objectives in the Context of Macroeconomic Stability

An IMF-supported program consists of the objectives, targets, macroeconomic policies, and conditions, to which the borrower and the IMF agree. An IMF-supported program is intended to help a country achieve its objectives while maintaining or restoring macroeconomic stability. Although there may not be a distinct threshold between macroeconomic stability and instability, IMF documents have specified key characteristics that identify a country in a state of macroeconomic stability. These include, for example, a prudent fiscal policy; a sustainably financed trade deficit; low and stable inflation; and rising per capita Gross Domestic Product (GDP) (see figure 1).[16]

An IMF-supported program is defined by its objectives and the link between those objectives and the macroeconomic policies used to achieve them, with the specific content of a country's program reflecting the country's characteristics and circumstances. For example, IMF-supported program objectives in low-income countries are broadly geared toward the long-term goals of increasing economic growth and reducing poverty. In middle- and high-income countries, particularly those experiencing acute crises, IMF-supported programs generally aim to stem capital outflows, restore confidence, and bring about a recovery in the short- to medium-term.

The macroeconomic framework used to develop the IMF-supported program consists of the following elements as illustrated in figure 1:

- *Targets for key macroeconomic variables:* IMF-supported programs include targets to help achieve a country's objectives. In low-income countries, programs may include quantitative targets to limit the growth of the money supply and the budget deficit to lower inflation and maintain debt levels consistent with macroeconomic stability. In middle- and high-income countries, an IMF-supported program may include targets to stabilize the exchange rate, raise interest rates, and tighten credit conditions to stem the outflow of capital and restore investor confidence.[17]

- *Macroeconomic policies:* Four types of macroeconomic policies—monetary, fiscal, external, and structural reforms—may be used to help a country achieve its objectives. Monetary policy is used to affect the growth of the money supply and interest rate levels. Fiscal policy sets the amount and composition of government expenditures and government revenue to affect the size of the budget deficit. External policies concern the size of the trade deficit and the exchange rate, which can influence the amount of exports and imports and the buildup of international reserves. IMF-supported programs also are likely to include "macro-critical" structural reforms intended to help countries establish sound financial sector regulatory systems.

- *Conditions:* IMF-supported programs may contain quantitative performance criteria (QPC) and macroeconomic structural conditions, which the country has agreed to implement to receive IMF disbursements.[18] Examples of QPCs that address macroeconomic policy variables include (1) limits on government borrowing to curb the public debt, (2) a ceiling on the expansion of the money supply to manage the interest rate or contain inflation, or (3) a floor on international reserves to stabilize the exchange rate and weather shocks. According to the IMF, a country's performance criteria are frequently revised during the course of a program as external conditions evolve in a way not initially foreseen. Structural conditions are measures that the IMF and country authorities consider critical for the successful implementation of the program. Structural conditions may include specific measures to strengthen banking supervision, reform the tax system, improve fiscal transparency, and build up social safety nets. Although structural conditions are no longer used as performance criteria, the structural reforms that the IMF sees as critical to a country's recovery will continue to be monitored.

Various Combinations of Policies and Variables Are Consistent with Macroeconomic Stability, Allowing for Negotiations

Because of the extensive linkages among the various economic sectors[19] and the mutual dependence of policy instruments and targets,[20] designing an IMF-supported program is complex, iterative, and requires economic judgment. The process of designing the program begins when country authorities contact the IMF due to impending or ongoing macroeconomic instability or crisis. The IMF staff and country authorities establish the country's need for borrowing based on the specific underlying macroeconomic problems to be addressed and discuss program objectives and policies. Using a macroeconomic framework as an analytical basis for the IMF-supported program, IMF staff and country authorities use an iterative process to set targets for key macroeconomic variables, such as real GDP growth, inflation, and the budget deficit, and identify specific economic policies intended to achieve these targets.[21] The framework is intended to ensure consistency of the target values for the macroeconomic variables among the various sectors of the economy and to align the IMF's macroeconomic and structural policy advice with the program's objectives, while incorporating country-specific factors. For example, the macroeconomic framework might be used to inform discussions about how to achieve the target of a lower budget deficit by weighing policy options that include reducing expenditures, raising revenues, obtaining grant financing, or modifying the goal. The process for designing the program usually culminates with country authorities and IMF staff agreeing on the goals, targets, and policies for a program that is both technically feasible and politically acceptable. Then, they seek agreement on the conditions, including QPCs and structural reforms, needed to complete the program. The IMF Board is then asked to discuss and approve the program.

In designing an IMF-supported program, a government has to make difficult trade-off decisions among different priority objectives and policies consistent with macroeconomic stability. The trade-offs required reflect the specific country circumstances and the severity of the macroeconomic imbalances. According to an IMF/World Bank document, there is a substantial gray area for a combination of levels of key macroeconomic variables, including growth, inflation, fiscal deficit, current account deficit, and international reserves that lies between macroeconomic stability and instability, where a country could enjoy a degree of stability, but where macroeconomic performance could clearly be improved (see figure 1). This gray area allows for negotiation between the country authorities and the IMF staff.

This process can be illustrated in the following hypothetical example. A country can be adversely affected by the global recession in a number of ways, including through declining export revenue as the price and volume of exports fall. The decline in exports is likely to lead to a rise in unemployment as private sector activity declines, contributing to increased poverty. Any effort on the part of the government to increase spending to counter this fall in aggregate demand is likely to increase the budget deficit, especially in the context of falling revenues. The increased spending also may contribute to inflationary pressures.[22] If the country, prior to the crisis, was already experiencing a high debt level and an elevated inflation rate, the way forward can be quite complicated. If the budget deficit were to rise by too much, inflation could increase to a point where the country would be at risk of macroeconomic instability, while insufficient domestic spending could lower economic growth, worsening the unemployment situation and increasing poverty.

Financial assistance through an IMF-supported program can help mitigate the situation, but the government of the hypothetical country in this example still faces a difficult policy trade-off—how to reduce the impact of the recession on the poor without risking high inflation. Within this overall context, the discussions between IMF staff and government officials are likely to explore targets for the budget deficit and inflation that attempt to balance these two concerns. While the range of discussion regarding these targets is limited to what will achieve or maintain macroeconomic stability, country officials and IMF staff may have different perspectives on the risks of macroeconomic instability, the degree to which spending cuts will harm the poor, and the political feasibility of gaining parliamentary approval for significant spending cuts. These different perspectives could provide the basis for negotiation for the targets contained within the program.

Four IMF-Supported Programs Were Negotiated Based on Countries' Circumstances

IMF-supported programs in each of the four countries we reviewed contain different sets of objectives, targets, and conditions that reflect each country's individual circumstances, trade-offs, and negotiations with IMF staff. The program in postconflict Liberia focuses on rebuilding capacity, whereas the program in Zambia, a country with significant natural resources, but substantial poverty, centers on increasing economic growth. Hungary, a middle-income country, faced a risking risk of debt default; thus, the program concentrates on restoring investor confidence and reducing debt and expenditures. A banking and currency collapse precipitated Iceland's request for a program, which focuses on recapitalizing the banks and stabilizing the currency. While IMF staff and country officials in all four countries generally agreed with the programs and have made progress in implementing the programs, each country has encountered some challenges in implementing conditions or achieving targets. Figures 2, 4, 6, and 8 show country background information for Liberia, Zambia, Hungary, and Iceland. Table 2 summarizes the context, circumstances, and objectives of the IMF-supported programs we reviewed.

Table 2. Context, Circumstances, and Objectives of Four Current IMF-Supported Programs

Country	Context	Circumstances	Objectives
Liberia	Low-income, postconflict	Economy and society devastated by years of civil war and government mismanagement	Rebuild basic capacity, including economy, government, and infrastructure
Zambia	Low-income, adversely impacted by global crisis	Despite significant natural resources, including copper as the mainstay of exports, substantial poverty remains	Increase economic growth, reduce poverty, and improve governance
Hungary	Middle-income, risked defaulting on debt payments	Years of over-spending and easy credit led to massive debt accumulation	Restore investor confidence by reducing debt and expenditures
Iceland	High-income, banking system and currency collapsed	Economic meltdown, currency crash	Recapitalize banks, stabilize currency

Sources: GAO review of IMF and country documents.

Liberia's Program Focuses on Rebuilding Basic Capacity after Years of Devastation

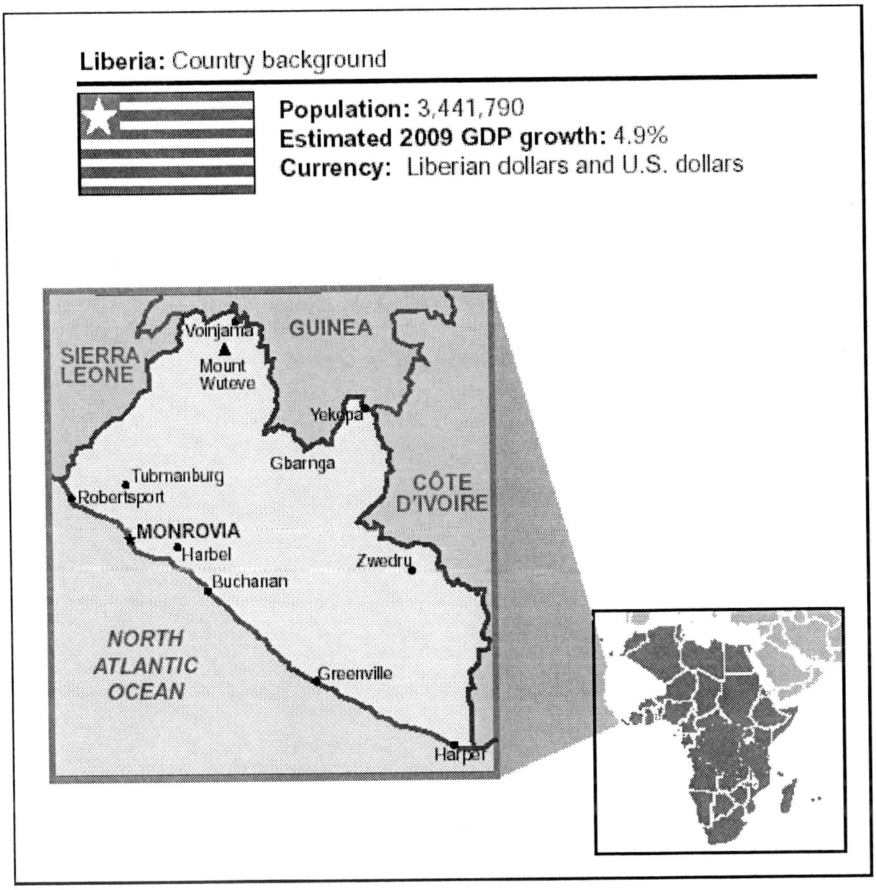

Sources: IMF and CIA World Factbook 2009.

Figure 2. Liberia's Country Background.

Liberian Government Is Working to Rebuild Devastated Capacity

Although recovering from civil wars that spanned 1989 to 2003, Liberia remains one of the world's most impoverished countries. Devastated by past war and government mismanagement, the country suffers from minimal basic infrastructure, limited health care, a largely unskilled labor force, and a population with a low literacy rate. Liberia also has a weak rule of law and widespread corruption, according to the documents we reviewed and Liberian officials we interviewed. Liberian government officials emphasized the need to address social issues, such as building basic infrastructure and providing health care and education.

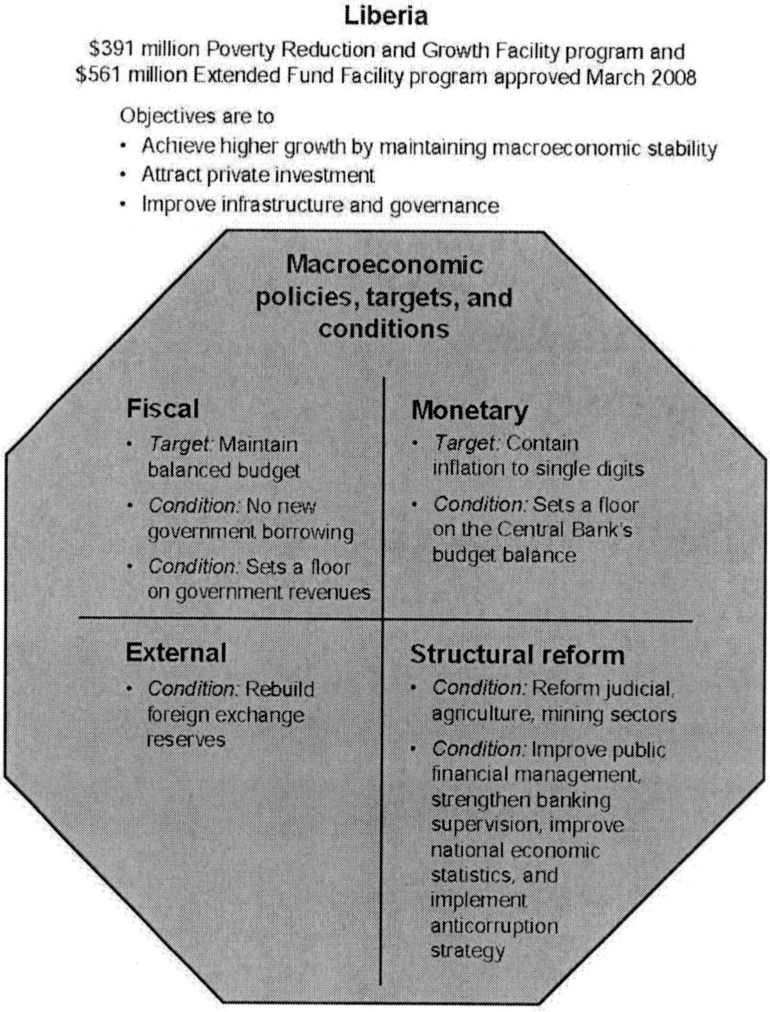

Source: GAO analysis of IMF documents.

Note: Program amount was the approximate U.S. dollar amount at the time of program approval.

Figure 3. Elements of Liberia's IMF-Supported Program

In the last 3 years, the country has made significant progress in strengthening its economy and government. For example, the GDP has been rising; the exchange rate remains relatively stable; and government revenue has increased. In 2006, the government requested IMF technical assistance to develop a program to support economic reconstruction, begin building a track record of policy implementation, resolve its arrears to creditors, and lessen its significant debt burden. Under this IMF staff-monitored program, in which the IMF provided no financial assistance, the IMF found that the Liberian government made satisfactory progress. Specifically, the IMF reported that the government has facilitated the rebuilding of public institutions, restored credible macroeconomic management, and supported implementation of important structural reforms to improve financial management and the financial sector. In 2008, Liberia cleared its long-standing overdue obligations, including obligations to the IMF that initially precluded the country from IMF assistance, and met requirements to begin receiving debt relief under the enhanced Heavily Indebted Poor Countries (HIPC) Initiative.[23] More than 100 IMF member countries participated in a fund-raising effort for Liberia, securing sufficient commitments to finance the IMF's debt relief to the country.

To make further reforms to help ensure a sustainable recovery over the long term, the government received a new 3-year IMF-supported financial assistance program in 2008. Figure 3 shows elements of the program, including its overall objectives and the policies, targets, and conditions intended to help achieve these objectives.

Government Endorses Program but Questions Fiscal Constraints

Liberian authorities and IMF staff said they generally agreed on the program but continue to negotiate its fiscal constraints. Liberian officials stated that they welcome IMF assistance, have open dialogues with IMF officials, and have a sense of ownership of the program. When the IMF began its support to Liberia in 2005, Liberia had significant external and domestic debt. In addition, the country did not have the financial resources to service any new debt, and its creditors sought evidence that Liberia could control its fiscal position in advance of providing comprehensive debt relief. Therefore, the IMF's focus was on efficiently securing government resources. To accomplish this, IMF staff said the program focused on the government achieving a balanced budget, in which expenditures equal revenues. Given Liberia's dire situation, the country has few options available for implementing its program objectives, according to Liberian officials and IMF staff. For example, under the program target to maintain a cash-based, balanced budget, the country is precluded from borrowing to finance additional spending. Both Liberian officials and IMF staff said that the typical trade-off decisions—for example, between larger budget deficits and increased public expenditures—are not as relevant under this program target. Rather, policy decisions in Liberia generally centered on the country's need to have a balanced budget, one of the program targets. Some Liberian authorities we met with said that they preferred to have more flexibility in spending to address some urgent needs, such as increased public spending on roads, health care, and education. IMF staff agreed with these views but recommended that the country prioritize having a balanced budget to ensure that it would not incur additional debt. IMF staff informed us that, while maintaining a balanced budget, Liberian officials and not IMF staff determine the composition of the country's expenditures.

Despite the existing program target of zero borrowing to maintain a balanced budget, IMF staff made an exception to this target in response to a Liberian government request. In May 2009, IMF staff supported the Liberian request for limited, highly concessional—or below market-rate—borrowing to invest in critical port infrastructure. According to an IMF review, Liberia's main port in Monrovia was badly damaged during the civil war, and further deterioration could have far-reaching ramifications on economic growth through lower exports, import shortages, and rising prices. The IMF review concluded that the proposed borrowing would not undermine debt sustainability and is directed at an urgent and important facility needed to increase trade and economic activity. IMF staff stated that they accepted Liberia's request in part because the government had thus far performed well under its IMF-supported program.

Program Is on Track, but Challenges Remain

In its June 2009 report, the IMF stated that Liberia's program remains on track while noting challenges. The government met most of its performance criteria and continued to advance structural reforms. For example, the IMF concluded that Liberia's fiscal performance through the end of 2008 was solid. The IMF said that Liberian officials remain strongly committed to a balanced cash-based budget. Furthermore, the Liberian government established an anticorruption commission that became operational in December 2008.

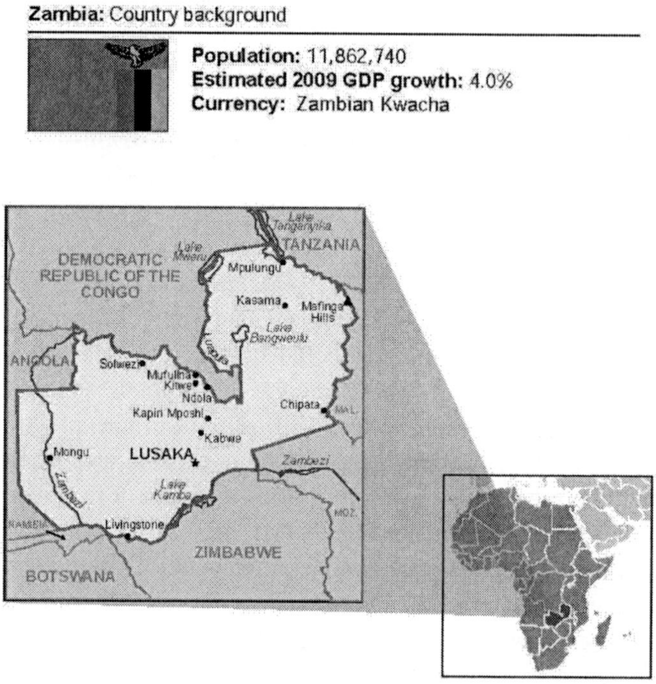

Sources: IMF and CIA World Factbook 2009.

Figure 4. Zambia's Country Background

The government continues to face some challenges that may affect the progress of its reforms. Notably, the global recession has slowed Liberia's economic recovery and may further pose risks to Liberia's achievement of its program objectives. A sharper-than-projected slowdown in global growth or a decline in world commodity prices could reduce demand for Liberia's key exports, or delay investment activity in these sectors, to a greater degree than projected. Liberian officials also stated that the political process presents a challenge in implementing reforms and legislation tied to the IMF-supported program's goals. For example, Liberian government officials said they plan to strengthen public financial management, a stated goal of the IMF-supported program. However, the passage of legislation to improve public financial management was delayed due to lengthy political debates in Liberia's legislature. This legislation was submitted to the legislature in December 2008 but not passed until August 2009. Furthermore, the government encountered a 3-month delay in setting up a functioning commission to address corruption due to late passage of the law to establish it.

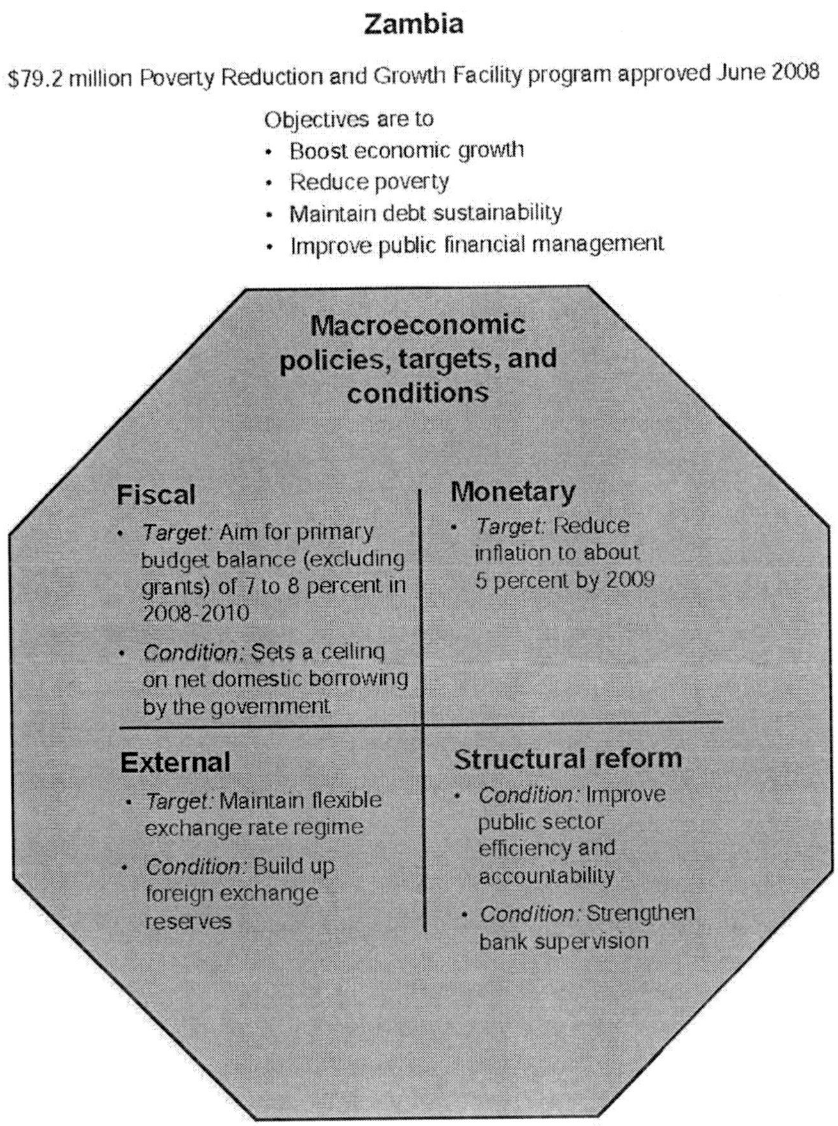

Source: GAO analysis of IMF documents.
Note: Program amount was the approximate U.S. dollar amount at the time of program approval.

Figure 5. Elements of Zambia's IMF-Supported Program

Zambia's Program Focuses on Increasing Growth and Strengthening Governance

Zambia Has Significant Natural Resources, but Substantial Poverty Remains

Zambia, a country endowed with natural resources, has performed well economically, but poverty, aggravated by the global economic crisis, remains widespread. The country's economy, afflicted by high debt and inflation through the 1990s, grew strongly in the early

2000s. The country's prior PRGF program, begun in 2004, identified reforms intended to help Zambia achieve a sustainable level of debt and reduce its 30 to 40 percent inflation rate, according to IMF staff. In 2005, Zambia qualified for debt relief under the HIPC Initiative and has begun to benefit from approximately $6 billion in debt forgiveness. As of 2007, its economic growth was robust, inflation remained in the single digits, the currency was relatively stable, and its strong external position allowed a further increase in international reserves. Zambia also benefited from the revof mining in the wake of privatization and the higher world prices of copper, the mainstay of the Zambian economy. In 2008, copper accountedfor an estimated 74 percent of Zambia's export earnings, according to an IMF document. The IMF reported that Zambia's 2008 budget maintained the prudent approach to fiscal policy of recent years. Despite increased spending, including on capital projects, the fiscal position was expected to strengthen with rising revenue from the mining sector.

Nonetheless, the lack of sufficient infrastructure—including power, transportation, and telecommunications—impedes rapid economic grow and development in Zambia. In addition, poverty has been reduced but remains exceptionally high, especially in rural areas where 80 percent of the population lives in poverty, according to an IMF document. To address economic challenges, the Zambian government received a new 3-year IMF supported financial assistance program in 2008. Figure 5 shows elements of the program, including its overall objectives and the policies, targets, and conditions intended to help achieve these objectives.

Government Generally Agrees with Program but Debates Spending Limits

IMF staff and Zambian officials stated that they had reached agreement on the initial and revised targets in the current IMF-supported program. IMF staff and Zambian officials said that they maintain a constructive relationship, which has improved during the implementation of the current IMF-supported program compared with past IMF-supported programs. Fexample, through negotiations with country officials over the years, the IMF relaxed its targets related to government wages and inflation rates. According to IMF staff, Zambia's government wages were relatively high, causing the IMF to limit wages of Zambia's civil service employees in an earlier IMF-supported program. From 2003 to 2004, some NGOs criticized the IMF's role in determining the budget limits on the size of the Zambian government wage bill. The IMF advised the Zambian government that such a high wage bill would not leave sufficient room in the budget for spento support the government's poverty reduction strategy. After holding further discussions, IMF staff reached agreement with Zambian officials about this issue. In Zambia's current IMF-supported program, the IMF no longer sets targets related to civil service wages. In addition, IMF staff aZambian officials discussed and revised the inflation target in Zambia's current program. Zambian officials stated that they thought the progrtarget of 7 percent inflation, set in June 2008 at the beginning of the program and based on the IMF's projections, was too ambitious. After some external factors that were out of Zambia's control (such as food anfuel price increases) caused the country's inflation rate to accelerate to 16.6 percent at the end of 2008, IMF staff and Zambian officials deemed the initial inflation rate target to be infeasible within the specified time frame. During the IMF's June 2009 review, the inflation rate target was revised to 10 percent by the end of 2009, with a goal to further reduce the inflation rate to single digits in 2010.

Significant elements of Zambia's negotiations with IMF staff have centeron fiscal policy and the trade-offs between increasing priority spending and reducing excessive debt. IMF staff and Zambian officials stated that they discussed policy options, such as the extent to which the government can undertake additional spending and what recourse Zambia has withoutborrowing to finance the additional spending. Zambian officials said ththey would prefer to use greater deficit spending to stimulate growth, particularly to address the impact of the economic crisis. However, IMF staff suggested restraint and reform to guard against wasteful spending and maintain macroeconomic stability. According to IMF staff, the country faces the ongoing risk of returning to its previous unsustainable debt levels if the government does not spend effectively.

Program Was Broadly on Track, but External Shocks Have Slowed Progress

In June 2009, the IMF reported that Zambia's program was initially broadlyon track, but slippages occurred later mainly due to three factors that had an adverse impact on the economy. First, rising world food and fuel prices early in 2008 pushed inflation to 16.6 percent, above the program target of 7 percent for the end of 2008. Second, a transition in political leadership delayed decisions on the budget and structural measures central to Zambia's economic program. Finally, the global economic crisis negatively affected the economy and exacerbated poverty, most directly through precipitous fall in the price of copper, a commodity on which Zambia overwhelmingly relies for earnings. The IMF review noted that copper prices have declined by about two-thirds since they peaked in mid-2008Export proceeds, government revenue, and capital inflows have been reduced as a result. The slump in copper prices will inevitably have a detrimental effect on Zambia's economic prospects in view of the mining sector's central role in the economy. As a result of these shocks, Zambia's real GDP is projected to slow down, and its balance of payments position has weakened.

IMF staff noted that Zambian officials have responded appropriately to these external shocks. For example, the IMF found that Zambia's fiscapolicy had struck the right balance between maintaining high-priority infrastructure spending to promote medium-term economic growthsafeguarding short-term macroeconomic stability by scaling back investment and recurrent spending. IMF officials noted that spending cuhave not reduced priority social spending. Furthermore, IMF staff saidZambia's public debt sustainability outlook is favorable. Specifically, Zambian officials have adopted a new public debt management policy and strategy to help ensure that the amount of public debt remains sustainable.

Hungary's Program Focuses on Reducing Debt and Expenditures

Hungary Risked Defaulting on Its Debt Payments

In fall 2008, Hungary's government secured financing from the IMF and other creditors due to a rising risk of default and unsustainable debt. Hungary was among the first emerging market countries to suffer from the fallout of the global financial crisis. As financial difficulties in advanced economies led to a decline in global liquidity and an increase in investors' concern about the risk of their investments, investors increasingly started differentiating among emerging markets. Hungary's high debt levels negatively affected investor interest in its assets. Hungary experienced an earlier short episode of financial stress in March 2008, then its financing conditions deteriorated sharply in mid-October 2008.

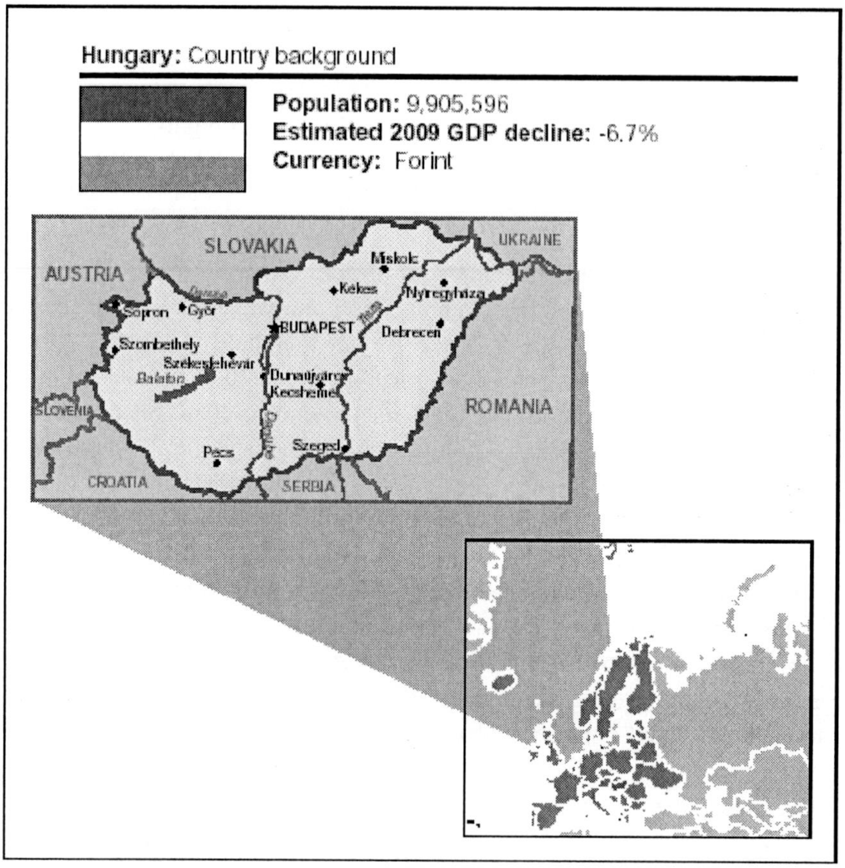

Sources: IMF and CIA World Factbook 2009.

Figure 6. Hungary's Country Background

Prior to the crisis, Hungary's large fiscal deficits led to rising government debt. The general government deficit averaged more than 8 percent of GDP from 2002 to 2006. As a result, public debt rose to about 75 percent of GDP in 2008, the highest level of similar countries in Eastern and Central Europe, according to the IMF.

With easy access to foreign currencies, foreign-owned and Hungarian banks made domestic loans in foreign currencies, which carried lower interest rates attractive to Hungarian borrowers. The rise in such lending eventually resulted in about two-thirds of the lending to Hungarian households and corporations being denominated in foreign currency, according to the IMF. The risk of such loans is that a reduction in the value of Hungary's currency, the forint, makes loans more expensive for borrowers to repay. In March 2009, the currency reached an all time low relative to the euro, according to the IMF. In the 5 months between October 2008 and March 2009, the forint depreciated by 26 percent against the euro.[24] This reduction stressed borrowers and translated into credit risk for banks that faced difficulty collecting loans.

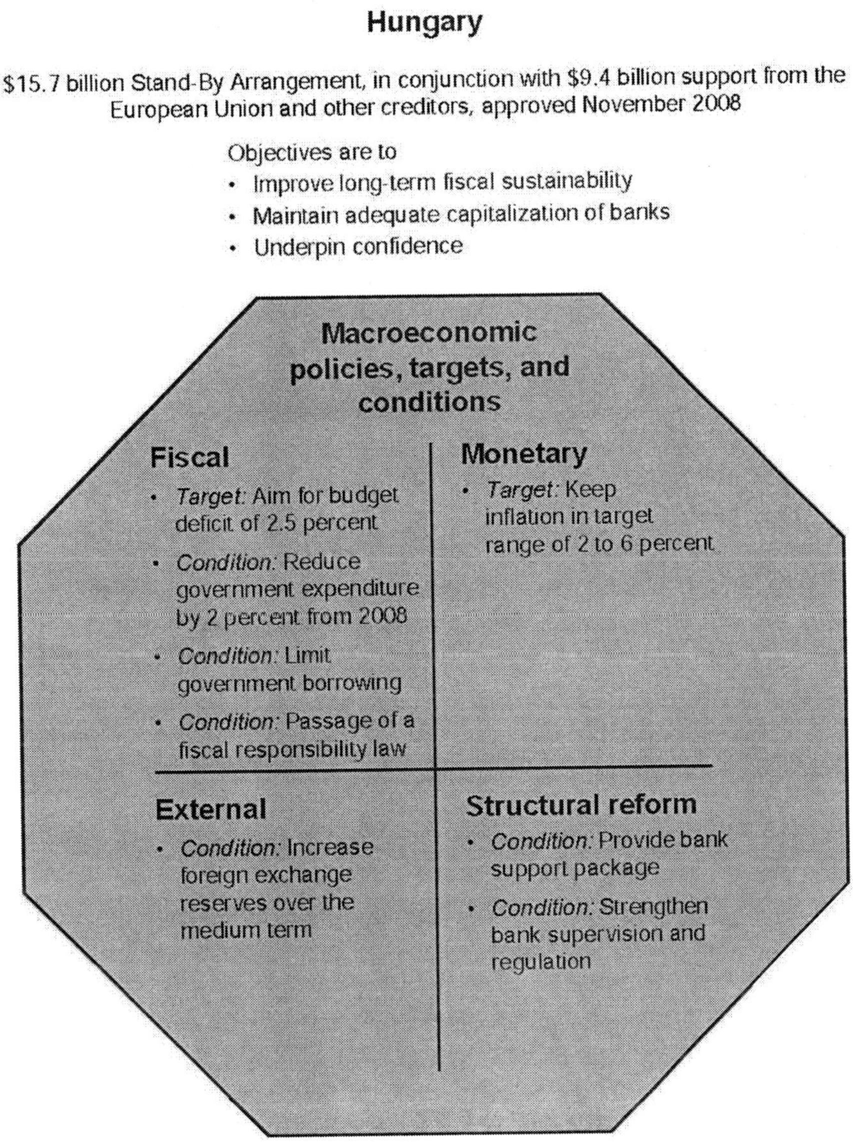

Source: GAO analysis of IMF documents.

Note: Program amount was the approximate U.S. dollar amount at the time of program approval.

Figure 7. Elements of Hungary's IMF-Supported Program.

To address the increasing risks, the initial objectives of Hungary's IMF-supported program focused on restoring investor confidence and reducing government expenditures. Figure 7 shows elements of the program, including its overall objectives and the policies, targets, and conditions intended to help achieve these objectives.

IMF and Hungarian Officials Mainly Concur, but Spending and Banking Challenges Remain

IMF and Hungarian authorities generally agree on the elements of the IMF-supported program, but determining how to achieve the deficit target and support the banking system remain challenges. Country authorities stated that they broadly concur with the goals of the program and accept the need for reform due to the crisis. In addition, they indicated that IMF staff are cooperative, helpful, and unobtrusive, providing latitude for the policy response to be defined and owned domestically.

Stabilizing the economy requires the Hungarian government to restore investor confidence by decreasing the amount of government debt, mainly by reducing expenditures and achieving the deficit target, according to the IMF. While government officials said they plan to meet the deficit tarthey have yet to determine the necessary policy changes. Debate in Hungary now centers on spending decisions for 2009. Because taxes are already high to support a large government budget, increasing revenue by raising taxes is not considered a viable option, according to IMF staff.While spending cuts are not expected to be popular with the general public, Hungarian officials acknowledge that the spending cuts consistenwith the IMF-supported program are necessary. However, IMF staff and Hungarian authorities have disagreed on the target for the budget deficit as a percentage of GDP, a key metric. In the beginning, IMF staff called fa lower budget deficit than authorities said was reasonable. Later, their positions reversed, with IMF staff recommending a wider budget deficit target than the Hungarian authorities' suggestion of 2.9 percent, a figurethat would allow them to stay within European Union guidelines.[25] The latest target, 3.9 percent, was reached after IMF, European Union, and Hungarian officials agreed that deteriorating economic circumstancemerited a higher target. Moreover, if the recession lasts longer than expected or if the government officials are unable to agree on sufficient spending cuts, fiscal consolidation efforts could be hampered.

Hungarian officials and IMF staff reached agreement in addressing the domestically controversial area of regulatory oversight of the banksystem but expressed different views on how to proceed. Country authorities indicated that a debate continues on formulating a new approach to banking supervision. Currently, the powers of the agencharge of that responsibility, the Hungarian Financial Supervisory Authority (HFSA), are limited, according to the agency's officials. The HFSA must conduct on-site investigations, which take 45 to 60 days, ancan only recommend remedial action for individual banks. The HFSAargues that it should be able to impose regulations in a more timely fashion and on the entire sector. For example, it should be able to issuebinding regulations for the entire banking system, including on capitallevels. The HFSA also favors greater independence, suggesting that it report to Parliament rather than the Ministry of Finance, as it currently does. IMF staff support greater independence for the HFSA and seek to strengthen and integrate weak and fragmented segments of the financial supervisory structure. IMF staff outlined details in a paper and provided technical assistance to explore options. The authorities have decided to support the HFSA as an independent agency with the right to issue regulations. However, implementing the change is sensitive and requires political support that may or may not materialize.

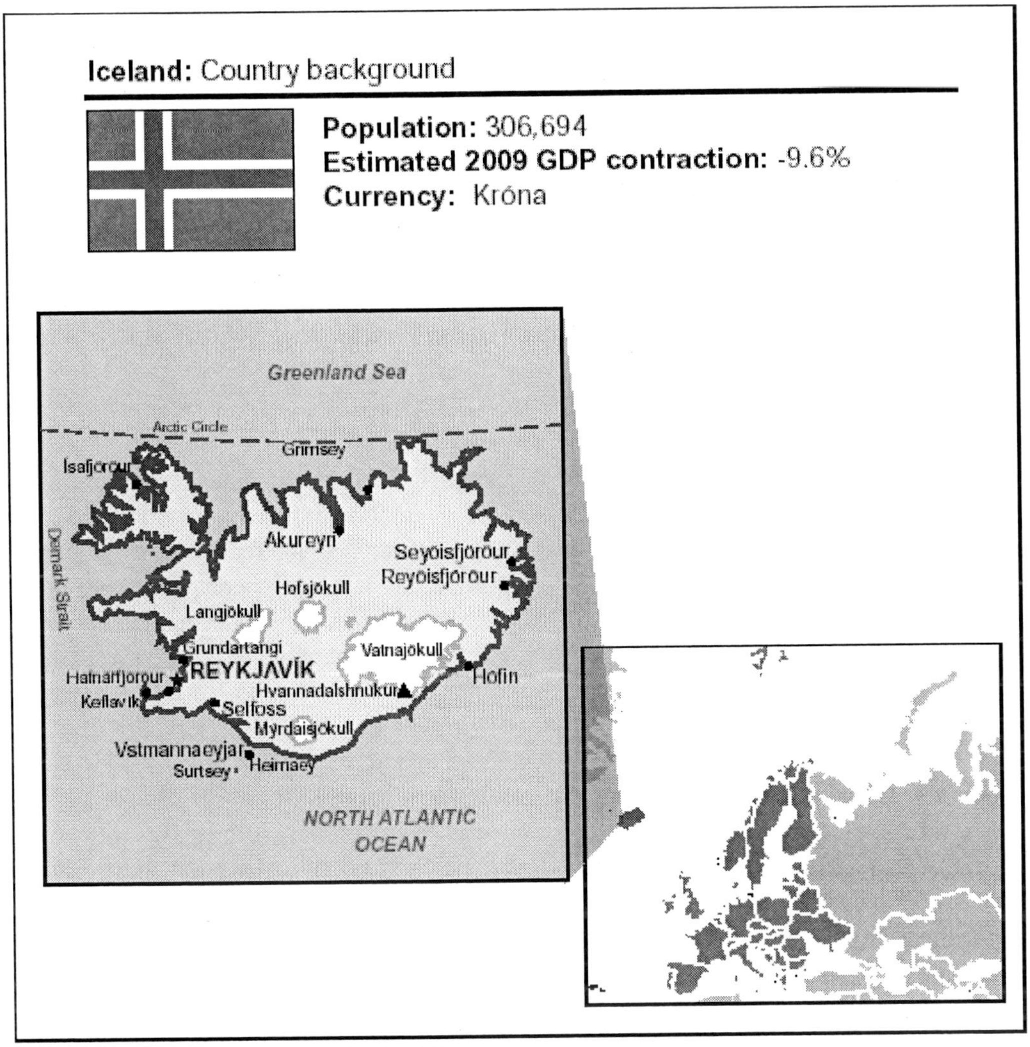

Sources: IMF and CIA World Factbook 2009.

Figure 8. Iceland's Country Background

Regarding the stability of banks, according to Hungarian authorities, initially IMF staff were concerned that banks did not have sufficiecapital and could be at risk of insolvency or collapse. As a result, according to authorities, IMF staff argued for a preemptive bank recapitalization that would provide additional capital to key Hungarian banks. While IMF staff stated that preemptive recapitalization was not thintention, banks were uneasy about the potential of greater government involvement because recapitalization would occur through a capitaenhancement fund established with government funds that wouldpurchase ownership shares of the banks. Although the IMF held discussions with authorities to dispel concerns, Hungarian authorities disagreed with the idea of preemptive capitalization, indicating that the banks were healthy and well-capitalized. In addition, one bank executivexpressed concerns that preemptively and massively recapitalizing thebanking system would be overly cautious and potentially harmful. He added that it could be counterproductive because it would reduce return on equity for local Hungarian banks and may put foreign parent banks isituation where they would be unable or unwilling to provide support, resulting in a banking collapse, the very outcome the IMF seeks to aln its June 2009 review of the program, the IMF concluded that the banking sector was resilient during the early part of the year, but that the possible need for additional capital could not be ruled out. In September 2009, the IMF completed its third review stating that, while policies are on track, continued implementation of program policies remains essential to strengthen macroeconomic stability.

Iceland's Program Focuses on Recapitalizing Banks and Stabilizing Currency

Iceland Is Struggling to Address a Severe Banking Crisis

Iceland's struggle to address a severe banking crisis led it to seek financing from the IMF and other creditors in fall 2008. In the wake of international financial turmoil, Iceland's economy faced a banking crisis of extraordinary proportions. Triggered by a loss of investor confidence and fuelled by the financial sector's high debt and dependence on foreign financing, the crisis led to the collapse of Iceland's three main banks, accounting for around 85 percent of the banking system. The economy continues to experience a deep recession and a dramatic surge in public sector debt, reflecting the unprecedented cost of restructuring the banking system.

In Iceland, an oversized banking system developed that significantly outstripped the authorities' ability to act as a lender of last resort when it ran into trouble. Banks increased their assets from slightly more than 100 percent of GDP in 2004, after the privatization of the banking sector was completed, to close to 1,000 percent of GDP. Iceland was one of the first victims when declining investor confidence intensified in fall 2008 because investors realized that the banking system was too big relative to the economy's size and thus started to pull assets out of Icelandic banks. Within a week, Iceland's three primary banks collapsed, the króna's value dropped by more than 70 percent, and the stock market lost more than 80 percent of its value.

To address its significant banking crisis and plummeting currency, Iceland's government, in fall 2008, received a $2.1 billion IMF-supported program, which also depended on significant financing from other creditors. Figure 9 shows elements of the program, including its overall objectives and the policies, targets, and conditions intended to help achieve these objectives.

In the short run, the IMF-supported program has been narrowly focused on stabilizing Iceland's currency, the króna. Iceland has a significant amount of debt that is either denominated in foreign exchange or indexed to inflation. Therefore, when the króna depreciates, debt servicing becomes much more expensive, which would likely lead to a wave of defaults in the corporate and household sectors, further harming the economy.

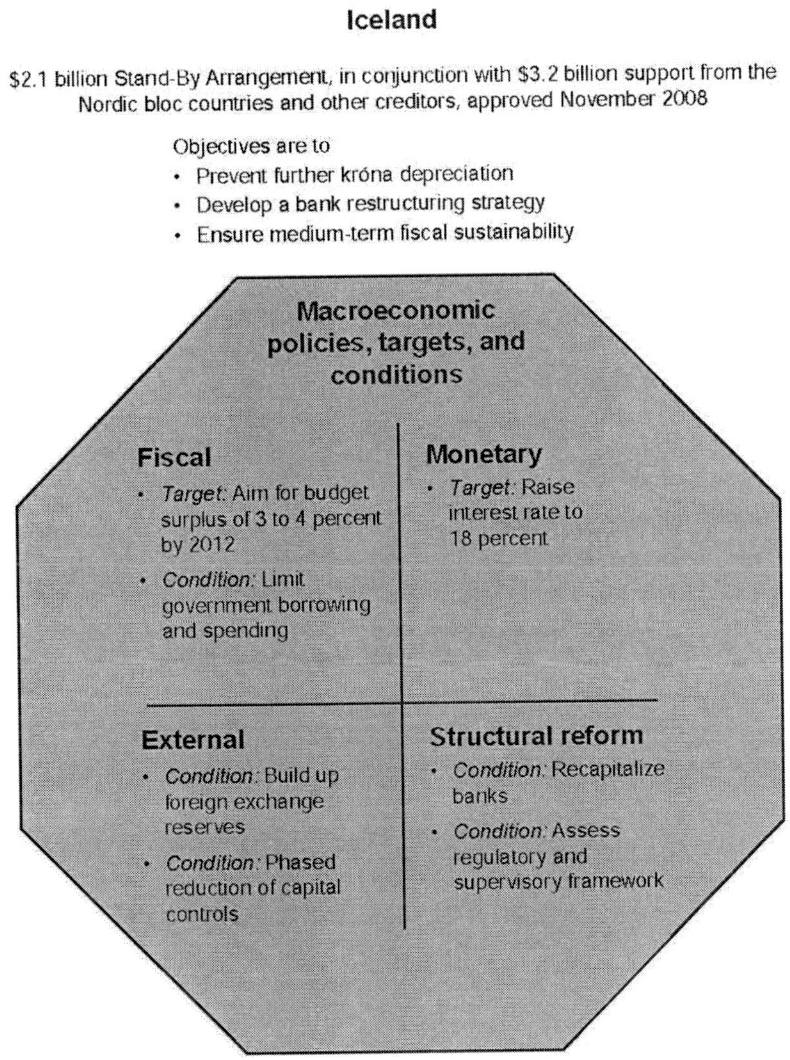

Source: GAO analysis of IMF documents.

Note: Program amount was the approximate U.S. dollar amount at the time of program approval.

Figure 9. Elements of Iceland's IMF-Supported Program.

Government Generally Endorses the Program, but Some Critical Issues Remain

Country authorities said they generally endorse the IMF-supported program and recognize the need for fiscal austerity. They said they are fully committed to the program and acknowledge that economic reform and reduced government spending will be painful but necessary measures that must be taken to address the economic crisis. Government efforts are under way to generate more revenue through higher taxes and to decrease expenditures by freezing civil service wages and adjusting some social services. Authorities said stakeholders, including unions, politicians, and households, are involved in the dialogue on austerity, which is critical because any retrenchment will be difficult and unpopular. According to authorities, Iceland is a Nordic welfare state in which its citizens have come to expect a high standard of living and generous social benefits. However, due to the scale of the economic catastrophe, traditional assumptions may be challenged as the government cuts spending.

Regarding fiscal policy decisions, country authorities indicated that IMF staff provide only broad direction and do not get involved in the details, unless asked to provide expertise or input on a specific measure. For example, IMF staff have not recommended cuts in certain government transfers, such as unemployment or parental leave benefits, or stressed that specific taxes be raised. Although budget choices and priorities are left to the government, IMF staff emphasize the need for changes that are durable over time and that will lead to a long-term improvement in the fiscal position. In contrast to the perception that the IMF always imposes fiscal restraint, Iceland's program was designed to provide an increase in the budget deficit initially to mitigate the macroeconomic shock and then to turn the focus to gradually reducing the deficit over a period of time.

Country authorities also stated that relations with IMF staff generally are cooperative, and negotiations involve a fair amount of give and take. In addition, they said that IMF staff have been helpful overall, particularly regarding fiscal and monetary policy, surveillance, and technical assistance. Moreover, authorities said they own the program and take responsibility for the crisis and the steps that must be taken to resolve it. They acknowledged that asking for IMF support was initially highly controversial, and many Icelandic citizens and some members of Parliament still do not want the government to implement the program.

Government authorities and IMF staff expressed different views on how to resolve continuing interest rate, capital controls, and banking issues. Authorities prefer earlier interest rate reductions than IMF staff suggest. Although Iceland's interest rate is high by international standards, IMF staff said the higher rate is necessary to stabilize the króna and is normal policy in the context of a currency crisis. However, a high interest rate is a drag on the domestic economy because the elevated cost of domestic credit hurts some companies and households. Authorities argue that the interest rate should be reduced to relieve pressure on residents struggling to make payments on home mortgages and business loans. IMF staff caution against reducing the interest rate too quickly due to the risk that such action may lead to renewed currency depreciation, which would increase the cost of the large stock of Iceland's foreign currency debt and could cripple recovery prospects. However, authorities contend that many residents are already facing bankruptcy and question whether a high interest rate does in fact help stabilize the króna. They suggest that interest rate reductions so far have not resulted in significant currency depreciation. Although IMF staff have not questioned the need to lower rates eventually, they differ with the authorities on how quickly the interest rate should be lowered. IMF expressed concern that if interest rates come down too far too fast, Iceland may see excessive depreciation in the exchange rate, which would be difficult to reverse. IMF staff have warned that the current level of uncertainty necessitates a slow and cautious approach.

Icelandic authorities imposed capital controls to restrict the movement of financial assets between countries in October 2008 and maintained them as part of the IMF-supported program approved in November 2008. In addition, Icelandic authorities acknowledged that the controls were necessary to stabilize the economy, at the time, due to the crisis but view them as a drastic measure and favor loosening them as soon as possible. Like a high interest rate, capital controls help limit the outflow of money and reduce downward pressure on the króna. Icelandic authorities view the combination of high interest rates and capital controls as redundant— a "belt and suspenders" approach. In addition, imposing capital controls was a shock to both the domestic and external sectors. Moreover, capital controls created dual exchange rates, one officially sanctioned by the Central Bank, and one determined by market forces off-shore. This enabled foreign importers of Icelandic goods to buy króna more cheaply in currency markets abroad, weakening the system. As a result, authorities created a new rule to stop the practice. International investors, traders, and business people continue to try to identify loopholes and work-arounds, so efforts to update and revise the capital controls structure continue.

Discussion of lifting capital controls is ongoing, but the details of exactly when and how remain controversial. Bank industry representatives we spoke with expressed frustration with capital controls, criticizing them as a harsh measure. Authorities prefer to loosen capital controls as soon as possible and assert that gradual removal of the controls is an important step toward normalizing economic conditions. Icelandic businesses view access to capital markets, international funding, and investments as one of the main preconditions for economic recovery. Both authorities and IMF staff envision a gradual lifting of capital controls, but only when the conditions are right. The concern is that billions of dollars worth of króna-denominated bonds, amounting to about 60 percent of GDP, are held by foreigners. Allowing sudden repatriation of those funds could lead to a massive outflow and currency depreciation. Therefore, IMF staff caution that confidence must be restored through fiscal consolidation and banking sector reform before phasing out capital controls.

Differences also remain on a critical banking issue, particularly who will bear the losses related to certain foreign obligations. Iceland's collapsed banks had several overseas branches and subsidiaries, mainly in other European countries. For example, "Icesave" is a vehicle in which residents of the United Kingdom, Denmark, and other countries deposited billions of dollars worth of savings. When Iceland's banks failed, money to cover these deposits disappeared. Opinion in Iceland about whether and how to ensure the value of the accounts is divided. Critics argue that Icelandic citizens should not have to bear the enormous cost of mistakes made by a few private bankers. However, two IMF Board members, with a deep stake in the issue, argued that Icesave deposits must be honored. While this was not an explicit condition of the IMF-supported program, resolution of the Icesave issue was linked to the provision of $2.5 billion in support from a bloc of Nordic countries,[26] a source of funding critical to, and in addition to, financing provided by the IMF-supported program.

Originally scheduled for completion in early 2009, the first review was delayed, in part to provide more time to address banking issues, and was completed in October 2009. Following the delay in completing the first review, the IMF Board granted the Icelandic authorities' request to extend the program by 6 months (to May 2011), to allow time to achieve objectives that will take longer than expected. The IMF review noted that, in the context of Iceland's financial crisis, Iceland's economy has shown some positive signs. For example, according to the IMF review, inflation has decreased; the program's main objective, stabilizing the króna, has been met; the financial sector restructuring objective was achieved; and external financing has been secured.

Macroeconomic Policies in IMF-Supported Programs Are Broadly Consistent with Findings of Academic Literature

For low-income countries, empirical evidence suggests inflation is detrimental to economic growth after it exceeds a critical threshold, which is broadly consistent with the inflation targets included in the IMF-supported programs we reviewed. Similarly, for middle- and high-income countries, the academic literature identifies weaknesses in macroeconomic policies that often precede economic crises that are consistent with the policies in the IMF-supported programs we reviewed.

Empirical Evidence Evaluating the Complex Relationship between Inflation and Growth Is Broadly Consistent with IMF-Supported Programs in Low-Income Countries

Empirical Research Suggests a Complex Relationship between Inflation and Growth; Inflation Harms Growth above a Critical Threshold

Inflation targets are a prominent feature of IMF-supported programs in low-income countries, but there has been considerable debate about appropriate targets for these countries. Some believe that the IMF may have gone beyond the existing empirical evidence in targeting very low inflation, potentially compromising economic growth. Although the precise relationship between inflation and economic growth in low-income countries remains uncertain, the empirical literature over the past 10 years has reached consensus about some aspects of this complex relationship. For example, there is general agreement about the following in low-income countries:

- The relationship between inflation and growth varies depending on the level of inflation and potentially on other country-specific variables.[27]
- Inflation is detrimental to medium- and long-term economic growth after it exceeds a critical threshold, implying that inflation can compromise growth if it is "too high."
- Inflation does not negatively affect economic growth at low levels—in fact, the relationship can be positive for this limited range.[28] Reducing inflation below this critical threshold produces no additional economic growth or may cause a country to sacrifice some long-term growth benefits.

These findings are represented in figure 10, which provides an illustrative summary of the impact of rising inflation on economic growth in low-income countries. The central finding from the literature is that relationship is nonlinear with a critical point (point 1) where the relationship between inflation and growth changes significantly.

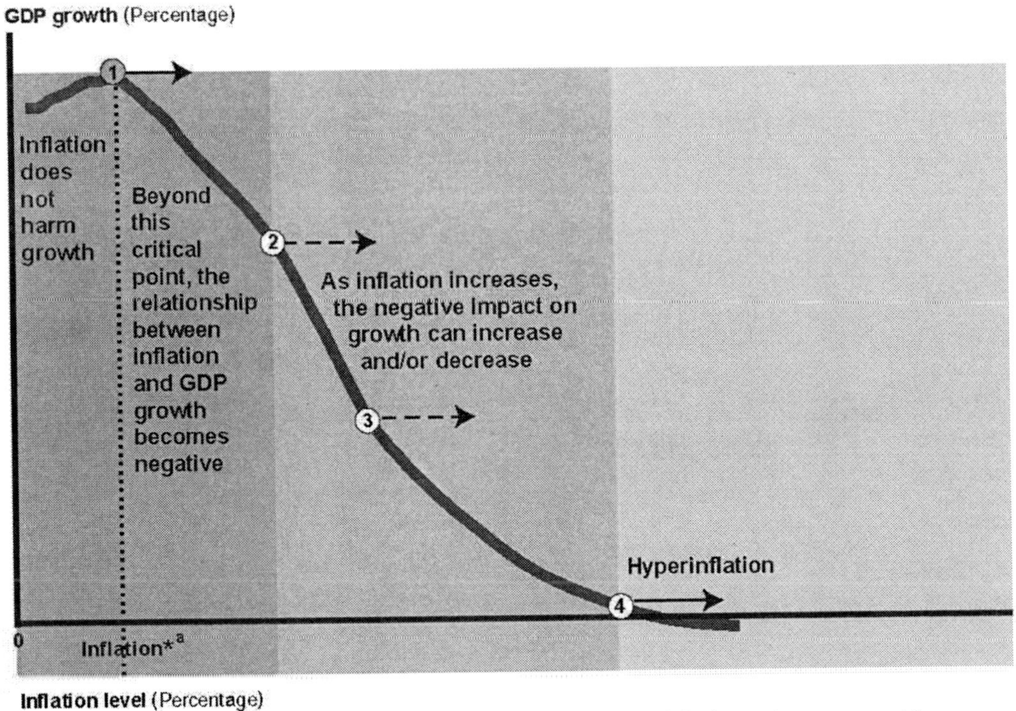

Source: GAO analysis of empirical research on inflation and growth in lower income countries.

Note: Although based on the literature, the relationship depicted here should not be considered definitive.

[a] Inflation* represents the rate of inflation beyond which inflation is harmful to growth. Estimates for this critical threshold rate range from 3 to 18 percent for low-income countries in the empirical literature.

Figure 10. Relationship between Inflation and Economic Growth in Low-Income Countries as Described in Empirical Literature.

To the left of point 1 in figure 10, inflation does not harm economic growth and, in most cases, a positive relationship is established.[29] Beyond point 1, countries face a trade-off between the short-term cost associated with lowering inflation to achieve higher medium- and long-term growth and the cost of accepting higher inflation and therefore lower future growth. Anti-inflationary policies in the region left of point 1 can be counterproductive since the potential costs of reducing inflation are not offset by increases in economic growth or, at worst, can be compounded by declines in long-term growth rates.[30] However, as inflation rises and the critical threshold is breached, the negative effects of inflation surface. Beyond this point, any increases in the inflation rate result in additional declines in economic growth. As points 2 and 3 show, the marginal costs to long-term growth can either increase or decrease as inflation rises, although empirical research does not reach a consensus as to whether the relationship changes for moderate inflation rates. As a country approaches hyperinflation (point 4), it likely faces a complete breakdown in economic functioning.

However, examining the inflation-growth relationship under these conditions generally goes beyond the scope of the literature we reviewed.[31] Earlier academic literature raised doubts about whether moderate to high inflation was costly to economic growth, but recent literature suggests that the cost of inflation was understated because researchers failed to acknowledge the complex, or nonlinear, naturrelationship between inflation and econom

Table 3. Inflation Targets in IMF-Supported Programs for 31 Low-Income Countries, as of July 2009

Low-income country	Medium-term inflation target	Type of IMF arrangement
Afghanistan	6%	PRGF
Burundi	6%	PRGF
Gambia, The	5%	PRGF
Guinea	5%	PRGF
Haiti	7%	PRGF
Kyrgyz Republic	Single digit	ESF
Liberia	Single digit	PRGF
Madagascar	Under 10%	PRGF
Malawi	5%	ESF
Mauritania	5%	PRGF
Mongolia	9%	SBA
Mozambique	Single digit (7%)	ESF
Nicaragua	7%	PRGF
Pakistan	5%	SBA
Rwanda	Single digit (7%)	PRGF
Sao Tome and Principe	Single digit	PRGF
Sierra Leone	Single digit	PRGF
Tajikistan, Republic of	Single digit	PRGF
Tanzania	5%	ESF
Zambia	5%	PRGF
Currency unions (or currency board)		
Benin	Below 3%	PRGF
Burkina Faso	3%	PRGF
Central African Republic	Below 3%	PRGF
Congo, Republic of	3%	PRGF
Cote d'Ivoire	Below 3%	PRGF
Djibouti	3%-3.5%	PRGF
Grenada	Below 3%	PRGF
Mali	Below 3%	PRGF
Niger	Below 3%	PRGF
Senegal	Below 3%	ESF
Togo	Below 3%	PRGF

Sources: GAO analysis of recipient countries' letters of intent and IMF's Article IV reports.

Note: For Mauritania, Mongolia, and Grenada, no clear target was articulated, and therefore we have taken the long-term inflation projection for the country as the implicit target.

Current IMF-Supported Programs Generally Target Single-Digit Inflation That Is within the Bounds of the Existing Empirical Estimates

Although not definitive, the empirical literature supports the focus of IMF-supported programs on containing inflation in low-income countries. Excluding those with countries in currency unions, or with currency boards, IMF-supported programs in low-income countries consistently target inflation in the 5 to 10 percent range.[32] The 31 IMF-supported programs in low-income countries, as of July 2009, are designed to help the countries achieve and maintain macroeconomic and financial stability, including targeting single-digit inflation to avoid the risk that rising prices pose to economic growth. According to IMF documents, inflation above 10 percent is generally considered harmful to medium-term growth, while targeting inflation below 5 percent may not be appropriate given the potential benefits of modest inflation on product and labor markets. Of the 31 IMF-supported programs, the 20 programs that did not involve countries participating in currency unions all targeted single-digit inflation at no less than 5 percent (see table 3). In some cases, we found shorter-term inflation targets above 10 percent. For example, Sao Tome and Principe, and Guinea both have short-term targets in low double digits as part of the longer-term objective of gradually reducing inflation to the single digits.

The 11 other countries with IMF-supported programs participate in common currency unions (or operate a currency board) with inflation targets of 3 percent or lower that are set indirectly by the choice of exchange rate arrangements, not the IMF.[33] Inflation targets in the common currency unions in table 3 are driven by the decision to maintain a fixed exchange rate that requires member countries to keep the range of inflation close to inflation levels in the developed country or area to which the common currency is fixed.[34] Almost all of the countries included in the lower half of table 3 belong to currency unions that peg their currency to either the euro or, in the case of Grenada, the U.S. dollar. The only exception is Djibouti, which is not part of a currency union but operates a currency board tied to the U.S. dollar. As a result, the inflation targets for these countries are largely independent of IMF inflation policy and tend to approximate the inflationary experiences of the euro area or the United States.

Inflation Targets in IMF-Supported Programs within the Bounds of the Existing Empirical Studies

The empirical literature we reviewed, consisting of nine studies, provides estimates of the inflation rate (ranging from 3 to 18 percent) beyond which inflation hampers long-term growth for low-income countries. Inflation targets in IMF-supported programs, although at the lower end of the 3 to 18 percent range, are generally consistent with estimates in empirical studies. (See figure 11.)

Eliminating the lowest and two highest estimates produces an approximate range of 5 to 12 percent for the threshold, which is roughly consistent with the inflation targets of 5 to 10 percent in the 31 IMF-supported programs for low-income countries we reviewed.[35] Across the studies, the estimated threshold is generally found to be higher for low-income than for high-income economies, providing some support for inflation targets in IMF-supported programs that tolerate higher inflation in low-income countries. (The bibliography for inflation-growth literature contains a full listing of the studies.) While there is some disagreement on where the critical threshold lies, there is consensus that it is lower than the level suggested by some studies prior to 2000. These studies provided some evidence that inflation did not significantly hurt economic growth until it reached the 20 to 40 percent range, but these findings have not proven robust for a number of reasons. Specifically, some of the threshold calculations were based on judgment rather than empirical estimation.[36]

Flexibility in the Selection of an Inflation Target for a Particular Country Is Prudent

The complexity of the relationship between inflation and economic growth uncovered by the literature indicates it may be inappropriate to set a uniform policy target applicable to all countries. The empirical literature illustrates that combining countries at different levels of development can produce unreliable results both in the estimating of the threshold in the inflation-growth relationship and the effect of low and high inflation on economic growth. This calls for flexibility in the implementing inflation targets in individual countries because the "growth-maximizing" rate of inflation might be expected to differ, at least somewhat, even across low-income countries at various stages of development. For example, after increasing the sample of low-income countries, some researchers found that the estimated inflation threshold increased from 6 to 17 percent.[37] Similarly, another study found no clear-cut threshold for developing countries and attributes this finding to the differences across countries grouped under the "developing" country label.[38] One interpretation of these findings is that, even though the literature generally supports inflation targets in IMF-supported programs, the gains from a given reduction in inflation to single digits from somewhat higher levels might by the cost in some cases. As a result, the relationships and trade-offs should be carefully evaluated for each country.[39]

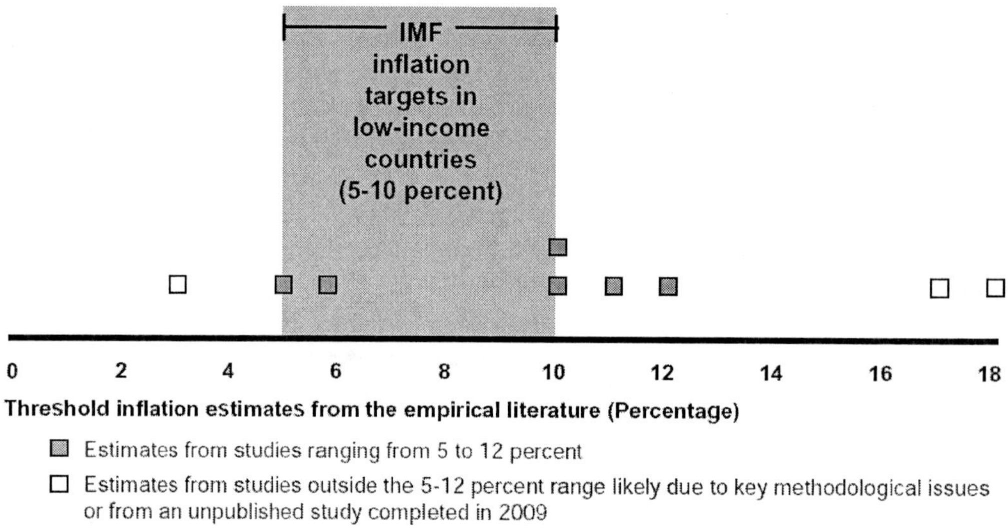

Sources: GAO analysis of empirical research on inflation and growth in lower income countries and IMF documents.

Note: Threshold estimates indicate the inflation rate where growth is negatively and significantly affected by further increases in the inflation rate. Figure 11 only includes threshold rates of inflation that were estimated empirically using low-income, developing, or nonindustrial countries.

Figure 11. Inflation Targets in IMF-Supported Programs Are within the Estimates from Nine Studies

Table 4. Indicators of Crisis Vulnerability from the Academic Literature

Indicator	Nature of vulnerability
Real exchange rate	A high real exchange rate relative to historical averages indicates that the currency may be overvalued and the economy uncompetitive.
M2/international reserves[a]	Low international reserves relative to the supply of money indicates that the currency has only limited backing.
Inflation	High inflation can indicate monetizing the budget deficit or monetary policy inconsistent with the exchange rate, which may trigger a loss of confidence in the currency
Short-term debt/ international reserves	Low international reserves relative to short-term debt indicates that the central bank only has limited capacity to mitigate the effects of rapid capital flight.
Measures of public indebtedness[b]	High public debt indicates that fiscal policy may be unsustainable and that investors may lose confidence in the ability of the government to meet its obligations.

Source: GAO analysis of academic literature.

[a]M2 is a measure of the money supply that includes currency and bank deposits.

[b]Measures of public indebtedness in the literature include the budget deficit and external debt/GDP.

Moreover, the methodologies and the validity of the estimates vary across studies, and none should be viewed as definitive. Although recent empirical literature is informative and addresses a number of methodological issues that plagued earlier studies, other limitations remain. Important limitations of the literature analyzing the relationship between inflation and economic growth include (1) potential biases due to the omission of important variables; (2) biases resulting from the failure of some studies to address the fact that, in addition to inflation impacting economic growth, economic growth may also affect inflation; (3) issues with small samples and outlier effects; and (4) technical issues related to the modeling procedures employed. Moreover, the negative effects on the economy may extend beyond the effects on economic growth. As a result, studies that investigate only the impact of inflation on economic growth may understate the total negative effects of inflation. Finally, there are relatively few systematic analyses of the critical threshold beyond which inflation hampers long-term growth; therefore, there is likely to be continued disagreement on where the threshold lies.

Academic Literature Identifies Weaknesses in Macroeconomic Policies That Often Precede Economic Crises, Consistent with IMF-supported Programs

Academic Literature Identifies Weaknesses in Macroeconomic Policies Preceding Currency, Banking, and Debt Crises

The academic literature identifies weaknesses in macroeconomic policies preceding economic crises. We focused on this aspect of the academic literature because, as previously noted, middle- and high- income countries have sought significant IMF financial assistance due to stress associated with the global financial crisis. Empirical academic literature we reviewed, focused on anticipating and explaining economic crises, attempts to identify leading indicators of crises, including weaknesses in macroeconomic policies. This body of research is known as the crisis "early warning system" literature. Economic crises include in particular (1) currency crises, which involve a speculative attack or large depreciation of a currency; (2) banking crises, which involve the widespread failure of critical financial institutions; and (3) sovereign debt crises, which involve the default or near default of a government on its debt obligations. Economic crises can involve one or more of the types of crises described above and often precipitate moderate to severe recessions involving substantial losses of jobs, income, and production.

By analyzing a broad history of crises—crises that have occurred in dozens of countries over the last several decades—researchers have tried to identify common precursors of crises that may provide "early warning" that a crisis is coming. We reviewed 19 published or widely cited studies, identified in economic research databases, or in citations of other studies, written since 1998.[40] For each study, we documented the variables that were predictive of an economic crisis. Across the studies, several macroeconomic policy variables (and many variables unrelated to macroeconomic policy) consistently predict currency, banking, or debt crises. These variables suggest a number of specific policy weaknesses that make countries more vulnerable to crises, especially high inflation, high public indebtedness, and an overvalued currency. These vulnerabilities can represent unsustainable monetary, fiscal, and exchange rate policies, such as (1) high money growth, inconsistent with the government's commitment to a fixed exchange rate or broad exchange rate stability; (2) large and persistent budget deficits that significantly increase the stock of public debt and jeopardize the ability of the government to meet its obligations; or (3) a significant inflow of foreign capital without the central bank accumulating a buffer of international currency to guard against sudden capital outflows. Table 4 contains the specific macroeconomic policy variables identified by the literature and the nature of the related vulnerabilities.

Several factors unrelated to macroeconomic policy also often precede crises, including external events (e.g., a crisis in a neighboring country), private sector behavior (e.g., significant private sector borrowing), and institutional or political factors (e.g., weak law enforcement). Crises are not singularly caused by unsustainable macroeconomic policies; there are often other factors or triggers that increase the likelihood of a crisis. Nevertheless, crises do not strike at random, poor macroeconomic policy management can greatly increase a country's vulnerability to crisis.

While the crisis "early warning system" literature can inform the development of macroeconomic policy, it has limitations and provides qualitative rather than precise quantitative guidance.[41] Conceptually, the literature identifies certain costs associated with loose macroeconomic policies that are important considerations to include in the full accounting of the costs and benefits associated with macroeconomic policies, but these are not the only considerations. Furthermore, the literature has a number of methodological limitations. Specific limitations that we identified during our review of the crisis literature include selecting a sample of countries in a way that overstates the predictability of crises, analytical approaches that fail to account for multiple causes of economic crises, and crisis definitions that may not correspond to severe economic consequences (e.g., the inclusion of speculative attacks that did not result in actual currency depreciation in the definition of currency crises). The limitations we identified may introduce biases into estimates of policy effects in studies where they are present. The exclusion of noncrisis countries in some analyses may, for example, overstate the level of international reserves necessary to guard against crises in some countries. These limitations suggest caution in interpreting the precise numerical results of the literature.

Macroeconomic Policies Are Focused on Critical Vulnerabilities in IMF-Supported Programs in Middle- and High-Income Countries

The central macroeconomic policy weaknesses identified by the literature closely correspond to the macroeconomic policy areas upon which IMF-supported SBA programs focus. The IMF-supported programs in middle- and high-income countries we reviewed have macroeconomic program requirements (generally QPCs) designed to limit money growth and inflation, limit public debt, and accumulate international reserves. Similarly, high debt, high inflation, and low international reserves are important macroeconomic policy weaknesses that make a country more vulnerable to crises.[42] We reviewed certain quantitative macroeconomic program requirements in all SBA programs in which governments have drawn IMF funds, which included 13 countries for which program documents were available as of July 2009.[43] Because SBA programs are for countries considered to have temporary balance-of-payments needs, these countries are generally middle- or high-income countries that have been adversely affected by the global financial crisis. In each of the 13 programs, we found that quantitative program requirements supported the broad goals of (1) limiting money growth and inflation, (2) limiting public debt, and (3) accumulating international reserves.[44]

To support the broad goals identified above, IMF-supported programs often used a variety of specific policy variables. To limit money growth and inflation, SBA programs featured QPCs and other program requirements for a number of macroeconomic policies. These included ceilings on the net domestic assets of the central bank, inflation consultations, and ceilings on the amount of credit the central bank may extend to the government or the private sector.[45] To limit public debt, 11 of the 13 SBA programs had QPCs for the government's budget deficit, and some had restrictions on the government issuing new external debt, and short-term external debt in particular.[46] To accumulate international reserves, 12 of the 13 SBA programs had floors for either net international reserves or net foreign assets.[47] With respect to our case study countries, we have noted above that a large stock of public debt was a key factor driving the crisis in Hungary. In Iceland, the IMF noted in 2007 that the króna was overvalued by 15 to 25 percent, and inflation rose sharply before the banking crisis ensued. The focus of IMF-supported programs on the central policy weaknesses should assist countries in regaining investor confidence and addressing the underlying crisis vulnerabilities.

AGENCY COMMENTS

The Department of the Treasury provided written comments on a draft of this chapter, which are reprinted in appendix III. Treasury stated that it fully concurs with our conclusions that IMF-supported programs are shaped by negotiations with local officials in the context of country circumstances. In addition, Treasury noted our finding that the underlying economic literature on growth, inflation, fiscal and external sustainability, and financial stability, drive IMF policy advice in lending programs. Treasury also emphasized that it encourages the IMF to work with low-income countries to increase spending in areas such as health and education. Furthermore, we received technical comments on a draft of this chapter from Treasury and the IMF, which we incorporated as appropriate.

Appendix I. Scope and Methodology

To examine the process for designing an International Monetary Fund (IMF)-supported program, we reviewed and analyzed IMF's public documents and data. These documents include IMF Articles of Agreement; countries' letters of intent; IMF consultation reports and assessments of country progress under IMF-supported programs, including the Article IV consultation reports; program design papers; strategy papers; policy documents; and IMF's Independent Evaluation Office reports. We also met with officials representing the IMF and the U.S. Department of the Treasury (Treasury) in Washington, D.C., to discuss the process of designing of an IMF-supported program and the typical trade-offs associated with the program's policy decisions. Specifically, we used IMF policy documents and countries' letters of intent to identify the primary objectives and key targets of low- and middle- to high-income countries. We also reviewed the letters of intent provided to the IMF by countries receiving current IMF-supported financial programs, as well as updates of program reviews conducted by the IMF for these programs, available as of July 2009, to obtain examples of macroeconomic target variables, quantitative performance criteria, and structural reforms. We utilized interviews with IMF officials, as well as IMF policy papers, including IMF institute documents, to clarify and explain the process of designing an IMF-supported program.

To examine the IMF-supported programs in recipient countries, we selected four case study countries—Hungary, Iceland, Liberia, and Zambia—and reviewed documents and interviewed officials regarding these countries' IMF-supported programs. Our selection of these four countries include criteria to examine how IMF-supported programs may differ in low-, middle-, and high-income countries with geographic diversity that had relatively large amounts of IMF financing as of April 2009. Our choice of countries was meant to be illustrative, not representative or generalizable to the population of IMF-supported programs. Documents we reviewed include the letters of intent provided to the IMF by these four countries; IMF reviews, reports, and press releases regarding these countries' IMF-supported programs; and country background documents provided by U.S. embassies in these four countries. In addition, we interviewed IMF and Treasury officials in Washington, D.C., to discuss the context of the four recipient countries and the countries' IMF-supported programs. In Hungary, Iceland, Liberia, and Zambia, we met with U.S. embassy officials, IMF staff, officials representing foreign governments, academics, and nongovernmental organizations to obtain their views about the IMF-supported programs.

To examine the extent to which the findings of empirical economic studies are consistent with the IMF's macroeconomic policies, we reviewed IMF documents and empirical studies. Using published or widely cited empirical studies identified in economic research databases EconLit, Social Science Research Network, and Google Scholar, we identified key relationships between macroeconomic policies and economic growth and crises, and compared them with macroeconomic policies in IMF-supported programs. Specifically, we reviewed two parts of the academic literature relevant to the macroeconomic policy decisions in IMF-supported programs, namely the literature that links inflation with economic growth, and the crisis "early warning system" literature that identifies leading indicators of currency, banking, and debt crises. For the inflation and growth literature, we reviewed empirical studies isolating the threshold level of inflation explicitly for lower-income countries identified in economic research databases and published since 1999. Due to the lag between publication and submission, we also included working papers produced during the last 2 years. Although we found these studies to be reliable for the purposes of identifying the range of estimates and comparing them with targets in IMF-supported programs, their inclusion in this chapter does not imply that we deem them to be definitive. (The bibliography contains a full listing of the studies linking inflation with economic growth that we reviewed.) To determine the inflation targets in all 31 IMF-supported programs in low-income countries, as of July 2009, we reviewed countries' letters of intent and IMF Article IV reports and recorded the target for each country. To ensure the data were collected consistently and accurately, each recorded target was independently reviewed and verified. In a few cases where no clear target was articulated, we used the long-term inflation projection for the country as the implicit target. For the crisis "early warning system" literature, we reviewed 19 published or widely cited studies, identified in economic research databases, or in citations of other studies, written since 1998. We chose 1998 as the starting year because of the large volume of research explaining or predicting economic crises that was performed after the Asian financial crisis. For each study, we documented the variables that were predictive of an economic crisis. Where possible, we used a conservative standard for identifying key predictor variables. Under the signals method, we selected only variables that had a noise-to-signal ratio (NTSR) of 0.5 or less (less than 1 indicates more signal than noise). Noise indicates an incorrect prediction while a signal indicates a correct prediction, so a NTSR of less than 1 implies more correct than incorrect predictions. Under traditional regression methods, we selected only variables whose coefficients had p-values less than 0.05. (Several studies we reviewed reported coefficients that were statistically significant at the 10 percent level.) (The bibliography contains a full listing of studies in the "early warning system" literature that we reviewed.) Similar to our identification of inflation targets in IMF-supported programs in low-income countries, we determined certain quantitative macroeconomic program requirements in all Stand-By Arrangements in which governments have drawn IMF funds, which included 13 countries for which program documents were available as of July 2009. We reviewed these countries' letters of intent, determined and recorded the policies associated with the macroeconomic program requirements for each country, then independently verified that the requirements data were collected consistently and accurately.

We conducted our work from November 2008 to November 2009 in accordance with all sections of GAO's Quality Assurance Framework that are relevant to our objectives. The framework requires that we plan and perform the engagement to obtain sufficient and appropriate evidence to meet our stated objectives and to discuss any limitations in our work. We believe that the information and data obtained, and the analysis conducted, provide a reasonable basis for any findings and conclusions in this product.

Appendix II. Countries Approved to Receive IMF Financial Arrangements as of August 31, 2009

Table 5 shows the countries that have been approved to receive financial assistance from the IMF as of August 31, 2009. The recipient countries are categorized by type of IMF lending arrangement.

Table 5. Countries Committed to IMF Financial Arrangements as of August 31, 2009

Type of IMF lending arrangement	Countries approved to receive funding
Poverty Reduction and Growth Facility	Afghanistan
	Burkina Faso
	Burundi
	Central African Republic
	Congo, Republic of
	Cote d'Ivoire
	Djibouti
	Gambia
	Ghana
	Grenada
	Guinea
	Haiti
	Liberia
	Mali
	Mauritania
	Nicaragua
	Niger
	Sao Tome and Principe
	Sierra Leone
	Tajikistan
	Togo
	Zambia
Exogenous Shocks Facility	Ethiopia
	Kyrgyz Republic
	Malawi
	Mozambique
	Senegal
	Tanzania
Stand-By Arrangement	Armenia
	Belarus
	Bosnia and Herzegovina
	Costa Rica

Table 5. (Continued)

Type of IMF lending arrangement	Countries approved to receive funding
	El Salvador
	Gabon
	Georgia
	Guatemala
	Hungary
	Iceland
	Latvia
	Mongolia
	Pakistan
	Romania
	Serbia
	Seychelles
	Sri Lanka
	Ukraine
Flexible Credit Line	Colombia
	Mexico
	Poland

Source: IMF.

Appendix III. Comments from the Department of the Treasury

DEPARTMENT OF THE TREASURY
WASHINGTON, D.C. 20220

October 26, 2009

Mr. Thomas Melito
Director, International Affairs and Trade
Government Accountability Office
441 G St., NW
Washington, DC 20548

Dear Mr. Melito:

I would like to commend the Government Accountability Office (GAO) on the quality of the forthcoming report titled "International Monetary Fund Lending Programs Allow for Negotiations and Are Consistent with Economic Literature". The report distills the complex, iterative process used by the IMF in its negotiations with country authorities into a concise and accessible description of the factors that drive IMF program design. The Treasury Department fully concurs with GAO's conclusions that IMF-supported programs are shaped by negotiations with local officials in the context of country circumstances and that macroeconomic policies in IMF programs are consistent with empirical economic studies.

As the GAO report highlights, the macroeconomic frameworks at the heart of IMF programs naturally involve trade-offs between different policy objectives. Local authorities' prioritization of any given issue may impact other aspects of the macroeconomic framework. Striking an appropriate balance between different priorities is not easy and requires careful judgment. The IMF faces the added challenge that governments often avoid requesting IMF assistance until imbalances are clearly unsustainable and policy options are limited. Nonetheless, as the report shows, the conclusions of the underlying economic literature on growth, inflation, fiscal and external sustainability, and financial stability drive IMF policy advice in lending programs.

Besides supporting broad macroeconomic stability and economic growth, IMF policy advice and financing can also play an important role in protecting the poorest, especially in low-income countries. The poorest are often the most vulnerable to macroeconomic volatility like high inflation or financing crises. We strongly encourage the IMF to work with low-income countries to increase pro-poor spending (such as on health and education).

Again, I thank GAO staff for its fine job in tackling this complicated issue.

Sincerely,

Mark Sobel

Mark Sobel
Acting Assistant Secretary for International Affairs

Bibliography of Empirical Studies Reviewed in the Inflation-Growth Literature

To examine the relationship between economic growth and inflation in low-income countries, we reviewed the following academic articles. Our review of the literature included academic studies, using data from low-income countries, published from 1999 to 2009. Due to the lag between publication and submission, we included working papers produced in the last 2 years. The studies indicated with an asterisk (*) provided empirical estimates of the threshold level of inflation for low-income, developing or nonindustrial countries that serve as the basis for figure 11 in the report. The list includes widely cited studies published prior to 1999, although they either combine low-income and high-income countries when estimating the threshold inflation rate or determine the threshold on the basis of judgment.

Barro & Robert. (1996). "Inflation and Economic Growth," *Federal Reserve Bank of St. Louis Review, 78.*

Bruno & Michael and William Easterly. (1998). "Inflation Crises and Long-Run Growth," *Journal of Monetary Economics, 41.*

Bruno, Michael & William Easterly. (1996). "Inflation and Growth: In Search of a Stable Relationship," *Review of Federal Reserve Bank of St. Louis, 78*, no. 3.

*Burdekin, Richard C. K., Arthur T. Denzau, Manfred W. Keil, Thitithep Sitthiyot & Thomas D. Willett. (2004). "When Does Inflation Hurt Economic Growth? *Different Nonlinearities for Different Economies," Journal of Macroeconomics, 26.*

Fischer & Stanley. (1993). "The Role of Macroeconomic Factors in Growth," *Journal of Monetary Economics, 32.*

Ghosh, Atish & Stephen Phillips. (1998). "Warning: Inflation May be Harmful to Your Growth," *IMF Staff Papers, 45.*

*Gillman, Max, Mark Harris & Laszlo Matyas. (2004). "Inflation and growth: explaining a negative effect," *Empirical Economics, 29*, no. 1.

Gylfason, Thorvaldur & Tryggvi T. Herbertsson. (2001). "Does Inflation Matter for Growth?," *Japan and the World Economy, 13.*

*Khan, Mohsin S. & Abdelhak S. Senhadji. (2001). "Threshold effects in the Relation Between Inflation and Growth," *IMF Staff Papers, 48.*

*Kochar, Kalpana & Sharmini Coorey. (1999). "Economic Growth: What Has Been Achieved So Far and How?", in Hugh Bredenkamp and Susan Schadler (eds), *Economic Adjustment and Reform in Low-Income Countries* (Washington, D.C.: International Monetary Fund.

*Kremer, Stephanie, Alexander Bick & Dieter Nautz. (2009). "Inflation and Growth: New Evidence from a Dynamic Panel Threshold Analysis," *Sonderforschungsbereich Discussion Paper, 649*, Humboldt University, Berlin, Germany.

*Kremer, Stephanie, Alexander Bick & Dieter Nautz. (2008). "Inflation and Growth: New Evidence from a Panel Data Threshold Analysis," *Goethe University Working Paper*, Frankfurt.

*Pollin, Robert & Andong Zhu. (2006). "Inflation and Economic Growth: A Cross-Country Non-linear Analysis," *Journal of Post Keynesian Economics, 28*, no. 4.

Sarel, Michael. (1996). "Nonlinear Effects of Inflation on Economic Growth," *IMF Staff Papers 43*.

*Sepehri, Ardeshir & Saeed Moshiri. (2004). "Inflation-Growth Profiles Across Countries: Evidence from Developing and Developed Countries," *International Review of Applied Economics, 18*, no. 2.

*Vaona, A. & Schiavo, S. (2007). "Nonparametric and Semiparametric Evidence on the Long-run Effects of Inflation on Growth," *Economics Letters, 94*, no. 3.

Bibliography of Empirical Studies Reviewed in the Crisis "Early Warning System" Literature

We reviewed the following empirical studies in the crisis "early warning system" literature written since 1998. For each study, we documented the variables that were predictive of an economic crisis. Where possible, we used a conservative standard for identifying key predictor variables. Under the signals method, we selected only variables that had a noise-to-signal ratio (NTSR) of 0.5 or less (less than 1 indicates more signal than noise). Noise indicates an incorrect prediction while a signal indicates a correct prediction, so a NTSR of less than one implies more correct than incorrect predictions. Under traditional regression methods, we selected only variables whose coefficients had p-values less than 0.05. (Several studies we reviewed reported coefficients that were statistically significant at the 10 percent level.)

Berg, Andrew & Catherine Patillo. (1999). "Predicting Currency Crises: The Indicators Approach and an Alternative," *Journal of International Money and Finance, 18*.

Borio, Claudio & Philip Lowe. (2002). "Assessing the Risk of Banking Crises," *BIS Quarterly Review* (December).

Burkart, Oliver & Virginie Coudert. (2002). "Leading Indicators of Currency Crises for Emerging Countries," *Emerging Markets Review, 3*.

Bussiere, Matthieu & Marcel Fratzscher. (2006). "Towards a New Early Warning System of Financial Crises," *Journal of International Money and Finance, 25*.

Ciarlone, Alessio & Giorgio Trebeschi. (2005). "Designing an Early Warning System for Debt Crises," *Emerging Markets Review, 6*.

Davis, E. Philip & Dilruba Karim. (2008). "Comparing Early Warning Systems for Banking Crises." *Journal of Financial Stability, 4*.

Demirgüç-Kunt, Asli & Enrica Detragiache. (1998). "The Determinants of Banking Crises in Developing and Developed Countries," *IMF Staff Papers, 45*, no. 1.

Edison, Hali J. (2003). "Do Indicators of Financial Crises Work? An Evaluation of An Early Warning System," I*nternational Journal of Finance and Economics, 8*.

Esquivel, Gerardo & Felipe Larrain. (1998). "Explaining Currency Crises." Harvard Institute for International Development.

Hemming, Richard, Michael Kell & Axel Schimmelpfennig. (2003). "Fiscal Vulnerability and Financial Crises in Emerging Market Economies," Occasional Paper 218 (Washington, D.C.: International Monetary Fund,).

Kamin, Steven B., John Schindler & Shawna Samuel. (2007). "The Contribution of Domestic and External factors to Emerging Market Currency Crises: An Early Warning Systems Approach," *International Journal of Finance and Economics, 12.*

Kaminsky & Graciela L. (2006). "Currency Crises: Are They All the Same?" *Journal of International Money and Finance, 25.*

Kaminsky, Graciela, Saul Lizondo & Carmen Reinhart. (1998). "Leading Indicators of Currency Crises," *IMF Staff Papers, 45* (March).

Kaminsky, Graciela L. & Carmen Reinhart. (1999). "The Twin Crises: The Causes of Banking and Balance of Payments Problems," *American Economic Review, 89.*

Komulainen, Tuomas & Johanna Lukkarila. (2003). "What Drives Financial Crises in Emerging Markets?" *Emerging Markets Review, 4.*

Kumar, Mohan, Uma Moorthy & William Perraudin. (2003). "Predicting Emerging Market Currency Crashes." *Journal of Empirical Finance, 10.*

Manasse, Paolo, Nouriel Roubini & Axel Schimmelpfennig. (2003). "Predicting Sovereign Debt Crises," *IMF Working Paper WP/03/221* (November).

Manasse, Paolo & Nouriel Roubini. (2005). "'Rules of Thumb' for Sovereign Debt Crises," *IMF Working Paper WP/05/42* (March).

Shimpalee, Pattima L. & Janice Boucher Breuer. (2006). "Currency Crises and Institutions," *Journal of International Money and Finance, 25.*

End Notes

[1] For the purposes of this chapter, lending includes arrangements and amounts that the IMF has committed to lend to recipient countries. The recipient countries may not have drawn these committed amounts. Unless otherwise noted, we use the August 31, 2009, U.S. dollar to SDR exchange rate of 1.56606 to convert IMF-reported SDR values to 2009 U.S. dollars throughout the report. The currency value of the SDR is determined daily by the IMF by summing the values in U.S. dollars, based on market exchange rates, of a basket of four major currencies—the euro, Japanese yen, pound sterling, and U.S. dollar.

[2] Balance-of-payments problems occur when countries have difficulty obtaining the financial resources needed to meet their payments to nonresidents.

[3] The G-20 is an organization of Finance Ministers and Central Bank Governors representing industrialized and developing economies.

[4] SDR is an international reserve asset created by the IMF in 1969 as a supplement to existing reserve assets, or quasi-currency that borrowing nations can draw upon if needed.

[5] Supplemental Appropriations Act, 2009, Pub. L. No. 111-32, June 24, 2009. The legislation made available the dollar equivalent of up to 75 billion SDRs, but also included that if the United States agrees to an expansion of its credit arrangement in an amount less than the dollar equivalent of 75 billion SDRs, any amount over the United States' agreement shall not be available until further appropriated. According to the Department of the Treasury, there is an understanding between the Department of the Treasury and the U.S. Congress, which is supported by the administration's public statements, that the United States would only commit up to $100 billion.

[6] Agreement on an IMF-supported program requires the IMF Executive Board's approval. This board comprises 24 Executive Directors who are appointed or elected by member countries or by groups of member countries.

[7] We use the word target to mean a goal or objective of an IMF-supported program, rather than a formal target or program requirement.

[8] Letters of intent are prepared by the member country. They describe the policies that a country intends to implement in the context of its request for financial support from the IMF.

[9] The Article IV consultation is an annual review of members' macroeconomic circumstances. Typically, an IMF staff team visits the country, collects economic and financial information, and discusses with officials the country's economic developments and policies. The staff prepares a report, which forms the basis for discussion by the Executive Board.

[10] In May 2009, the IMF announced reforms to its policy on conditions. For example, the IMF eliminated structural elements as performance criteria. These structural performance criteria (SPC) are changes in the underlying

makeup of an economy, such as fiscal systems, social safety nets, and measures to strengthen the financial sector. Though eliminated as criteria, the IMF will continue to monitor structural reforms as part of the overall review of country progress.

[11] The G-20 also called for urgent ratification of a long-pending amendment to the IMF's Articles of Agreement. The Fourth Amendment was proposed to enable all IMF members to participate in the SDR system on an equitable basis and correct for the fact that countries that joined the IMF after 1981—now more than one-fifth of the current IMF membership—had never received an SDR allocation.

[12] Pub. L. No. 111-32. The legislation appropriated the dollar equivalent of 4,973,100,000 SDRs.

[13] Pub. L. No. 111-32. The legislation made available the dollar equivalent of up to 75 billion SDRs.

[14] These provisions are included in Pub. L. No. 111-32, Sections 1403(d) and 1404.

[15] Statement on Signing the Supplemental Appropriations Act, 2009, June 24, 2009. The provisions noted in the signing statement included Sections 1403 and 1404.

[16] The IMF identified these conditions for low-income countries. Macroeconomic instability can be characterized by large trade deficits financed by short-term borrowing, high and rising levels of public debt, double-digit inflation rates, and stagnant or declining GDP.

[17] Limiting the budget deficit may also be crucial for middle- and high-income countries, and stabilizing the exchange rate may also be important for low-income countries.

[18] Conditions may also include prior actions, which are measures that a country agrees to take before the IMF approves financing or completes a review. Examples of prior actions include adjustment of a country's exchange rate, elimination of a country's price controls, or formal approval of a government budget consistent with the IMF-supported program's fiscal framework.

[19] The key sectors of the economy are real (output growth), monetary and financial (money and banking system), fiscal (government deficit), and external (balance of payments).

[20] For example, the projections for GDP growth, inflation, and the current account influence are influenced by monetary, exchange rate, and fiscal policy instruments. GDP growth and inflation are thus important inputs into determining government revenue and expenditures. However, the size of the deficit has an effect on economic activity, as well as the method of financing the deficit influences inflation and interest rates.

[21] IMF staff use the financial programming model, which consists of accounting identities, behavioral relationships, and economic judgment, as a consistency check on the macroeconomic framework. This process allows targets and policies to be adjusted and reformulated in light of changing outcomes. The process may undergo multiple iterations as IMF staff strive to ensure internal consistency across the various sectors of the economy.

[22] If the increase in government spending is financed by borrowing from the central bank, the effect on the price level may be significant.

[23] In 1996, the World Bank and IMF launched the HIPC Initiative to create a framework in which all creditors, including multilateral creditors, can provide debt relief to the world's poorest and most heavily indebted countries, and thereby help reduce constraints on economic growth and poverty reduction due to the countries' debt burdens. Countries begin receiving debt relief on an interim basis until they complete the initiative, which Liberia may do in 2010. According to IMF staff, Liberia has been receiving interim debt relief from its main creditors, but full debt relief will only be secured when it reaches the HIPC completion point. For more information, see GAO, *Developing Countries: The United States Has Not Fully Funded Its Share of Debt Relief, and the Impact of Debt Relief on Countries' Poverty-Reducing Spending Is Unknown,* GAO-09-162 (Washington, D.C.: Jan. 26, 2009).

[24] Foreign exchange data obtained from Thomson Reuters Datastream, a large financial statistical database.

[25] Hungary aspires to join the group of European countries that share a common currency, the euro, in the future, which requires it to meet a set of criteria, including a budget deficit of less than 3 percent.

[26] The countries included Norway, Denmark, Finland, and Sweden.

[27] In technical terms, this means the relationship has been found to be nonlinear. This implies that the trade-off between higher inflation and lower economic growth—or the marginal growth costs of inflation—can differ as inflation rises.

[28] Theoretically, inflation can positively and negatively affect growth through various channels. For example, high rates of inflation reduce the value of savings and distort price signals, interfering with the efficient allocation of resources and the functioning of the financial system. On the other hand, at low levels, inflation can help foster capital accumulation, contribute to labor and product market flexibility, and make an economy less vulnerable to prolonged recessions.

[29] While the relationship is found to be positive, in most cases it is also statistically insignificant.

[30] IMF and other researchers suggest a need for caution in setting very low inflation targets in low-income countries.

[31] Given that hyperinflation is clearly detrimental to economic growth, the literature we reviewed focused on the effects of moderate to high inflation.

[32] A currency union is a group of countries that adopt a single currency and a uniform monetary policy. In the case of the currency unions discussed in this chapter, the unions also peg the common currency to the euro or the

U.S. dollar. A currency board is a monetary arrangement that pegs the currency of a country to a more widely used and dominant currency and typically backs all currency in circulation with international reserves.

[33] For example, the West African Economic and Monetary Union pact sets a 3 percent inflation threshold as a convergence requirement for participating countries. The Central African Economic and Monetary Union pact has a similar convergence criterion. Grenada is part of the East Caribbean Currency Union, which pegs to the U.S. dollar. Djibouti operates a currency board tied to the U.S. dollar.

[34] If inflation were allowed to deviate significantly from the levels in the developed country or area, the real exchange rate would become increasingly misaligned and undermine the goals of the fixed-rate currency system.

[35] Given the state of the literature, a 5 to 12 percent range is a reasonable interpretation of the literature since two of the three estimates outside the 5 to 12 percent range are likely due to methodological issues and the remaining estimate (17 percent) is from a June 2009 study that addresses a number of the methodological issues in the existing literature but has not been peer reviewed. Of the published studies, one estimates a 3 percent threshold using a specification that is now used infrequently in the literature because it allows a few outliers to drive the results. The other study estimates a threshold of 15 to 18 percent using a simple nonlinear model that may not accurately estimate the threshold inflation rate. However, none of the studies should be interpreted as having identified the exact inflation level beyond which inflation hampers long-term growth, and this exercise is not meant to imply that literature is conclusive.

[36] For example, two widely cited studies prior to 1999 impose thresholds ranging from 15 to 40 percent. See Michael Bruno and William Easterly, "Inflation Crises and Long-Run Growth," *Journal of Monetary Economics* 41 (1998); and Stanley Fischer, "The Role of Macroeconomic Factors in Growth," *Journal of Monetary Economics* 32 (1993). To the contrary, the threshold models that dominate recent literature are designed to estimate inflation thresholds as opposed to imposing them.

[37] See Stephanie Kremer, Alexander Bick, and Dieter Nautz, "Inflation and Growth: New Evidence from a Dynamic Panel Threshold Analysis," *Sonderforschungsbereich Discussion Paper 649*, Humboldt University, Berlin, Germany (2009).

[38] See A. Vaona and S. Schiavo, "Nonparametric and Semiparametric Evidence on the Long-run Effects of Inflation on Growth," *Economics Letters* 94, no. 3 (2007). It is important to note that this study exploits techniques that have some positive methodological features but are extremely sensitive to outliers.

[39] Even if inflation above 10 percent is believed to be harmful to long-term growth in a country, there are still trade-offs to be considered for negotiation. For example, if there is only a small benefit to moving from 12 percent to 9 percent inflation, it may not justify the potential cost of disinflation.

[40] See appendix I for our complete literature review methodology and the bibliography for crisis "early warning system" literature for a list of the studies reviewed.

[41] The lack of consensus in the crisis "early warning system" literature as to the appropriate way to estimate the effects of policies (and other variables) implies that it is difficult to obtain precise quantitative guidance from researchers' estimates of policy effects. This lack of consensus is reflected in the two different methods, which we denote as (1) the signals approach and (2) the marginal approach, which researchers have used to assess potential leading indicators of economic crises. The signals approach assumes that there are thresholds beyond which relevant indicators "signal" that a crisis is more likely. The marginal approach assumes that changes in relevant indicators increase or decrease the likelihood of a crisis, irrelevant of particular thresholds. As an example of the divergent predictions from the two approaches, consider the real exchange rate. As discussed above, a higher real exchange rate can indicate an overvalued currency, an uncompetitive economy, and an increased likelihood of crisis. According to one study using a marginal approach, a 10 percent increase in the exchange rate would increase the likelihood of a currency crisis by approximately 3.6 percentage points. According to a study using a signals approach, the real exchange rate signals that a crisis is likely only when its value exceeds the 90th percentile.

[42] Another leading indicator of crises, an overvalued currency, does not correspond to common quantitative macroeconomic program requirements in SBA programs. However, the crisis events that precipitate IMF-supported programs are likely to involve a significant depreciation of the currency. As a result, the likelihood of overvaluation to be present once a crisis ensues is diminished.

[43] See appendix I for more information on our methodology.

[44] The IMF-supported program in Bosnia-Herzegovina did not have a QPC or other program requirement to facilitate the accumulation of international reserves. However, Bosnia-Herzegovina operates under a currency board in which it must hold foreign exchange reserves not less than domestic currency in circulation, under domestic law. Maintaining this currency board is also a structural benchmark of the program, but not a performance criterion.

[45] An inflation consultation is a program requirement that triggers a meeting with IMF staff or the IMF Board if inflation falls outside of certain bounds.

[46] Short-term debt has a maturity of 1 year or less.

[47] Net international reserves are a subset of net foreign assets. Net international reserves are the foreign exchange reserves of the central bank, less liabilities. Net foreign assets is a broader concept that includes the foreign currency assets and liabilities of the banking system.

CHAPTER SOURCES

The following chapters have been previously published:

Chapter 1 – This is an edited, excerpted and augmented edition of a United States Congressional Research Service publication, Report Order Code R40578, dated January 29, 2010.

Chapter 2 – This is an edited, excerpted and augmented edition of a United States Congressional Research Service publication, Report Order Code RS22976, dated February 4, 2009.

Chapter 3 – This is an edited, excerpted and augmented edition of a United States Congressional Research Service publication, Report Order Code R40977, dated December 9, 2009.

Chapter 4 – This is an edited, excerpted and augmented edition of a United States Congressional Research Service publication, Report Order Code RS22729, dated January 29, 2008.

Chapter 5 – This is an edited, excerpted and augmented edition of a United States Congressional Research Service publication, Report Order Code RL33626, dated January 29, 2008.

Chapter 6 – This is an edited, excerpted and augmented edition of a United States Congressional Research Service publication, Report Order Code RS22658, dated January 26, 2010.

Chapter 7 – This is an edited, excerpted and augmented edition of a United States Government Accountability Office publication, Report Order Code GAO-10-44, dated November 2009.

INDEX

D

J

K

L

M

Q

R

S

T

U

V

W

Y